PENGUIN BOOKS

FIRE IN THE MIND

Pupul Jayakar was born in Etawah, Uttar P̶. has been closely involved with the development of indigenous culture, handicrafts and textiles since the country achieved independence in 1947. She has been the Chairman of the All India Handicrafts Board, Chairman of the Governing Body of the National Institute of Design, Chairman of the Handicraft and Handloom Exports Corporation of India, Chairman of the National Institute of Fashion Technology, Chairman of the Crafts Museum of India, Chairman of the Calico Museum of Textiles and Chairman of the Festival of India in Great Britain, France, USA and Japan.

She was Chairman of the Krishnamurti Foundation, India, and published a bestselling biography of Krishnamurti in 1986. She has written several other books, including *Indira Gandhi: A Biography*, *The Earth Mother*, *The Children of Barren Women*, *The Buddha* and *God is Not a Full-Stop*, a volume of short stories.

At present, she is the Chairman of the Indian National Trust for Art and Cultural Heritage (INTACH) and a member of the Krishnamurti Foundation India.

Pupul Jayakar is currently working on her memoirs, and lives in Bombay.

# FIRE IN THE MIND

## DIALOGUES WITH J. KRISHNAMURTI

## Pupul Jayakar

PENGUIN BOOKS

Penguin Books India (P) Ltd., 11 Community Centre, Panchsheel Park, New
Delhi 110 017, India
Penguin Books Ltd., 80 Strand, London WC2R 0RL, UK
Penguin Putnam Inc., 375 Hudson Street, New York, NY 10014, USA
Penguin Books Australia Ltd., 250 Camberwell Road, Camberwell, Victoria
3124, Australia
Penguin Books Canada Ltd., 10 Alcorn Avenue, Suite 300, Toronto,
Ontario, M4V 3B2, Canada
Penguin Books (NZ) Ltd., Cnr Rosedale and Airborne Roads, Albany,
Auckland, New Zealand
Penguin Books South Africa Pty. Ltd., 24, Sturdee Avenue, Rosebank 2196,
South Africa

First published by Penguin Books India 1995

Copyright © Krishnamurti Foundation Trust Ltd., 1995

10    9    8    7

Typeset in Times Roman by FOLIO, New Delhi

For more information please contact:
Krishnamurti Foundation India
64/65 Greenways Road
R.A Puram
Chennai 600 028

www.kfionline.org

Made and printed in India by Swapna Printing Works (P) Ltd.

# Contents

# PART II

# Foreword

*Sceptical research, sceptical investigation is the true spiritual process. This is true religion.*

Madras, 14 January 1981

This collection of J. Krishnamurti's dialogues is my homage to a profoundly religious revolutionary, affirming a teaching of compassion and freedom.

Krishnamurti—Krishnaji to his friends—negated all spiritual authority. He sought a holistic perception and a freedom of the mind from reactive responses. He regarded all beliefs and ideals as crippling illusions which distorted man's relationship with nature and humanity and generated conflicts at all levels of life.

Krishnaji's approach to the discovery of truth is as relevant today as it will be in centuries to come.

*

It was in October 1947, two months after Independence, that Krishnaji returned to India from Ojai, California, after an absence of over nine years. A new India awaited him. The partition had left a trail of massacres and hatred that had traumatised the nation's psyche.

Krishnaji was staying in Bombay and, unlike on his previous

visits to India, he made himself available mornings and evenings. Seekers came to sit around him and question him on problems they felt were crucial to an understanding of their own lives and to the country's new awakening. Most of them were young people—freedom fighters disillusioned in the aftermath of freedom, confused and in despair at the ambitions, hunger for power, sycophancy and double talk that had surfaced soon after Independence. Many creative people came to him: poets, painters, monks and sannyasis—eager to probe, eager to discuss the true and the creative. There were also those burdened with sorrow who came to the sage to be healed.

The majestic presence of Krishnaji and the myths and legends that surrounded his early life overwhelmed many of us, young and old. With great simplicity and denying all hierarchy, Krishnaji spoke to us directly. He brought us into the perceptive field of his concerns, making it possible for us to ask questions and reveal our sorrows, our fears and our hopes.

It was during these months in Bombay that dialogue emerged as a way of exploration into consciousness. It was an approach that was to become central to Krishnaji's teaching.

There is an ancient tradition of religious discourse in India which stresses dialogue and doubt as crucial to the discovery of truth. But Krishnaji negated the hierarchy inherent in a dialogue between guru and disciple. There were no anchors. No guru, no book, no tradition could give answers to life's questions, nor free the human mind from bondage. The seeker, the questioner, the human being in sorrow had to accept total responsibility.

At first we who listened found it difficult to follow what lay behind his words. There were a few who were aware that there was a within that could be discovered or explored. With immense patience Krishnaji repeatedly stressed the need to slow down the mind, to pause, to ponder, to question relentlessly, to observe thought without judgement and to perceive thought as 'what is'.

We had been nurtured on an educational tradition which stressed reason and the perception of the outer world as the actual and we saw the religious mind as based on belief and faith. At first we found it impossible to listen and perceive what lay within us. There was, however, a yearning to seek that which lay hidden at the root of the human mind.

Spontaneously a form was taking shape. Krishnaji sat with us in a circle, listening with great intensity to the questions asked by the participants. There was never an immediate answer, he paused, posed a counter-question, threw the question back to the questioner. He found that in this situation be could directly contact the minds of his companions, draw them close and understand the nature of the obstacles they faced in perceiving thought without distortion. He was aware when questions were asked from direct perception or, when in the process of listening a counter-question born of memory was taking shape as thought in the brain, then consciousness was fragmented, then there was no deep listening.

It was essential to listen with intensity to Krishnaji, to listen critically, even to challenge him. For it was only when challenged that Krishnaji's responses held the light of vast insights. And yet if our minds failed to understand, with grace, with ease, without effort, Krishnaji would say: 'Let us begin again. That is patience. That patience has no time. Impatience has time.'

The approach of Krishnaji was entirely new, demanding from us the energy to listen, to perceive, to question and be questioned. For Krishnamurti too it was a challenge. It is possible that new insights were arising as he investigated. He was eager to awaken in us an intelligence that had not crystalised, that was not conditioned by words. It was with such a mind that we could journey with him into the depths of consciousness. 'In the very act of listening without effort, miracles happen, light penetrates darkness.'

Sensing our confusion and aware of our inability to listen, he asked: 'What is self-knowing? How do you know yourself? Is it in the observing of a thought springing up? We are reluctant to let go the first thought and so there is a conflict. Or is self-knowing to extinguish the first thought and perceive the second thought and then the third, then dropping the third and following the fourth, so that there is a constant alertness and awareness of the movement of thought and an energy that comes alive born of attention?'

Unfortunately there are hardly any records of those early dialogues except for the few notes kept by some of us gathered around him.

Throughout the 1950s—every year, in fact—Krishnaji travelled to India and the West. He returned from the West in the early 1960s afire with the ferment in the scientific and technological world and the volcanic energy being released that would inevitably transform human consciousness and generate explosive pressures on humankind. With the eye of prophesy, he looked into the centuries that lay ahead and perceived the velocity of change that was to come about with the unlocking of the mysteries of nature and the birth of skills that could manipulate and structure what was discovered. He had intimations of a massive search for artificial intelligence that would render certain human faculties obsolete.

The dialogues had assumed a new weight and density; a subtlety of enquiry was transforming perceptive processes. Every cell in Krishnaji's brain seemed to be awake. Aware of every movement, every sound, in the outer and the inner, he was penetrating in depth into the nature of the scientific mind and the religious mind—the only two minds that could survive in the centuries ahead.

'Something new is going on, of which we are not aware,' he said. 'We are not aware of the significance, the flow, the dynamic quality of the change. There is no time.'

> The scientific mind with its logic, its precision, its enquiry, investigates the outer world of nature, but this does not lead to an inward comprehension of things; but an inward comprehension brings about an understanding of the outer. We are the result of the influences of the outer. The scientific mind is precise and clear in its investigation. It is not a compassionate mind, for it has not understood itself.

> *Bombay, 8 March 1961*

The religious mind is capable of thinking precisely, not
in terms of the negative and positive; therefore, that
mind can hold within it the scientific mind. But the
scientific mind does not contain the religious mind
because it is based on time, knowledge; it is rooted in
success and achievement. The religious mind is the real
revolutionary mind. It is not a reaction to what has
been. The religious mind is the only mind that can
respond totally to the present challenge and to all
challenges, at all times.

*Bombay, 1 March 1961*

There was passion and an urgency in his dialogues. He demanded
a mutation in the human brain so that automation and the artifacts
of technology could not take over the inhuman role of master. For
this the investigation into the within could no longer be ignored.
Yet it had remained unexplored by the scientific mind. The
wisdom humanity lacked was that the mind was the root of the
problem-making machinery. It was in this area of perception that
the ultimate freedom of humanity lay.

'What is needed,' Krishnaji said, 'is a new mind that functions
wholly. While the scientific mind is disciplined, the religious mind
explodes without discipline. Self-knowing is essential because it is
only a mind in self-knowing that withers away, allowing the new
mind to be.'

'The mutation of the human mind is not in the outer but in the
depths of consciousness,' in those dark caves and ravines of the
brain where the primordial, the ancient and the suppressed lie
dormant. With great intensity he asked; 'Can one live with eyes
and ears that hold the totality of the past, the yesterday and the
million years, the second before and the primordial? That is
mutation; that is revolution.'

Krishnaji was exploring his own mind, probing deeper and
deeper into consciousness, entering into darkness and the unknown. 'I
see,' he said, 'that entering into myself implies the same movement
as entering into space—as energy enters, it gathers momentum.'

In another dialogue, investigating further, he says: 'When the brain is deeply attentive, listening to what is being said—a state of the active present—and simultaneously self-examining then attention has the quality of fire.' This intensity of listening and simultaneous exploration cuts the Gordian knot. Perception no longer flows in a linear stream. 'Consciousness as the movement of time and measure is not.' The whole brain is operative.

In the West, he was holding dialogues with physicists, biochemists, genetic engineers and those engaged in designing computers and creating artificial intelligence. He was at the same time enquiring into problems of time and the scientific approach to the brain and consciousness.

On his return to India he continued his investigations. A series of dialogues were held on 'intelligence, computers and the mechanical mind'. Equally intent on exploring the ancient Indian mind, Krishnaji entered into dialogue with the surviving religious traditions of Buddhism and Vedanta. He sought to probe a religious psyche that had long served to nurture a quest for truth. Questioning and being questioned, new challenges emerged and extended the dimensions of enquiry.

*

The dialogues covering a vast sea of human concerns continued over the years. Fresh minds joined the old stalwarts. Krishnaji was using the mind to penetrate the mind. We were witness to the expansion of the limitless and its impact on the limited mind.

With his old comrades, with Buddhist monks and with scientists, Krishnaji was investigating at depth into the nature of time and dialogue itself. There were moments when the dialogues seemed to touch the very limits of thought and consciousness. There was an ending of time and thought—a state where the experiencer, the questioner, was not. A profound sense of sacredness permeated the mind, providing a totally new dimension to the whole field of religious enquiry.

In 1985, Krishnaji visited India for the last time. He was

desperately ill with cancer of the pancreas, but, in spite of the frailty of the body, he continued to hold dialogues. The last discussion was held at Vasanta Vihar, Madras, on 28 December 1985, a month and a half before his death in Ojai, California. In the dialogue he discussed the nature of time and he asked a question: 'Is there a time of non-movement? Is there a timeless activity which is infinite and measureless? We are using words to measure the immeasurable and our words have become time. Words have become time and with these words we are measuring a state which is not measurable and that which is not measurable is not of time.' He left India ten days later, with this question unanswered but alive in our consciousness.

\*

Today, a few years later, some of the finest minds in science, Nobel Prize winning geneticists and biochemists such as Gerald Edelman (*Bright Air, Brilliant Fire*) and Francis Crick (*The Astonishing Hypothesis*), have published books investigating not only intelligence but also consciousness. This was possible because the tools and technologies for probing into the brain and its functioning were now available for the first time.

Scientists are now beginning to seriously investigate questions such as: What is consciousness? How do we find out? How does the mind emerge from the brain? Can we construct an object which not only has intelligence but also consciousness? To do this, some scientists who have the knowledge of brain functions are constructing 'intentional objects' with intelligence and consciousness. Already scientific papers are being published on certain chemicals which can wipe out the memory of all distressing experiences, without affecting other memory.

The capacity to manipulate the mind—to programme it and change the nature of consciousness, so that the mind loses its power and its initiative—is now a possibility. This threatens the very existence of the rich and profound nature of human consciousness. It could make the birth of a new compassionate mind an impossibility. When we observe this, the dialogues of Krishnamurti and his exploration into the mind and consciousness become supremely relevant. For they uncover the nature of the within through self-knowing and so bring about a revolution in the mind's functioning.

\*

*Fire in the Mind* is divided into two sections. The first consists of fifteen dialogues between J. Krishnamurti and me. In some of these dialogues, a few of the listeners occasionally participated, but their intervention did not disturb the thread of the enquiry.

The second part consists of five dialogues between J. Krishnamurti and a group of friends who had held dialogues with him over the years. It reveals the nature of Krishnamurti's attention which enabled him to be questioned and to question a number of varied and conditioned minds, without the enquiry losing its power or direction.

In am deeply grateful to the Krishnamurti Foundation India for the opportunity given to me to cull together this book of J. Krishnamurti's dialogues. My profound gratitude is due to Asit and Clea Chandmal, from whom I learnt of the explosive growth in new scientific technologies, dealing with the brain, mind and consciousness. My gratitude is also due to Dr Geetha Varadan for the care and concern she gave to editing these dialogues. I would like to express my grateful thanks to Shri K. Krishnamurthy of the Krishnamurti Foundation India for putting together the dialogues published in this book. My affectionate thanks to my granddaughter, Maya Herzberger, for the critical eye with which she read my 'Foreword' and made very valuable suggestions.

The Krishnamurti Foundation would like to thank Mrs Mitter Bedi for her generous permission to use Krishnamurti's photograph taken by the late Mr Mitter Bedi on the cover of the book.

\*

*There is a reality which coming upon the mind transforms it, you don't have to do a thing. It operates, it functions, it has an action of its own, but the mind must feel it, must know it and not speculate, not have all kinds of ideas about it. A mind that is seeking it will never find it, but there is that state unquestionably. In saying this I am not speculating, nor am I saying it as an experience of yesterday. It is so. There is that state. And if you have that state, you will find everything is possible, because that is creation, that is love, that is compassion.*

Bombay, 23 December 1956

*Bombay*
*5 January 1995*

*Pupul Jayakar*

# PART I

# The Unfolding of the Teaching

**PUPUL JAYAKAR (PJ) :** I have been wanting to ask you a question for several years. It is a question that in a sense contains the totality of your Teaching and, I think, if we could discuss it, it might help clarify certain issues.

I have heard you for thirty years and I feel that through these thirty years there has been a movement in the Teaching. I am using the word 'movement' deliberately. I am not calling it a development, but rather an unfolding.

In 1948 when I first heard you, you were very concerned with the problem of the thinker and thought, with self-knowledge and the observation of one thought as it arises in consciousness, the pursuance of that thought to its end, the pursuance of another thought that intervenes, and so on, and so on.

You symbolically took the hand of the person who was with you and entered into the process of self-knowing.

To observe thought operate in consciousness ultimately appeared to be the key to your Teaching.

You then discussed the whole problem of judgement, condemnation, the observing of judgement and condemnation and the movement beyond. There were many other facets of this: there was the whole problem of the thinker and thought, whether the thinker was separate from thought or whether the thinker was part of thought itself. This awakening to thought, for me at least, has been the most crucial point of understanding. You went on to say that the pause between two thoughts was silence; that the ending of thought, rather, was silence.

Today, you do not say that. You hardly speak of the thinker and thought. You hardly speak of the observation of thought. You hardly speak of the movement of condemnation, the observation of condemnation and the movement beyond. You speak of a totality of seeing, a holistic seeing, which appears to wipe out the need for all the rest.

My question is: Has your Teaching moved from what it was to what it is today or is the 'movement' only a deepening of the Teaching? Or, is it that you can arrive at this holistic position without going through the whole process of observation and self-knowing? For you see, sir, you no longer take the person by the hand and enter into the process. I would like to know whether you have turned away from the earlier position.

**J. KRISHNAMURTI (K) :** No. But you used the word 'unfolding'; I think that is correct. You see, the questioning is in the same direction. It is a widening, a deepening and, as you said, a 'holistic' position, rather than a going minutely into detail as we did, if I remember rightly, and from what you say, thirty years ago.

So your question now is, correct me if I am wrong, whether K has moved away completely from the past Teaching to the present position, or whether the Teaching is now direct, simple and comprehensive. Would you accept that?

**PJ :** Sir, you say that it is nothing but a deepening, a widening. That may be from your point of view, but what about the person who listens? Is it possible, without moving through the other, to immediately jump?

**K** : Yes.

**PJ** : You speak today, as you never did before, of a total immobility in consciousness . . . .

**K** : Yes.

**PJ** : You speak of a total non-movement. You also make another statement. You say that the ending of thought is not silence. You have said, a number of times, that the space between two thoughts is not silence.

**K** : I would say that the space between two thoughts is not silence but that the total ending of thought is silence. This means the total ending of time. Time coming to a stop is complete silence.

**PJ** : The query is: Can a person who has not observed time in operation in consciousness, time as thought, time as judgement, time as becoming and, so, is not familiar with the process of becoming, suddenly leap from a state of becoming—a state whose implications he is totally unaware of—into the other?

**K** : Obviously not.

**PJ** : Then we are back where we were.

**K** : Not quite. Let's be clear. You are asking, Pupulji—aren't you?—whether there has been a radical change in the Teaching. You are asking whether there has been, after thirty years, a movement away from observation, a movement away from a questioning of the division between the thinker and thought and the whole content of consciousness. You are asking whether there is a difference or a fundamental change in the Teaching from that of thirty years ago to today. That is the basic question, isn't it?

**PJ** : Yes, that is the basic question.

**K** : Could we begin from today and look back to yesterday? That is, could we look not from yesterday to today, but from today to yesterday? Do you follow what I am saying?

**PJ** : Yes.

**K** : Could we do that?

**PJ** : But, a person like me looking from today to yesterday had a yesterday.

**K** : Yes, but you are looking at yesterday with a different mind, with a different eye which you hadn't yesterday.

**PJ** : I agree, sir, but my point is that without the yesterday . . . .

**K** : There would be no today.

**PJ** : Without the yesterday would it be possible for me, today, to look back at the yesterday?

**K** : Now, wait a minute. I haven't quite understood your question. Go slowly.

**PJ** : You said: Can you look back from today to yesterday? And I said: I had a yesterday and, therefore, from today I can look back at the yesterday . . . .

**K** : Yes, naturally.

**PJ** : But if I did not have the yesterday . . . .

**K** : Go slowly, go slowly. If you had no yesterday, you are saying, you could not look back from today to yesterday.

**PJ** : No, I make a further statement: I cannot *be* today.

**K** : You cannot be today, obviously. But Pupul, there is something else in what you are saying, something which we have to be clear about. You say: You had a yesterday, so from yesterday you can look at today. I said: Look from today to yesterday. To that you said: If I had no yesterday, I couldn't look from today. But I did not introduce the *not* having a yesterday. You carried on a little further. Don't, please, carry it further; wait; proceed slowly.

Thirty years ago, which is yesterday, there was a certain category or a certain expression of this Teaching. Now, after thirty years you are asking: Has that Teaching, of thirty years, undergone a deep change? To that I say: Can you as you are today look back to thirty years ago, and not the other way round? That's all I am asking. Don't bring in a new element into it for the time being.

Pupul, would you say from the position of today that there has been a change when you look back to thirty years ago? Please, don't think that I am turning the tables on you. I am only asking you this in order to find out how you look at the past from your position today, and not in order to catch you out, as it were. You see, I think how you look at yesterday is a valid question. *(Long pause)*

**PJ** : Yes, I will answer. There has been no change; basically there is no change.

**K** : Why do you say that?

**PJ** : Because in-built into this holistic seeing is the seeing and listening which I came to yesterday. The holistic seeing, or the immobility that you speak about, holds all that.

**K** : Wait, Pupul, wait. The past, or rather the present, holds the entirety of the past.

**PJ** : I do not speak of it as memory, Krishnaji. Please let me make it very clear; I am not speaking of it as memory.

**K** : I understand what you are saying. The present holds the past.

**PJ** : It holds the totality.

**K** : The totality of the past.

**PJ** : Sir, you asked me a question.

**K** : Yes. Can you look from today to yesterday? When you look from today to yesterday, you are looking not only with the memory of yesterday, but you are also looking at it with different eyes.

**PJ** : Yes, sir, but my query still is not answered.

**K** : No, perhaps not; but we will explore it as we go along. I was asking: Can you look from today to all the yesterdays? This is a very interesting question. I don't know what the others feel, but I think that this is an extraordinary question which invites a great deal of debate. Now, to come back. Thirty years ago there was a certain Teaching and today, I am saying, that it is a holistic Teaching. Let's put it that way for the time being. You are asking if this whole movement of thirty years has brought about a basic change. I would say that there is no basic change.

**PJ** : My query is: Without the process of self-knowing and the observation of 'what is', is this possible?

**K** : Yes, it is possible. Without those thirty years of exploration, without those thirty years of discussion and examination of consciousness and its content and so on and so on—without all that—one can comprehend, one can be aware of and have an insight into this whole thing immediately. How shall we explore this? Right?

**PJ** : Sir, you may not have felt it, but thirty years ago the people around you felt that you took them by the hand . . . .

**K** : Yes, I know; they have told me.

**PJ** : Now you have taken away your hands.

**K** : I understand and, perhaps, we are also a little more mature.

**PJ** : But what has brought about this maturity? The thirty years?

**K** : No. Let's go into this a little bit. *(Long pause)* Why do you, if I may ask, go back thirty years? I am not stopping you; I am just asking you, why do you go back thirty years?

**PJ** : I will tell you why, sir. I have been wanting to see, very objectively, what has been taking place in the Teaching over the last thirty years. I have been wanting to see what has been taking place not only as it has come through in the written word but as it comes through within me.

**K :** Yes.

**PJ :** As I was going into it for myself, certain things became very obvious. There are three distinct periods in your Teaching. These are periods when changes took place and a totally different position was evident.

**K :** Would you explain it a little bit?

**PJ :** There was the period when you spoke of self-knowledge and what I have discussed already . . . .

**K :** Yes.

**PJ :** Then around the sixties you moved away from there and you talked about this totality of seeing. You were concerned about this totality of seeing and yet you spoke of the ending of thought as being silence. Today, you have put all that aside. You never discuss any particular subject but take the whole. Today you have a more—forgive me for using this word—'cosmic' way of speaking.

**K :** Yes.

**PJ :** And you are more precise in the language you use. You ask, in almost scientific terms: Can the brain cells themselves hold the holistic?

**K :** Do I?

**PJ :** That's why I wanted to move slowly into this position.

**K :** So let's begin. What is the first thing you are asking? Leave the three things, we will come to them later.

**PJ :** Sir, if you say that the process of self-knowing, the process of going into the self, and that of observation are not necessary and that the holistic position is possible immediately, then the question is: What is it that triggers it? That is the major query.

**K** : Oh, my lord!

**PJ** : I understand the other position. I understand what careful observation is. I understand the process of becoming. I understand the movement of it. But today you are making a major departure. You are saying today that the holistic position, holistic seeing, is possible *now*. But what brings the maturity to the eye and the ear and the process of learning which makes it possible?

**K** : Pupul, what is it you are trying to tell me now?

**PJ** : Sir, you say that the holistic position is possible here and now. My major query is: Without the thirty years . . . .

**K** : I understand. So let's examine that statement. I may be wrong or I may be saying something which is not accurate, so one must go into this carefully.

Are you asking: How can a blind man see light or, to put it differently, how can one, without any preparation, have a holistic view? It comes to that, doesn't it? Without going through all the examination, all the exploration and detailed observation, without all that activity, can one see, immediately, the totality of all existence? Right? That is the basic question, isn't it?

**PJ** : Yes.

**K** : That is, without thirty years 'preparation', is it possible to see the totality of all existence, to see the wholeness of consciousness? Right?

**PJ** : Which means a totally empty consciousness.

**K** : No, no, not empty. Let's go slowly. Seeing the totality of consciousness . . . .

**PJ** : Which is the past.

**K** : Wait, wait, wait. I know it is the past. You are asking a question which is: Without preparation, without the drill, without all that examination, is it possible to see the total content of consciousness and move out of it? Right?

**PJ** : And be totally immobile.

**K** : That is the question. Is that possible? I say: Yes. Have I stuck my neck out? It doesn't matter. I still maintain that it is possible to see the whole content of consciousness which is the movement of thought, with all its different categories and types and characteristics instantly and to move out of it, reaching a point where thought comes to an end. Let's put it that way for the time being. Yes, I will stick to that, and I maintain it not out of obstinacy or stubbornness or because I think that as nobody else has said this it's good to say it. I don't maintain this because of any such absurd thing.

**PJ** : Was the position then not true?

**K** : No, I wouldn't say that it was not true.

**PJ** : The position then was true, because the perception of the thinker and thought was a total perception.

**K** : Yes, yes.

**PJ** : As total as this.

**K** : Yes, quite right. However, in explaining the totality of that perception, one had to go into details. But then, as now, it was a total perception.

**PJ** : But, if you had not spoken and there had not been a listening to that observing—observing the mind, judging, condemning, wanting—and if there had not been an actual perception, this would not have been possible. How does one proceed?

**K** : Without going through all that, Pupul, could we just say: Is it possible? That is the real crux of the question.

**PJ** : What you said then was as total and as true as anything you say today.

11

**K** : I agree. K may have said something out of totality, just as he is now saying something out of totality. In that saying there may have been a detailed examination.

**PJ** : Yes, yes.

**K** : But that examination was born from the totality of perception.

**PJ** : Yes.

**K** : And therefore it is still total.

**PJ** : I agree sir; I think it is so too. But, for the person who comes for the first time, the question as to whether that is still not necessary remains.

**K** : You see, Pupul, you are saying the same thing.

**PJ** : Must one not see the process of becoming?

**K** : Must you not go through school, through college, through university to reach the final examination? Without going through all that, can you come to this?

**PJ** : I know you will say no, because that would involve a process and it would involve time. I know that; but I say that was total and true then . . . .

**K** : As now.

**PJ** : As now.

**K** : Then what's the question?

**PJ** : For the person who starts, it's the most crucial thing.

**K** : I understand this.

**PJ** : If you say that you can plunge straight into this holistic position, the question then is 'how'. As you showed us then, sir, show us now.

**K** : Yes, all right; I understand. K is saying that there is no preparation necessary—the preparation of thirty years.

Now is that valid? That is: Can one observe without the past? Right? Can one have an insight without the weight of yesterday and can that insight be instantaneous? Am I stating the question correctly?

**PJ** : Yes.

**K** : The perception of the totality can only come about instantly.

**PJ** : Yes.

**K** : It cannot come through time, through thought, through exploration. That perception of the whole can only take place instantly. Now, if that is so, then what is the need for preparation?

**PJ** : Would you call all that preparation?

**K** : What?

**PJ** : The observing, learning . . . .

**K** : Pupul, thirty years; I am talking of thirty years.

**PJ** : If you see the thirty years as 'time', I want to drop the thirty years.

**K** : No, Pupul, I would like to point this out: It is only possible to have complete, total, insight immediately, instantly and that instant is not contained in time. Right?

**PJ** : Yes.

**K** : X cannot see this. He says: Tell me what I have to do in order to have this extraordinary insight immediately. And K tells him: Observe the thinker and the thought. He also says that there is no division between the thinker and the thought. Now, the question is, as this is being explained, is X listening, or is there a process of abstraction taking place which pushes X away from the instant action? K says that the thinker and the thought are identical; they are not separate. Can you see, instantly, the truth of it or do you say: I must think it over?

**PJ :** I understand. But, sir, the brain that has observed—and that observation has deepened—*is* capable of receiving when you speak.

**K :** No, Pupul, I question whether it is not capable of receiving *without* the thirty years.

**PJ :** If this is so . . . .

**K :** Why haven't people seen? That would be the normal question. They don't see because they are not actually listening.

Now just listen carefully. This person, K, says that the perception of the totality is instant. And the questioner then says: Tell me what to do; please help me to understand what you say.

**PJ :** The moment that question is asked, it is like asking someone—you—to give me insight.

**K :** Nobody can give it to you.

**PJ :** Then I am stuck.

**K :** No, wait a minute. Look at the question. You ask: Can you give it to me? And K says: No, it cannot be given by anyone. Wait a minute. What is your reaction to that statement, namely, that nothing and nobody—no guru, no time, no evolution, no experience—can give it to you?

**PJ :** To that I would say, yes.

**K :** Yes, but don't you also ask: Since it cannot be given and I haven't got that insight, what am I to do? That would be a normal, healthy reaction. *(Pause)* To that K says: Listen to what K is saying. Listen. Don't weave it into a theory or a speculative abstraction. Just listen to that statement: Nobody can give it to you. If you listen, and if it is the truth, it must have a tremendous effect on you because your whole attention is captured in listening to the fact that no time is necessary, no preparation is necessary.

**PJ** : But do you think, sir, that a person who has not delved into the self can listen like this?

**K** : He cannot, because even though he may delve into himself, he won't listen to this. Pupulji, listen. Would you listen to the fact that nobody can give it to you?

**PJ** : Yes.

**K** : What has happened to your mind? If you so listen, what has taken place?

If you are dependent on a guru or on an outside agency such as a God and so on, would you listen? Or would you say: I am too frightened to listen to what you are saying, because that means I have to abandon everything? There is fear and you say: I won't listen to you because that means I have to give up my whole dependency on something which I have cultivated for millennia. That is the difficulty, Pupul.

**PJ** : You have said something just now. But you still have not answered my first query whether there has been a deep change in your Teaching.

**K** : None at all.

He talked about authority, he still speaks about authority; he talked about fear, he still talks about fear; he talked about consciousness in different sets of terms, he still talks about it. He said thought must end, and he still speaks of it. He spoke of the nature of desire, and he still speaks of it.

**PJ** : May I ask a question, Krishnaji? Do you, during these years—I am hesitant to use the word 'years' because again you will say time, and so on—think that there has been any inner change in you? I am asking this very seriously.

**K :** Let me observe it. I have never been asked this question before. Has there been a deep change in me from thirty years ago or from when I started, in the beginning? To be really truthful and accurate: No. Yes, there have been changes in expression, changes in vocabulary, changes in language and gesture—you know all that—but there has been no fundamental change from the beginning till now.

**PJ :** So what we see . . . .

**K :** That is immobility. Have you got it? Let's go into this.

Listen to this statement, namely, that the perception of the total is immediate. Time is not necessary; preparation is not necessary. Examination, exploration, will not help you to perceive that instant totally. You say to me: What is your next instruction? What am I to do? Right? To which I naturally reply: Don't do anything, just listen. For if you listen, accurately, to the statement that time, preparation, the whole process of evolution is unnecessary, if you listen—not just accept or take it and observe it and say, 'Yes, I have understood it'—you will have instant perception.

Come, let's discuss it. You see, Pupul, the point is that our whole attitude, our whole way of life, is based on evolution—on becoming, on growing, on achieving, and on finally reaching God. I think that basic assumption, that basic conditioning, is radically false. Now do you see the falseness of it instantly, or do you say, 'Wait a minute; this, that, and the other'?

**PJ :** No sir, I would say that I see the truth of that.

**K :** Wait a minute; go slowly, Pupul. What do you mean when you say that you see the truth of it?

**PJ :** I can listen to that without a ripple, without a movement in consciousness.

**K :** If you so listen, what takes place? Let us say that the Buddha said to me, 'The ending of sorrow is the bliss of compassion'. I

16

don't examine this statement. I don't translate this statement into my way of thinking. I don't question it; I don't analyse it; I don't say, 'What do you mean by it?' I am only in a state of acute, total, attention of listening—nothing else—because that statement has enormous truth and there is tremendous content in that statement.

Then I would say to the Buddha, 'Forgive me, sir, but I am not capable of such intense action or non-action—whatever it is—of listening, so please help me'. Right? So the Buddha says, 'First listen to what I have said, namely, that no agency that the mind, that thought, has invented, will help you. Nothing will help you. There is not even an outside agency that will help you to have this tremendous "insight".' I listen and I am frightened. For that means that I must drop everything that I am attached to. And I ask, 'How am I to be detached?' You see, my reasoning is false. My reasoning—the questioner's reasoning—is false. The moment I ask, 'How am I to be detached?', I am lost.

He says, 'Be detached', but I am not listening. I have a great reverence for him, but I am not listening. I am not listening because attachment has been a tremendous thing in my life, and in one stroke he says, 'Throw it out'. And in one instant I must throw it out . . . .

**QUESTIONER (Q) :** Is the dropping also the moment of perception?

**K :** Yes. The moment you see the fact that you must be free of all knowledge . . . . But the man who has spent his life collecting knowledge from books and all the rest of it, says, 'What are you talking about?'

**PJ :** Krishnaji, may I ask one question?

**K :** You may ask lots of questions; we've got today and tomorrow, so come on.

**PJ :** A statement like, you say, the Buddha makes: Is it a question—I am putting it this way because I know of no other so, please, listen—of holding the totality of that statement without the word?

**K :** Yes, of course. The word is not the thing. The statement, the description, of the flowering, and all that, is not the thing; therefore there must be freedom from the word. And then the questioner says, 'Please help me to be free of the word'. You see, then one is lost. That's why I am saying that the intensity of listening is the real crux of it.

**PJ :** What is it that gives that intensity?

**K :** That intensity? Nothing.

Our whole way of thinking is based on growth; it is based on becoming, on evolving. I see a child and he grows to manhood. I see technological growth—it takes years and years for some scientific discovery or technique to be perfected. So everything is a growth. Everything is a becoming, a growing, an expanding. Now somebody comes along and says, 'That's right in certain places but it has nothing whatsoever to do with enlightenment'— let's use that word for the moment. The mind being heavily conditioned by the tradition of growth, man won't even listen.

You see, Pupul, you may say something which is totally accurate, totally true, something that is immovable, irrevocable. And what you say may have tremendous insight behind it. But the difficulty, Pupul, is that I cannot listen to it because I have commitments. I am attached. And because of this I don't listen to this extraordinary statement.

So, to answer your question whether there has been, between the thirties, the forties and now, a fundamental change in me, I say: No, there has been a considerable change in expression, in the way I use words and so on, but the basic Teaching is the same.

*Brockwood Park*
*11 June 1978*

# What is Consciousness?

**PUPUL JAYAKAR (PJ)** : Could we inquire into some of the terms that you use, for through the years these words have been used by you in different senses, with different meanings? The words I want to inquire into are 'consciousness', the 'mind', the 'brain cells' and 'thought'.

I feel that you use the words 'consciousness' and the 'mind' in various ways. Sometimes you use the words 'consciousness' and the 'mind' as if they were one, sometimes you use the word 'mind' as synonymous with 'thought', and sometimes you seem to suggest that the 'mind' contains thought but that it is, itself, not thought.

**J. KRISHNAMURTI (K)** : So, shall we begin with the word 'consciousness'?

**PJ** : Yes, but as long as we bring in all these four words.

**K** : Yes. Of course. Pupul, what does consciousness mean to you? What does the word and the content of that word mean to you?

**PJ** : It means the sense of existing, of being. It means the sense that one *is*. You see, one only discovers the fact that one is because of consciousness.

**K** : Are you using the word 'consciousness' as synonymous with existence? For you see, if I may point out, I think that I am using the word 'consciousness' in a different way. I am using the word 'consciousness' not only as mere existence but also to include the turmoil in that existence. All the mischief, all the trouble and anxiety, all the fear, the pleasure, the sorrow, the love, the hate, and the hurts that one receives—all that is implied in that word consciousness.

**PJ** : Yes, but that is existence. Why are you not prepared to accept that word?

**K** : I'm a little shy of that word because I don't think that existence conveys the totality of one's consciousness.

**PJ** : Doesn't it, sir?

**K** : I am not sure. It may but, as I said, I'm rather shy of that word.

**PJ** : Existence is everything. It is the want, the not-want. It is the looking, the listening; it is memory, desire. It is everything.

**K** : All right, we won't quibble over that word.

**PJ** : Yes. It means the total content of what exists.

**K** : It means the total content of one's life.

**PJ** : Yes.

**K** : Is one aware of the total content of one's life?

**PJ** : No, not in a total sense.

**K** : So is one aware of the total content of consciousness, or only aware, at different times, of different parts of consciousness? You see, one is aware that one is hurt psychologically; one is also aware that one is hurt physiologically—after all, they react upon each other and so on. One may be aware of that hurt for a certain period—say for a day or two—and then one moves away from that hurt to pleasure.

**PJ** : Yes.

**K** : So, you see, we are never concerned with the totality of consciousness; we are only concerned with parts of it.

**PJ** : Because that is how it reveals itself.

**K** : Does it? Does the part reveal the whole?

**PJ** : No, sir, I am not saying that the part reveals the whole. *You* are saying that, sir. I am only saying that the part is revealed in the mind as a fragment. Consciousness reveals itself in the mind as a fragment.

**K** : I am not sure. Wait a minute. I'd like to be clear on this point. Does *consciousness* reveal the part in the mind, or is it that as thought—please, let me go slowly—in itself is a fragment, we can only see the fragmentation of consciousness? Let us be clear about this.

**PJ** : I don't quite follow that, Krishnaji.

**K** : Wait, wait. I am hurt psychologically. Somebody says something brutal to me and I am hurt. That hurt is part of my consciousness.

**PJ** : Yes, it is.

**K** : Just a minute. Let us go slowly. Thought is part of consciousness. Thought is a fragment; it is a limited movement. Now that limited movement, that fragment, says, 'I am hurt'. Now remember, Pupul, thought being in itself a fragment, it cannot see the whole.

**PJ** : Sir, when thought says, 'I am hurt' . . . .

**K** : No, thought doesn't say, 'I am hurt'.

**PJ** : All right, when thought sees that it is hurt . . . .

**K** : No. *Thought* doesn't say, 'I am hurt'. *I* say, 'I am hurt'; *I* say, 'I am jealous', 'I am anxious'.

**PJ** : Yes. But that moment itself, that moment of 'I am', is a thought formation.

**K** : We have to go very slowly into this question of the 'I'. The 'I' is put together by thought.

**PJ** : Yes.

**K** : The name, the form, the attributes, the qualities, the characteristics—all that—thought has put together. That thing, that major structure—which is the 'me', the 'I'—has been put together by thought.

**PJ** : Yes.

**K** : So when somebody says something brutal, *I* say, 'I am hurt'; *thought* doesn't say that.

**PJ** : Who says it? Who says, 'I am hurt'?

**K** : The thing that thought has put together as the 'me'. Let us say, for example, that X calls me a fool. Now, in point of fact, I am a fool, but I don't know it. I think that I am awfully brilliant. But X comes along and says, 'Don't be silly; you are nothing but an ass; you are stupid'. I don't like it. I am hurt. In exploring that hurt thought comes into operation; in exploration, I discover that thought has built the 'me'.

**PJ** : Yes.

**K** : So thought is never aware that it is hurt. Thought thinks that I am hurt. Thought thinks that the 'I' is different from it. Thought actually thinks that.

**PJ** : Yes, thought thinks that it is different.

**K** : Thought thinks that it is different from the structure which it has built.

**PJ** : The structure which is hurt.

**K** : Which is hurt, yes. So, thought can never be aware of the total content of consciousness. It can only be aware of the fragments.

**PJ** : What is the total content of consciousness?

**K** : We are going to find out. We began by discussing the word 'consciousness', and you used the word 'existence'. You said that consciousness implies existence. I said that the word 'existence' doesn't quite give the full meaning. So, I am looking for a word that will give a holistic meaning to consciousness. Do you understand?

**PJ** : Has it a holistic meaning, sir? Can you put it within a holistic situation?

**K** : I think one can. First of all, what is the content of consciousness? The content is everything that thought has put there. Right?

**PJ** : Yes.

**K** : And thought, in examining consciousness, can only see the fragment.

**PJ** : Yes.

**K** : So, thought cannot fundamentally perceive or comprehend the totality of consciousness. That's simple.

**PJ** : Yes.

**K** : Now, when someone like me uses the word 'consciousness'— perhaps wrongly—it means the totality of life. You see, for me, 'consciousness' means not only my life, your life, and X's life, but the life of the animal and that of the tree; it encompasses the whole; it encompasses the totality of all that.

**PJ** : Sir, today you are using the word very differently.

**K** : Yes, I know; I'm sorry I'm moving away from what I said.

**PJ** : Yes. In this last sentence you've said that consciousness is the totality of life.

**K :** It is the totality of life.

**PJ :** So it includes the insect, the bird, the leaf . . . ?

**K :** They have their own feelings and I have my own—you follow? You see, Pupul, I think that consciousness is global but limited.

**PJ :** Global but limited?

**K :** Yes. I am just feeling around. What do you say? Nobody jumps on me here. I say that consciousness is . . . I won't go into this for a moment.

**PJ :** What you have said just now is very, very new and I'd like to pursue it. You have always said that consciousness is its content.

**K :** Yes.

**PJ :** The content is the past as experience. Now you are saying that consciousness is total, that it is the totality of life.

**K :** Yes.

**PJ :** Which is very different from my experience of life.

**K :** What do you mean 'your experience of life'? Just a minute. Your experience of life is the experience of every human being.

**PJ :** Yes, but there are many aspects which are different. I have many experiences which are mine. But you are implying, now, that the totality of all life . . . .

**K :** No, there may be different colours, different sounds, but they are all the same thing, in the same direction.

**PJ :** You are implying that what is 'within' may be the experiences of man.

**K :** Yes. Let's limit it to that. Your life is the life of man. Your life is the life of humanity. Right?

**PJ** : Yes.

**K** : So, you are not, basically, different from humanity. You might have different coloured hair, a different face, name, and so on. I am not talking about all that. Basically you are humanity; you are the rest of mankind.

**PJ** : Yes.

**K** : Your consciousness is the consciousness of mankind.

**PJ** : Yes, but you have said something different, Krishnaji.

**K** : Wait a minute. I'm coming to that; I'm coming to that. Mankind goes through all kinds of travail, all kinds of trouble. Every human being goes through the most terrible times.

**PJ** : Yes.

**K** : Now, doesn't everything else go through it also? Insects, birds, every animal and tree—all nature goes through various kinds of turmoil. I am using the word 'turmoil' in the sense of disturbance.

**PJ** : Do you mean by this, Krishnaji, that consciousness is the whole phenomenon of life?

**K** : Wait a minute; just wait a minute. I'll have to go awfully carefully here. What do you mean by the word 'phenomenon'?

**PJ** : The phenomenon is that which can be perceived by the senses.

**K** : By 'perceived' you mean touched, tasted, and so on.

**PJ** : Yes, open to the senses.

**K** : But that's only a part of it, isn't it?

**PJ** : What is the other part?

**K** : All the accumulated knowledge, experience and so on. All the psychological agonies of man, which you cannot touch, which you cannot taste. The psychological turmoil may affect the body, and then the organism tastes the pain of anxiety.

**PJ :** Yes, and it is the anxiety of mankind.

**K :** Yes. This is the process of mankind. So it is global.

**PJ :** You are using the word 'global' in a special way . . . .

**K :** I know.

**PJ :** You see, it is as though there is something . . . .

**K :** I withdraw that word. It is—what? Universal? It is common; it is the fate of man; it is what is happening in the world.

**PJ :** Why would you then object to the word 'cosmic'?

**K :** I think the word 'cosmic' means order—the cosmos as opposed to chaos.

**PJ :** But after all, sir, the cosmic is the totality of this; it's not the fragment.

**K :** No, no. If we use the word 'cosmic', we have to be very careful because, you see, the word 'cosmos' apparently means order. And the human mind is not in order; human consciousness is not in order.

**PJ :** Yes, but now—apart from the superficial, fragmentary movement of the human mind—you have brought in many other elements. You have brought in the whole of the racial past, the whole of this accumulated movement.

**K :** Yes, tradition.

**PJ :** You see, sir, you have brought in centuries and centuries which, when seen together . . . .

**K :** But I wouldn't say that it is cosmic. You see, one has to be very careful with one's words. 'Cosmos' means total order; it is opposed to chaos, which is disorder. And our minds are in disorder. Our consciousness is in disorder. Right?

**PJ** : Yes.

**K** : So it cannot be called cosmic.

**PJ** : The human mind cannot be called cosmic, but . . . .

**K** : No, no, Pupul, I am talking about human consciousness; that's all.

**PJ** : But then how do you bring into human consciousness the total content of life?

**K** : We have not understood each other.

**PJ** : Aren't you bringing in the totality of life?

**K** : No. I am just saying that consciousness, as we have just used the word, is the common factor of man. Consciousness is common to all mankind.

**PJ** : Yes.

**K** : That consciousness with its content is confusion, conflict, and all the rest of it. Right?

**PJ** : Yes.

**K** : That consciousness cannot be called cosmic.

**PJ** : No, I agree; that cannot be called cosmic.

**K** : That's all.

**PJ** : Yes, I agree. But you have gone much beyond that in what you have said about consciousness.

**K** : Yes.

**PJ** : It is not just the individual confusion . . . .

**K** : No, you see, I question whether there is individuality at all.

**PJ :** Well, remove the word 'individual'. But experience, confusion, chaos, anxiety, fear, anger—when you talk of the total fact of life . . . .

**K :** No, no. My point is: Can thought be aware of the totality of consciousness? That's what we said.

**PJ :** And we said that it cannot be aware.

**K :** Yes, it cannot be. So, now, what is the question you are raising?

**PJ :** You see, this has come about because we raised the initial question of what the distinction between consciousness, the mind, the brain and thought is.

**K :** Right. We have now, more or less, understood what we mean by consciousness.

**PJ :** Yes. And what we mean by thought also.

**K :** Wait a minute. I want to be clear. If thought cannot be aware of the total content of consciousness, then what is it that's going to perceive the totality? Do you follow? Because if I don't perceive the totality of my consciousness and I can only deal with the fragments of my consciousness—and the fragments are endless—there must come into operation a factor that sees the totality of consciousness. Right?

**PJ :** Yes.

**K :** So, what is that factor? Is it the mind? Wait a minute. We are questioning whether it is the mind. It certainly is not thought.

**PJ :** It's not thought.

**K :** It certainly is not the brain cells, the brain.

**PJ :** Now, when you say that it is certainly not the brain cells, you mean that it is certainly not the brain cells as they exist.

**K :** Wait, let's proceed slowly. I'm not a brain specialist, but I think that we can be sure when we say that the cells carry memory. Right?

**PJ** : Yes.

**K** : And the memories are part of thought. Therefore the brain, as it is now, the brain that we are using, employing, cannot perceive the totality of consciousness.

**PJ** : Yes.

**K** : Right. Thought cannot see it because thought is part of consciousness. Right? The brain, the activity of the brain, cannot comprehend the totality of consciousness.

Then, we come to the mind. Can the mind perceive the totality? But first, what is the mind? Look, Pupulji, let's be more, if we can use the word, practical—I don't like that word 'practical', but . . . .

**PJ** : Yes.

**K** : Now, let's get back. What is the mind?

**PJ** : Yes, what is the mind? I really would like to know.

**K** : You see, I want to find out whether there is a state, whether there is a movement, beyond consciousness. Do you follow?

**PJ** : Yes. That's basically the reason for inquiry.

**K** : That is the basic question here. Therefore I must understand the movement of thought. I must have an understanding of the activity of the brain, which is part of thinking.

**PJ** : Yes.

**K** : I must find out whether that brain can manufacture or invent or fabricate or produce a perception which is beyond this consciousness.

**PJ** : Yes.

**K** : I don't think that the brain, as it is now, can. So, we are asking: Can the mind perceive the totality of consciousness? From that question follows: What is the mind?

**PJ** : You have used the word 'mind' in several ways.

**K** : Yes, I know. Is the mind the intellect? It is part of it, of course. Can the intellect perceive the totality of consciousness?

**PJ** : Is the intellect separate from thought, separate from reason?

**K** : No, it's not; of course it's not. But we think that the intellect is the most extraordinary thing we have. Right? We worship the intellect.

**PJ** : Yes.

**K** : Yes, but we don't have to go into it now. So, to come back: Can the intellect perceive the totality of consciousness? Obviously not. Because the intellect is part of thought and the usage of thought whether brilliantly or negligently, or efficiently or loosely, is all the same.

So, the intellect is part of the mind. The mind is also part of sentiment, emotions, feelings. Right?

**PJ** : Yes.

**K** : Now, can sentiment, romanticism, emotions, perceive the totality?

**PJ** : But you are using the 'mind' as if it were an instrument. You see, you ask, 'Can it perceive?'

**K** : Can it become aware? Put it differently, it doesn't matter.

**PJ** : No, but I would like to ask you whether the mind is an instrument or whether it is a field.

**K** : Are you asking whether the mind is a field?

**PJ** : Yes. Is it a field or an instrument? That's what I am asking.

**K** : Does the mind cover the whole field or only a part, a segment, a tiny corner of the field?

**PJ** : You see, sir, I am pursuing this because I want to get a clarification from you on your usage of words.

**K** : We are finding clarity, Pupul.

**PJ** : No, sir, I might see the mind as synonymous with thought. *I* might see it as such.

**K** : Wait a minute, Pupul. The mind includes the intellect.

**PJ** : Yes.

**K** : The intellect is part of thought.

**PJ** : Yes.

**K** : Feelings, emotions, sentiment, romanticism, imagination—all that is also a part of thought.

**PJ** : And the senses?

**K** : No, the senses are not; but thought identifies itself with the senses.

**PJ** : What part do the senses play in all this? I mean, we know the process of perception, sensation, and all that.

**K** : I don't think emotions, sentiment, and all that can possibly bring about a perception of the whole. I don't think that sentiment, emotion and sensation can ever offer a perception of the whole.

**PJ** : So you would rule out the senses as such?

**K** : No, no. I don't rule out the senses. The senses exist.

**PJ** : Yes.

**K** : I feel pain when you stick a pin . . . .

**PJ** : Are they being wrongly used?

**K :** As I said, when thought identifies itself with the senses, then the sensation becomes the 'me'.

**PJ :** Yes, because then there is a movement outward; there is a movement towards.

**K :** Towards, yes. 'I want', 'I don't want', and all the rest of it. So, the mind, you say, is the field. Field of what? The matrix?

**PJ :** No, because the matrix, again, circumscribes it.

**K :** Yes. So the field, again, is circumscribed.

**PJ :** But you see, sir, then there is no word . . . .

**K :** So, I'm just asking whether the mind which includes the brain, thought, the emotions, the intellect . . . .

**PJ :** Yes.

**K :** Ah, wait a minute; wait a minute. Is love part of the field? Is love part of the mind?

**PJ :** So, if love is not part of the mind . . . .

**K :** I don't know. I'm asking, but I don't think it is. The senses are part of the mind and thought identifies itself with the senses. Is love different from consciousness?

**PJ :** See, the moment you bring in the word 'love', sir, you have . . . .

**K :** We'll go into it. That is very important. We'll go into it, because that is part of our consciousness. Love is part of our consciousness.

**PJ :** As we know it, it is part of our consciousness.

**K :** Yes, as we know it. So, I include that. Does the mind include love? Now, what we call love is based on sensation, desire, pleasure. I love you; I love something. So, love, as we know it, is part of our consciousness. Right?

**PJ** : Yes.

**K** : Love, with its jealousies, antagonisms, quarrels, and all the rest of it, is part of consciousness.

**PJ** : No, but you didn't use love in that sense. Because if you did use it in that sense, then it would be no different from any other emotion.

**K** : So, is there a love, or is there a quality which is not part of consciousness? *(Pause)*

**PJ** : You see, the problem arises because, while you have gone through all the other things—the intellect, the mind, thought, the brain—you only discuss the senses as identified with desire, which go to build up the structure of the self. My question is: Have the senses any other role?

**K** : Yes. Wait a minute, let's get it clear. I think I have got the germ of it, the kernel of it. When you observe with all your senses, there is no identification with a particular sense. Right?

**PJ** : Yes.

**QUESTIONER (Q)** : Are you implying that the senses become one?

**K** : No.

**Q** : You don't distinguish between one sense and another?

**K** : No, sir, that's not what I'm implying. I am asking you whether you can look at something with all your senses awakened.

**PJ** : Isn't it, sir, a question of whether you can look and listen in the same instant, the same moment, of time?

**K** : You see, the question is whether it is possible to observe with all your senses, and whether, in that state, there is a single movement of thought. When there is a movement of thought, then it is a particular sense operating.

**PJ** : Yes.

**K :** Let us pursue this further because as human beings there is a natural curiosity, a natural urge, to find out if there's a totally different dimension which is not the dimension of consciousness as we know it. I don't mean something that is invented by thought. Right?

**PJ :** Yes.

**K :** And it becomes important to find that out.

**PJ :** You see, you have examined and negated all the known instruments that we have and with which we operate.

**K :** Yes.

**PJ :** The only thing which you don't totally negate is the quality of sensory movement.

**K :** How can I negate the senses?

**PJ :** Yes. So, that being quite independent or, to put it this way, that having the capacity to contain in it no illusion . . . .

**K :** The illusion is created by thought.

**PJ :** Yes. So, that having in itself the capacity to be free of illusion . . . .

**K :** That is only possible when there has been an awareness of the movement of thought, when there has been an awareness of the activity of thought.

**PJ :** Yes.

**K :** That is possible only when there has been an awareness of the whole nature of thought. Then the senses do not produce the psychological structure as the 'me'. That's all.

Look, Pupul, let's come down to earth—not that this is theoretical. As a human being, one perceives that one's consciousness is in total disorder. Right?

**PJ** : Yes.

**K** : And any movement away from that disorder inevitably leads to illusions. Now my question is: Is it possible to bring about order? Let us go step by step. I am using myself as an example of a human being. My consciousness is in disorder. I am aware of it. I am aware of all the things that are going on endlessly in my consciousness : anger, jealousy, hatred, possessiveness, attachment, domination. I want to bring about order in my consciousness, because I see the necessity of order. Order means harmony. The question is: Is it possible to bring it about?

We've discussed consciousness; we've discussed thought; we've discussed the mind, the feelings, and so on. What instrument or what quality is necessary to move out of this enchaining circle of consciousness?

**PJ** : You see, sir, this last question is very valid. The previous statement, namely, that I want to bring about order, is one of the things I have never understood.

**K** : Just a minute, Pupul, let's be clear. I am using these words to convey that there must be total order for the cosmic to be. I don't know what the cosmos is, but I realize that there is total disorder in my life. There is disorder and, therefore, there is misery, confusion, uncertainty, quarrels, and all the extraordinary things that go on in everyday life. So, order is necessary. Now, who is to bring that order? That's my point. Will the mind bring order? Will feelings, sensations, imagination—all that—bring order? Will thought bring order? On the contrary, thought cannot.

**PJ** : All these are fragments.

**K** : Yes, fragments. So, what will? Let's discuss it; let's go into it.

**PJ** : That is why I say, sir, that there is only one instrument that you leave free. That is, you allow only one instrument the possibility of being free of taint.

**K** : The senses?

**PJ** : Yes, the senses. You have blocked every other instrument . . . .

**K** : Yes, we have blocked every hole that the human mind has invented. Have we also blocked the senses?

**PJ** : I see that when the senses identified with thought operate, they only strengthen the structure which is the basic cause of confusion.

**K** : So, is there a separation between thought and the senses, so that thought is not active but only the senses?

**PJ** : Isn't there?

**K** : I'm asking.

**PJ** : Krishnaji, isn't the nature of seeing quite different from the optical thing which says, 'This is a tree'? There is the seeing or listening *per se,* independent of what is seen or what is heard. If I may put it this way, sir, that instrument is in itself not corrupted. Now, I say . . . .

**K** : What are you saying? The instrument which is thought . . . .

**PJ** : No, no. I am saying that the instrument which is seeing, the instrument which is listening, is not corrupt. It gets corrupted when it gets identified with thought.

**K** : That's right. It gets corrupted when it is identified with opinions, with judgements, with evaluations. So, listening correctly, listening accurately, is incorruptible. Yes, that is so. But is that the instrument that will help human beings like us bring about order?

**PJ** : If you deny all instruments . . . .

**K** : I must be careful here. What do you mean by an 'instrument'? You are saying that the mind is an instrument, that thought is an instrument.

**PJ** : Yes, the brain is an instrument, thought is an instrument.

**K** : If we are using the word 'instrument' in that sense . . . .

**PJ** : You would deny it.

**K** : Yes, I deny it. Because this very instrument has become corrupt and that which is corruption cannot bring about something which is incorruptible.

**PJ** : And yet—I am bringing in something else—you say that there is the 'other'.

**K** : Oh yes, definitely. Now, wait a minute. I am a human being. My consciousness is in total disorder. I say, 'Help me, please, to move out of this realm, this dimension, altogether'. Mankind has said this for millennia. Do you follow? So, gurus have come and said, 'Do this, this, this, and that will help you', but that hasn't brought about order. So one rejects all that totally, completely. Right?

**PJ** : Yes.

**K** : So, having rejected all that totally, what is one to do?

**PJ** : What is actually meant by 'being a light unto yourself'?

**K** : Actually it means: Don't look to another; don't rely on another; don't depend on another; don't ask another to help you.

**PJ** : Is the word 'light' at all significant?

**K** : 'Be a light to oneself' in the sense: Don't live in the shadow of others. Don't be a second-hand human being. Don't rely on anything, on anybody. So, I don't rely on you; I don't rely on the church, on priests, on gurus, on scriptures; I don't rely on anything. But I rely on the common intention of man to find something beyond this chaos, something which is not the priest's invention. Do you understand? And that is *not* the reliance on another. It is a co-operative inquiry; it is not a matter of my personal salvation. You see, Pupul, 'personal salvation' is so silly.

So, to come back: What is to be done? We have abolished the mind, we have abolished the activity of thought, we have abolished the activity of the brain which, as we know it now, is limited. Right, Pupul?

**PJ** : Yes.

**K** : We have also denied any pressure of the environment, of tradition, of pity. We have denied all pressure, and we ask: How are we, as human beings, to discover the 'other'?

**PJ** : You see, sir, what I am trying to say is this—that the moment you use your capacities for something, you're finished.

**K** : Yes, of course.

**PJ** : So, you are saying that the moment I need the instrument in order to reach the 'other', it is over.

**K** : Quite.

**PJ** : But, sir, it does not deny the energy which it holds; and that energy is an unlimited energy.

**K** : Ah! You are theorizing, Pupul.

**PJ** : No sir, forgive me; I am not theorizing at this moment.

**K** : What are you trying to say? I don't quite understand it.

**PJ** : I am saying that the moment I use the senses for something, they are identified with thought.

**K** : Yes, that's obvious.

**PJ** : But I cannot deny the senses, and I cannot deny that the senses in themselves are not corrupt.

**K** : Yes. The senses in themselves are not corrupt. When the senses do not identify with thought which builds the 'I'—psychologically—then those senses are natural; those senses are healthy; those senses are normal. Now, will those senses which are

38

healthy bring about a different dimension?

**PJ :** I don't know, because now, the way one operates, they are never in that state.

**K :** Therefore is it possible for thought not to identify with the senses? It is possible, obviously. I see a beautiful object—human or non-human—and I can observe it without saying, 'I must have it'. Of course I can; there can be mere observation.

**PJ :** Yes, it's like having a discussion with you; then all the senses are operating. So there is the possibility of such a situation.

**K :** Oh yes, there is the possibility, but I am not interested in possibilities. Pupul, as a human being, my only problem is this: how to get out of this disorder.

**PJ :** But how do I posit the 'other'?

**K :** I don't know. I don't posit the 'other'. I don't know what order is. How can I know what order is when I'm living in total disorder? I can speculate; I can imagine; I can theorize; I can, cunningly, verbally, intellectually, spin a lot of theories about it, but actually they have no meaning. What has meaning is this— there is disorder. What is to happen to move from this dimension to a totally different dimension which is not the invention of thought? That is the question. Right?

**PJ :** Yes, that is the question, but we started out by defining each term as it came along so that we could have a clear picture.

**K :** Yes, quite so, and we are very clear now—at least I hope so. Now, what is the action or non-action necessary to move from this to that? *(Pause)* This has been the age-old problem, Pupul; it's not something new. And they have said, 'Fast; pray; be a celibate; go to church'. And mankind has done all that; mankind has done everything, but still there's nothing but disorder. So, what shall we do?

What is the action which is inaction that will negate, completely, this disorder? *(Pause)* Is there a total negation or is it always partial? Do you follow what I mean? Do I negate attachment, then negate jealousy, then negate all the hurt, and so on? You see, that way is endless. Right?

**PJ** : Yes.

**K** : So, is there a total negation of disorder? *(Pause)*

**Q** : Sir, you are speaking of an action—but that 'action' cannot be a movement, because movement implies time.

**K** : Yes, I know, but I just used that word. I used that word—I can use any word—to imply a negation of disorder which does not entail a wanting of order, which does not have a movement towards order. Do you understand what I am saying? Is there a negation of total disorder? Can one deny disorder totally?

**Q** : Is this the action of keeping or of being completely still?

**K** : No. Look, sir, I am in disorder as a human being. I can separate disorder. Right? There is disorder here, there is disorder there, and so on. And in the very denial of a part, there is a certain type of order. Right? But that is not total order. There is water in the harbour, but it's not the sea. Right?

**Q** : Yes.

**K** : It is the same water, but it is not the sea. So, I can deny the parts, but those denials are never the whole. Right? So, I'm asking: Can there be a total denial of disorder?

**Q** : But you are asking if there is any action that can lead to that.

**K** : No, no; I am speaking of denial, and not of action. Let me put it this way. Sir, do you first of all see that partial denial is no denial at all?

**Q** : Yes.

**K :** Is there a denial which is not partial? Is there a denial of the whole content of consciousness which is disorder?

**PJ :** Sir, the denial of total disorder is a concept. Sir, total disorder itself is a concept.

**K :** *(Forcefully denying)* It is not a concept.

**PJ :** Disorder as it operates within me, yes.

**K :** Disorder as it operates in you—is that operation partial, fragmentary?

**PJ :** Each disorder as it arises is fragmentary. Sir, the disorder is not fragmentary; the way I meet it is fragmentary.

**K :** Fragmentary denial is creating disorder; fragmentary denial is disorder. And all my life I've denied fragmentarily. Right? We say that partial denial is contributing to disorder. From there we ask: Is there no partial denial at all and, therefore, total order?

**PJ :** The 'other', namely, total order, one cannot even think of; so let us put it aside. Let us talk about whether it is possible to totally deny, that is to deny non-fragmentarily.

**K :** All right, let's stick to that; it's good enough. When the mind, when thought, when the intellect—which is itself fragmentary—says, 'I deny disorder', then it is still disorder. Right? Because they are all fragments. The intellect, the reason—they are all fragments. Now what is the action or inaction that will say, 'No partial denial at all'?

**PJ :** You use the word 'inaction'. Let me pursue it, please. Is it that one is incapable of inaction? Is one incapable of not doing a thing about it?

**K :** Yes. That's what I'm trying to get at. We have done everything possible to clean up the consciousness. Right? We pray; we fast; we beg; we follow; we sacrifice; we deny. There is this constant activity to bring about order. Right?

**PJ :** Yes, sir.

**K :** Now, the question really is whether there is an action which is non-action. You see, that is only possible when I really, totally, completely, negate everything.

*Brockwood Park*
*12 June 1978*

# The Mind of Krishnamurti

**PUPUL JAYAKAR (PJ) :** In listening to you over the last thirty years, I have observed a certain manner in which you approach a problem, a certain manner in which you unfold a problem during discussion. I know that you have maintained that there is no 'way' but, as I have observed, a certain 'process'—don't call it a 'way' if you like—has revealed itself. I use the word 'process' and not 'methodology' because 'methodology' is too hard a word.

I would like, sir, to investigate the way you receive a question, the actual way in which you penetrate into it. I would also like to know what follows after you receive a question. I would like to explore your mind. So can we, during this dialogue, explore your mind?

**J. KRISHNAMURTI (K) :** You want to explore my mind?

**PJ :** Yes; but please forgive me for putting it this way. You see, sir, in exploring your mind, I feel that we can, possibly, understand the way of exploration in which we get bogged down.

**K :** All right, let's begin.

**PJ :** Can we begin with the question: How do you receive a question which is put to you? What is the state of the mind—your mind—which receives?

**K :** The question is: How does K, when a question is put to him, receive it and proceed to answer it? Right? *(Pause)*

I think he would say that first he listens; he listens without any conclusions, without any barriers. And, you see, because there is no hindrance, the mind is—could I use the word 'empty'? The mind is empty in the sense that there are no preconceived answers and no—because answers have been given before—recording and remembrance of those answers. I am using the word 'empty' in that sense. There is a state of emptiness and out of that K answers. Yes, I think it would be right to say that.

**PJ :** Now, in this state, what is the function of attention? You see, sir, the function of attention is to search, but if attention does not search, what happens to the question? You may receive it in emptiness, but what actually happens to the question? Because you do respond.

**K :** Yes. The question is put, and there is a hearing of it—a hearing of it not only with the ear but also without the usual process of hearing. It is like a seed that is put into the earth—the earth acts upon the seed, and the seed acts upon the earth and, gradually, out of that comes a plant or a flower.

You see, Pupul, there is the normal, physical, state wherein a question is heard with the ear; but there is also a state in which the question is heard not with the ear, and out of that state there is the answer.

**PJ :** You say that there is a listening with the ear and that there is a listening without the ear. Is it that a new instrument comes into being—an instrument which is not a physical growth in the brain, but a new capacity, a new instrument? You see, sir, when one observes you, it is as if your eyes are participating in the listening process as much as your ears. You have, if I may say so, a 'listening' eye.

**K :** I think so. Now, I would like to answer that last question by bringing in the word 'insight'. 'Insight' is a state of mind in which there is no memory, no remembrance; there is no conclusion; there is no sense of anticipation; there is no quality of reaction. Insight is much more than all that.

Now when you ask a question, there is a hearing with the ear and there is also a hearing with the non-ear, which means that the mind is in a state where there is no remembrance, no conclusion, no previous recording of that question and, therefore, no replying to that question according to memory. All that—remembrance, conclusions, ready responses, and so on—being absent, there is an insight into the question.

**PJ :** Does this hearing with the non-ear come into being with the very ending of the processes of the mind, or is it something else?

**K :** When there is an insight the brain cells themselves undergo a change. When there is insight, the insight transforms the brain cells.

**PJ :** You have said that there is a hearing with the ear and a hearing with the non-ear. You say that insight brings about a change in the brain cells. Does insight arise because of the non-hearing?

**K :** Yes, because of the hearing with the non-ear.

**PJ :** Can we investigate this hearing with the non-ear or is it impossible to investigate it?

**K :** Let's find out. First there is the hearing with the ear—which we all know. *(Pause)* Then there is the hearing without the ear—with the non-ear—which is a state similar to that of dropping a stone into a tranquil, completely quiet, pond or lake. When you drop a stone into such a pond, it makes little waves which disappear.

A state of listening with the non-ear is a state of absolute quietness of the mind. Now, when a question is put to such a mind, it is like a little stone that is dropped into a tranquil pond. The response is the wave, the little waves. I don't know if I am making it clear.

**PJ** : Now, is the pond the matrix of the mind? Is it 'mind only'?

**K** : I don't quite follow. I will have to go into this. When you say 'mind only' what do you mean?

**PJ** : That it is the totality of what is and what has been. You see, consciousness, as you have said so often, is its content. And consciousness, as we know and use it, is fragmented.

**K** : Wait a minute; look at it. Suppose that the mind, consciousness, is fragmented. Naturally when you put a question to that fragmentary consciousness, the answer must be fragmentary.

**PJ** : The question, you say, is dropped like a pebble into a pool— is it the totality which receives?

**K** : It is. I think we should go into it a little bit because it is really quite interesting. You see, Pupul, can the mind be so extraordinarily receptive that the past has no place in it at all?

**PJ** : The past is a fragment?

**K** : The past is a fragment and, so, does not enter into it at all.

**PJ** : You say that there is a listening with the ear and that there is a listening with the non-ear. Has the listening with the non-ear the same quality as listening?

**K** : We know listening with the ear.

**PJ** : Yes, we know listening with the ear. Listening is a word heard; now is listening with the non-ear of a different nature?

**K** : Oh yes; obviously.

**PJ** : What is its nature?

**K** : Listening with the ear or hearing with the ear and the response from that listening to a question will necessarily be fragmented. Right? But when there is a listening without the ear, that state of listening is not fragmented.

Listening with the ear implies the recording and the remembrance and from that past knowledge, past experience, answering the question. However, as there is no past involved in the listening with the non-ear, there is no fragmentary answer. I think that is right.

**PJ :** Is the non-ear listening different from that which receives?

**K :** I don't quite follow this. Let us be clear.

**PJ :** Sir, the question is posed. You said that it is received with the non-ear. There is a non-ear listening. Is that non-ear listening the same as that which receives?

**K :** *(Pause)* Yes, of course; it must be. I think the simile of a mill-pond is very good. Now, we are saying that the pond is absolutely quiet, and that the pond is nothing but clear, clean water. The pond is totally without all the pollution that man has put into it—the pollution is the past, and all the rest of it—and the question is put into that pond just as a pebble is, and the reply is the wave. I think—at least with me—that is how it functions.

**PJ :** Now, as there is a non-ear listening, is there also a non-eye seeing?

**K :** Yes. If you are using the word 'eye' in the sense of the visual, the optical—yes.

**PJ :** Can we go into the nature of that?

**K :** Let's see whether the hearing with the non-ear and the visual seeing without the past interfering with it are the same. Yes, the hearing without the ear and the seeing—the visual, optical seeing—without remembrance are the same. That is, to put it simply Pupul, when the past does not interfere in either case, they are the same.

**PJ** : Sir, tradition maintains that the outward movement of the eye is the movement of focusing, of naming. The optic movement which turns backwards, breaks through the naming process; it breaks the naming process; it dissolves the naming process. Is that so?

**K** : Let me see if I have understood the question correctly. Are you saying that there is an optical vision going out and then there is a coming back from the outward movement to the inner movement?

**PJ** : No sir, that is not it. There is an outer movement which we all know; it is the movement of seeing, of registering, of focusing, etc. Then there is for the *sādhaka*—I am purposely using that word *sādhaka*, for it stands for a man who is on the path of search—a movement of the eye within. That is, the very optic seeing is thrown within and it breaks the naming process, the divisive process. In fact it is known as the 'backward flowing movement', and it is a term that is used in various ways also by the Chinese.

**K** : The forward movement and the backward movement.

**PJ** : No sir, it is not the forward movement turning backwards. There are the senses moving out and there is the 'sense'—I am using the word 'sense' within quotes—that does not move out.

**K** : Ah, that is entirely a different matter! I understand; yes, I understand. It is not like a tide going out and coming in. There is only the going out, and another movement altogether which is going in.

**PJ** : Which is 'optically' going in—that is what tradition says.

**K** : So that is what tradition—Chinese, and all the rest—says. But what do you say?

**PJ** : You see, the looking out—the looking at a tree—focuses, but the looking within ends focusing; it ends the very instrument which focuses. It is as if . . . .

**K :** I must understand this very clearly; it is not quite clear to me. That it is not like the tide going out and the tide coming in is clear. Yes, I understand that the looking in is not like the sea going out and coming in but that it is an entirely different way of looking inward.

**PJ :** Yes, the looking inward is not a tide, but it can be a tide.

**K :** Of course, of course; that's right; that is the danger of it. The tide going out and the tide coming in—it is the same water. Whereas this optical going out and the looking within are two entirely different processes.

**PJ :** Would you say that the seeing without the outer seeing is of this nature?

**K :** I question the whole thing. You see, Pupul, I wonder if there is a looking within at all.

**PJ :** Can we explore that, sir?

**K :** I wonder if there is any such thing as a looking within, because looking within may imply a movement of thought.

**PJ :** Yes sir, but not necessarily.

**K :** All right. Then if there is no movement of thought, what do we mean by 'looking within'?

**PJ :** By looking within I mean a seeing of that which exists at a particular instant, both within and without. There is no within and without in that state.

**K :** That's the whole point, you see, but let's be very clear. The tide goes out, the tide comes in. From what you are saying, tradition—it may be right, it may be wrong; I don't know—holds that the outward looking and the inward looking is not like the tide going out and the tide coming in; it holds that the inward looking is not the reaction of the outward looking; it holds that the inward looking is entirely different from the outward looking. Right? This is what you are telling me, isn't it? And you are also saying that the inward looking dispels the whole structure of thought. Right?

**PJ** : Yes.

**K** : *(Long pause)* I question that. I question whether there is an inward looking at all. I am just exploring, Pupul; I am not saying that it is so. What is there to look inward? One can look inwards, from what you say, into the whole movement of thought. Is that inward looking?

**PJ** : I would say it is inward looking. Because there is a physical looking . . . .

**K** : Yes, the outward looking.

**PJ** : This is a non-physical looking. Let me put it this way: the looking is physical, but what is seen is not physical. Thought is not something that can be 'seen' as such.

**K** : Pupul, all thought is a material process.

**PJ** : But it is so fleeting.

**K** : I know; but it is a material process. The recording of knowledge, the remembrance of it—all that is a material process.

**PJ** : Yes, you say that sir, but there *is* a distinction; there is a distinction between seeing a microphone and seeing a flashing movement of thought.

**K** : But that flashing movement of thought is still a material process.

**PJ** : Yes, all right; I agree that it is a material process, but its existence is in a dimension which we call the 'within'.

**K :** Yes, I know that you call it the 'within', and I question that whole thing.

**PJ :** It is somewhere, sir.

**K :** No, my point is why should it be either 'within' or 'without'.

**PJ :** Because, sir, it is not without; it is not something which is visible without.

**K :** I see what you are trying to get at. You are saying that thought is not visible; it cannot be perceived as one's face is in a mirror. Thought cannot be perceived in a mirror. So that which is not perceivable you call the 'inner'.

**PJ :** Yes, it is not perceivable and, yet, it exists.

**K :** But I would question whether it is the inner at all.

**PJ :** Sir, you can take away the word 'inner' and use another word, but still the thing remains. Where is it?

**K :** Pupul, I believe that when the Eskimos use the word 'thought' they mean something outside.

**PJ :** Sir, I am talking of myself.

**K :** Look at it carefully, Pupul; think about it.

**PJ :** I understand, sir. What I am saying is that there is something which I can see outside—which is the physical seeing. I am also saying that I can never see, with the same optical eye, the nature of thought itself.

**K :** Yes, I can see my face in a mirror, but I can't see my thought in a mirror. That is simple.

**PJ :** Then where do I see it? What is the seeing then?

**K :** You know, Pupul, I don't think there is a seeing at all.

**PJ :** And yet, sir, you have kept on speaking of 'seeing'.

**K :** Yes, seeing—seeing the flower.

**PJ :** Seeing also anger.

**K :** No.

**PJ :** You said something just now: I don't think there is 'seeing' at all. Can we investigate that statement, please?

**K :** Yes, but we must go slowly, for we must be very clear on this point which is rather interesting.

First there is a hearing with the ear, and then there is a hearing without the ear. The hearing without the ear is like a mill-pond that is absolutely still. It is without a single movement; there is no air that ruffles it. Now the question is like a stone that is popped into that still pond, and the answer is the waves. Yes, the waves are the answer to the question.

**PJ :** Which it—the question itself—throws up.

**K :** That's right. He, K, has said so. Right from the beginning he has said that you must approach the question afresh, and all the rest of it, so that the very throwing of the question into the mill-pond produces the answer. There is no entity that answers; that is very important to understand.

Now, let us go back to your question regarding the 'seeing' of thought. There is no problem with regard to the seeing of your face in the mirror, right? You can see your face in the mirror, but the seeing of thought in the mirror is not possible. Right? So your question is: What then is the 'seeing' of thought? You see, Pupul, I don't think there is a 'seeing' of thought.

**PJ :** Then what actually takes place, sir?

**K :** That's what we are going to find out, but first let's be clear. It is clear that there is no seeing of thought, for 'seeing' implies that there is a 'seer' and that there is 'thought', and that the 'seer' and 'thought' are separate. The seer *is* thought. So there is only thought which cannot be seen in the mirror. So, for me, there is no inward looking.

**PJ** : Then what do you mean, sir, when you talk of the seeing of 'what is', for you say that thought cannot be seen?

**K** : Thought cannot be seen with the inward look.

**PJ** : Then by what is thought seen, if it is not seen by the inward look, and can't be seen as one sees one's face in a mirror? I ask this question because there is a seeing.

**K** : I wouldn't use the word 'seeing'.

**PJ** : Then what word would you use, sir?

**K** : I would use the word 'aware'. Yes, I would say that thought becomes aware of itself, of its own activity.

**PJ** : But you have been talking all these years of the *seeing* of 'what is'.

**K** : The seeing of 'what is' is the seeing of what is actually happening inwardly which is not the observation of what is happening with the optical eye or with another thought. 'Seeing' implies that.

**PJ** : What is that state, sir?

**K** : We are inquiring into that state. If you say that that state is one of 'seeing inwardly', I say that it is not possible. I say that it is not possible because then you would be bringing about a dual state—a state of 'seeing' and a state of 'that which is seen'. Right?

**PJ** : Can there be a 'seeing' without a dual state?

**K** : Yes. 'Seeing' implies that there is no opposite.

**PJ** : Yes, of course, because it has the same quality as the lake.

**K** : Yes. That's why, Pupul, I went back to that carefully. When you speak of 'inward looking', it sounds, to me, artificial and—forgive me—traditional. I think the thing works like a lake, like a tranquil mill-pond. Thought itself has to be quiet; it has to be as quiet as the lake. When you put a question to that lake, the question is answered from the lake.

**PJ :** But, sir, jealousy arises. Jealousy is a material thing.

**K :** Yes, absolutely.

**PJ :** I grow aware; but it is already over. You see, sir, I cannot see that which is over.

**K :** No, you see jealousy arise and there is the watching of it.

**PJ :** One of the things which has always puzzled me is this: Can there be a watching of the actual state of jealousy arising? For in such a state it would not arise.

**K :** There is jealousy. The fact of jealousy is a reaction, which you name 'jealousy'. The question is: Before you name it as 'jealousy', can there be a watching of that reaction without the watcher? Can there be a watching in which there is no opposite? Do you understand what I am saying? Can one just 'see' the reaction?—And I mean by that word 'seeing' an observation without the eye or the ear.

**PJ :** Could you please say that again, sir?

**K :** The observation of the arising of that reaction—of jealousy, in this instance—is the hearing without the ear, the seeing without the eye. Does it sound crazy?

Let's be clear, Pupul, about what we are saying. We are saying, first, that a question is asked and that question is like a stone dropped into a mill-pond, a mill-pond that is absolutely still. Now, what we are saying is that not only the question but the very answer is the dropping of the stone into the pond. You see, Pupul, the answer comes out *because* of the stone—for otherwise the mill-pond is absolutely quiet, right?

54

What we are talking about is not the tide going out and the tide coming in, but an observation of 'what is' without the previous remembrance associated with 'what is'; that's all.

**PJ** : You say that it is neither optical nor aural.

**K** : Yes.

**PJ** : And yet you use the word 'observing'?

**K** : Yes, I use the word in the sense that in the observation there is no remembrance of the thing which is being observed. I am right in this, but let me go slowly.

In the process of observation there is no centre from which something is observed—the centre being memory, various conclusions, hurts, and so on. So, there is no point from which it is being observed. And in the observation there is no conclusion, there is no association with past events, which means the seeing is as quiet as the mill-pond. And the question, or 'what is', is a challenge and the challenge drops into the mill-pond which is absolutely quiet and which responds. I am very clear about this, but I don't know if I am conveying this.

**PJ** : Sir, according to me, you have said a number of new things.

**K** : Quite right. Let's go ahead.

**PJ** : Sir, you just implied that the ripple is the response.

**K** : Yes, the ripple is the response. It is a marvellous idea.

**PJ** : I have observed you, sir, and I feel that you listen to your own responses with the same attention as you listen to a question that is put to you. Do you listen to your response?

**K** : Yes, I listen to it to see if it is accurate.

**PJ** : That's what I see; I see you listen to your own response so that your response and what the other person is saying—as far as this non-ear is concerned—are at the same level.

**K :** I have to understand your question; please make it clear.

**PJ :** Sir, when a person responds, he normally never listens to his own response.

**K :** No, he never listens.

**PJ :** He is always listening to what the other is saying. He never listens to his own response. At least I don't listen to it. I am watching myself, and I see that I don't listen to my own response. I listen to my own response afterwards.

**K :** If you are talking casually, you don't listen. But if you are talking seriously, you are listening to the questioner and you are listening. You see, Pupul, there is an act of listening which is not 'me' listening to my responses. There is only listening.

**PJ :** Yes, but when you listen and if what is said is not so, you move away from it. There is a total flexibility, if I may say so. You see, sir, with you there is no holding to an answer.

**K :** You see, if the pebble is very light, the ripple is just two waves. But if it is a rock it goes down and causes a great many waves. If the challenge is great, the waters must move in a series of waves; but if the challenge is very small, there is just a ripple. So the act of listening is not only to the person who questions, who challenges, but also to the answering. It is, in other words, a total state of listening—a listening to both the questioner and the person who replies. And, yes, when the answer, the reply, is not quite as it should be, there naturally is a movement away. *Because* you are listening, there is a withdrawal from that and, then, you change the movement.

So I have discovered that there is no inward looking; there is only looking.

**QUESTIONER (Q) :** Sir, what is the mill-pond?

**K :** I told you, the mill-pond is dead quiet; there is no ripple in it. If you drop a tiny little pebble into that tranquil pond there will be just a mild ripple, but if you drop a really heavy stone the ripples will go on.

Now, all this—the analogy of the mill-pond and so on—came about because Pupul began by asking: Can we investigate your mind, K's mind? If you ask, however, what is that mill-pond which is your—K's—mind, you will be entering into something else, and I don't know if I would investigate that.

**PJ** : You would not, sir?

**K** : I am not sure, I said.

**PJ** : But I think it is a thing which has to be raised with you. Of course, it would take another dialogue; I do not want to raise it today.

**K** : Raise what?

**PJ** : What is that mill-pond, sir?

**K** : First of all, Pupul, whose mill-pond? Is it the mill-pond of K's mind or the mill-pond of a person who is agitated and all the rest of it? You see, an agitated mind is not a mill-pond.

**PJ** : We are talking of K's mill-pond. I mean, what is being attempted here is to see how far one can go into throwing open K's mind.

**K** : Yes, I understand; I know what you are saying. You are asking: What is the state of the mill-pond that, apparently, K has? I don't think K is aware of the mill-pond.

**PJ** : What are you aware of, then, sir?

**K** : No, wait, wait, this is important to understand: If K is aware of it, it is not a mill-pond.

**PJ** : Sir, if I may ask, what is the inner nature of your self?

**K** : I am being asked what the inner nature of K's mind, of K, is.

If I were to reply I'd say: Nothing, which means not a thing. Yes, there is nothing. Would that be acceptable? Would you comprehend this state of K's mind, K's inner being, which says that there is nothing, absolutely nothing?

**Q :** Sir, you said that K cannot be aware of the mill-pond. Would I be correct in saying that that is because any examination would be . . . .

**K :** It is like measuring the immeasurable, you follow? I am not saying that K's mind is unmeasurable, but it is like measuring the immeasurable.

**Q :** But you said that the mill-pond only shows itself in those ripples.

**K :** Yes.

**Q :** Otherwise nothing else could be said about it?

**K :** You see, sir, the word is not the thing. *(Laughs shortly)* I have fallen back on an old trick.

**Q :** Are you saying that any examination of it is at a totally different level?

**K :** You *can't* examine it; it can't be examined. First of all, with what would you be examining it?

You see, the ordinary person's mill-pond—I am using that word even though it strictly can't be applied—is constantly in agitation. Now, from that agitation you are asking questions about the examination, what the tools, and so on, are of that—K's—mill-pond. I am telling you that that mill-pond just cannot be examined.

Pupul raised the question regarding the state of K's mind. And K says that there is a state of absolute nothingness, and that that nothingness cannot be examined—because examination implies measurement, and there is no measurement of nothingness; full stop.

You see, obviously, *you can only perceive nothingness if your mind is also that. (Pause)*

**PJ** : Sir, may I please ask you something? I find that in your dialogues, in your discussions, there is a great use of the pause. You pause. What is the significance of the pause?

**K** : What is music, Pupul?—Space between two notes, right? K pauses—why does he pause? I don't know. I have never thought about it. *(Pause)* I've got it. K pauses probably to see that the answer is from the mill-pond.

**PJ** : I understand. Now, to come back. During a dialogue it appears to a person who observes—and I may be wrong—that you start at the same level as the person with whom you are discussing.

Now, I have a very serious question to ask you here. Is it that the mill-pond that is K's mind, the mind which is nothing, enters the state of the mind of the person who is in duality?

**K** : No, no, no. There is no remembrance of nothingness. Do you understand? Pupul, just go into it a little bit, please. If K remembers nothingness, it is not then nothingness. All we can say is that it is there; we cannot enter into that. *(Pause)*

**PJ** : How do you, sir, comprehend my duality?

**K** : By listening to what you are saying.

**PJ** : But you don't know the nature of duality.

**K** : No, but I am listening to you asking: How can I be rid of jealousy? How can I be rid of something or the other? And I say that you can't get rid of it. My instant reply is that there is no riddance of any thing.

**PJ** : No, but there is also another thing. I make a statement. You will immediately see whether that is a theory or a fact. You see, sir, there is a capacity within you to see the truth.

**K** : Obviously, everybody has that.

**PJ** : Not always, sir.

**K** : No, not always.

**PJ** : Sir, you have been questioned for the last fifty years or so. Now, out of this questioning, which grows intense, you suddenly say, 'I see'. My question is: What is it that brings about that insight, what is it which suddenly makes everything clear?

**K** : As I told you, I listen; K listens. Somebody is talking; I listen. There is listening and, suddenly, there comes, out of nothingness . . . .

**PJ** : So are you saying, sir, that it arises in the very listening?

**K** : Yes. Because, to me what is important is the act of listening. There is a listening to the question—the question that is dropped like a pebble into a tranquil pond. It is simple.

**PJ** : Is this state the same as what takes place when you have an interview and when you sit on a platform?

**K** : No, no. When K sits on the platform it is quite different. In an interview the person is the problem; so both of us discuss. You see, it is a different matter . . . .

No, no; I am not sure that it is different. It is just that there it is much more concentrated. Yes.

**PJ** : I would like to explore that with you, sir, for the one thing that a person sees very clearly when he or she is having an interview with you—with K—is that he or she really sees nothing.

**K** : What?

**PJ** : If I may say so sir, for those of us who have had an interview with you it is like facing a totally empty state.

**K** : Yes.

**PJ** : There is nothing except the self reflected. You see, sir, you throw back on the person exactly what is in the person.

**K** : Yes. *(Long pause)* I am now Pupul and you are K. I ask you: How did you come to this extraordinary quality of the mill-pond? That would be my inquiry. How did you capture, how did you come by it? What are its characteristics? How did it happen to you and not to me? Tell me the things that prevent the mill-pond?

**PJ** : Please proceed, sir, because you alone can be the questioner as well as the one who answers. No one else can answer.

**K** : That's what I am doing—answering. This is great fun . . . .

All right, how did I—sorry, you—get to it? First of all you have no comparison; you have no sense of it at all. You don't even feel that you have got it and that I haven't got it. That-you-have-it-and-I-haven't means comparison. So you tell me first of all, 'Don't compare'. You ask me, 'Can you be totally free of comparison'? Now that is something new to me; it is a statement that I don't quite understand. So I say, 'I have lived all my life by comparison and you are now asking me to throw away all the things that I have learnt through comparison'. You tell me that the struggle, the pain, the envy, the jealousy, the drive—all that—must completely be dissipated. And you also tell me, 'Don't take time over it. Don't say, "I will do it tomorrow", for then that will never happen. It must be done instantly'. That's what you tell me.

Now, because I have listened to you very carefully—with the hearing and the non-hearing ear—I am very alert to what you are saying. I see it and say, 'Yes, I can't possibly dissipate it through time. It must be so now'. Your very challenge makes me respond. Your challenge being very vital, very urgent, very forceful, awakens in me the quality of urgency and, so, I understand. I understand completely.

And you also tell me, 'Don't accumulate; don't accumulate problems; don't accumulate hurts, memories, names, forms; just don't accumulate'. Again because my whole being is listening to you, I understand it instantly. You say to me, 'Every problem must be resolved instantly'. Now that, of course, would require a great deal of back and forth, but at the end of it I would see what you mean. And I would understand the ordinary things. I would understand fear; I would understand pleasure. I would not suppress it, but understand the whole movement of it. And with the understanding would come the ending of sorrow; the whole thing would be wiped away.

I think, if you were to put it to me, that's how I would act . . . .

You see, Pupul, I am in a state where I am surrounded by an immense stretch of water—water that is warm, healthy, sane. I am swimming in that marvellous water, and I won't leave you. Do you understand?

If somebody were to ask me, 'Why does Mrs Rao or Mrs Williams come and listen to you every year?' I would reply, 'I don't know, but if I were Mrs Rao or Mrs Williams or Mr Smith I would come and listen every year and, if possible, every day—because the flower is different every day. Beauty is different every day'.

*Rishi Valley*
*15 December 1978*

# Energy and Attention

**PUPUL JAYAKAR (PJ)** : Most people see that because of the various pressures which operate on the human mind—violence and terror—there is a shrinkage of space available to us to explore and an incapacity to face complex situations. I would suggest that we do not go into specific problems but lay bare the structure of the human mind, thus bringing us face to face with the structure of thought, for only then will it be possible for each one of us to investigate into the complexities which occupy our consciousness.

**J. KRISHNAMURTI (K)** : We have talked over the movement of fear together, in words which are common and easily understood. How have you listened to those statements? How have you read those statements and what has been the impact of those statements on you? We said that desire, time, thought, the various hurts—the whole of that—is fear. What has been the impact of that statement? Has it had merely a verbal, logical impact or has the impact been real, deep? Have we talked at a level where you have seen the truth of what has been said?

Pupul, let us say that you communicate to me not the verbal

---

Previously published as 'The Future of Man—III' in *The Way of Intelligence*, Madras : Krishnamurti Foundation India, 1985, pp 84–92.

description of it but the very truth of the whole thing. How would I listen to that statement? You see, I would not oppose it or compare what you say to something I already know, but I would actually listen to what you say. It would enter into my consciousness; it would enter that part of consciousness which is willing to comprehend entirely what you are saying . . . .

**PJ** : Sir, we are speaking of the future of man, of the danger of technology taking over man's functions. Man seems paralysed. You have said that there are only two ways open to him: either the way of pleasure or the way of an inner movement. I am asking you the 'how' of the inner movement.

**K** : When you ask 'how', you are asking for a system, a method, a practice. That is obvious. Nobody asks 'how' otherwise. How am I to play the piano? How am I to do this or that? In the word 'how' a method, a mode of acting—all that—is implied. So when you ask 'how', you are back again to the same old pattern of experience, knowledge, memory, thought, action.

Now, can we move away from the 'how' for the moment and observe the mind, or the brain? Can there be a pure observation of it, an observation which is not analysis? Observation is totally different from analysis. In analysis there is always the search for a cause; there is the analyser and the analysed. That means that the analyser is separate from the analysed. That separation is fallacious; it is not actual—the actual is that which is happening 'now'.

Observation is totally free of analysis. Is it possible just to observe without any conclusion, without any direction, any motive? Is it possible to have just pure, clear looking? Obviously, it is possible when you look at these lovely trees; it is very simple. That is, I can look at that tree without any distortion because I am looking optically, and in that observation the process of analysis has no place. I go beyond it. But to look at the operation of the whole movement of existence, to observe it without any distortion, is—usually—entirely different.

Now, the question is: Can I look at or can there be an observation of the whole activity of fear without trying to find the cause, or asking how to end it, or trying to suppress it, or running away from it? Is it possible just to look and stay with the whole movement of fear? I mean by 'staying with it' to observe without any movement of thought entering into one's observation. I say that with that observation comes attention. That observation *is* total attention. It is not concentration; it is attention. It is like focusing a bright light on an object, and in the focusing of that energy, which is light, on that movement, fear ends. Analysis will never end fear; you can test it out. So the question is: Is my mind capable of such attention, an attention which brings all the energy of my intellect, emotion, nerves, so as to look at this movement of fear without any opposition or support or denial?

**PJ** : Thought arises in observation, and does not stay with the observation of fear. Then what happens to thought? Does one push it aside? What does one do? Thought does arise, which is also a fact.

**K** : Just listen. The speaker explained not only personal fears but also the fears of mankind which is this stream, the stream in which is included thought, time and the desire to end it, to go beyond it. All that is the movement of fear. Can you look at it, observe it without any movement? For any movement is thought.

**PJ** : You may say that movement is fear, but in that observing, thought arises, which is also a fact.

**K** : Please listen. I spoke of desire, time, thought; I said that thought is time, and that desire is part of thought. You have shown the whole map of fear, in which thought is included. You see, Pupul, there is no question of suppressing thought; that is impossible. So you have to first look at it. But, unfortunately, we don't give attention to anything.

Pupul, you have just said something about thought. I listened to it very, very carefully; I attended to what you were saying. Can you so attend?

**PJ** : For an instant of attention, thought is not; then thought arises. This is the state of the mind. There is no doer because that is pretty obvious. It is neither possible to remain immovable nor to say that thought will not arise. If it is a stream, it is a stream which flows.

**K** : Are we discussing what observation is?

**PJ** : Yes, we are discussing observation. In that observation I have raised this problem because it is the problem of attention, of self-knowledge, the problem of our minds, the problem that in observing, thought arises. So, then what? What does one do with thought?

**K** : When in your attention thought arises, you put fear aside totally, but you pursue thought. I do not know if I am making myself clear. You observe the movement of fear. In that observation, thought arises. The movement of fear is not important. What is important is the arising of thought and the total attention on that thought. There is this stream of fear. You say, 'Tell me what to do. How am I, caught in fear, to end it? Tell me not the method, not the system, not the practice, but the ending of it.' You see that analysis will not end it; you see that that is obvious. So, the question is: What will end it?—A perception of the whole movement of fear, a perception without direction?

**JAGANNATH UPADHYAYA (JU)** : You made a statement about observing the movement of fear. I do not accept the distinction you have made between analysis and observation. I do not agree with your rejection of analysis. It is only through analysis that the entire structure of tradition and the weight of memory can be broken. It is only when that is broken that an observation is possible. Otherwise, it would only be a conditioned mind which would be observing. By your insistence on observation as distinct from analysis, perhaps there is the possibility or probability of the type of accidents or sudden happening occurring, of which other people have spoken. Therefore there arises the opportunity in which the *sákti* or transmission of power, takes place.

**PJ :** Is that the nature of looking at fear? I am answering part of the question. Is the nature of observing or looking at fear or listening to fear of the same nature as looking at a tree, or listening to a bird? Or are you talking of a listening and a seeing which is an optical observation, plus? And if it is plus, what is the plus?

**ACHYUT PATWARDHAN (AP) :** I see a great danger in what Upadhyayaji has said. He says that there cannot be an observation unless it is accompanied by analysis, and that if there is an observation without analysis then that observation may have to depend upon an accidental awakening of an insight. He speaks of that as a possibility. I feel that unless observation is cleansed of analysis, it is incapable of freeing itself from the fetters of the conceptual, the process in which we have been reared—the process where observation and conceptual understanding go together. Now, observation that is not cleansed of verbal or 'word' comprehension distinguishes itself from pure observation. Therefore, in my opinion, it is very necessary to establish that analysis is an obstacle to observation. We must see, as a fact, that analysis prevents us from observing.

**K :** Sir, do we clearly understand that the observer is the observed? I observe that tree, but I am not that tree. I also observe various reactions and name them 'greed', 'envy', and so on. Now, is the observer separate from greed? The observer himself is the observed, which is greed. Is it clear, not intellectually but actually? Do you see the truth of it as a profound reality, a truth which is absolute? When there is such observation, the observer is the past.

I am afraid. That fear is me; I am not separate from that fear. So the observer is the observed. And in the seeing of that truth which is absolute there is only the fact: the fact that fear is me and that I am not separate from fear. Then, what is the need for analysis?

You see, in that observation—if it is pure observation—the whole thing is revealed, and I can logically explain everything from that observation without analysis.

We are not clear on this particular point that the thinker is the thought, the experiencer is the experience. The experiencer, when he experiences something new, recognizes it. I experience something. To give to it a meaning, I must bring in all the previous records of my experience; I must remember the nature of that experience. Therefore I am putting it outside me. But when I realize that the experiencer, the thinker, the analyser, is the analysed, is the thought, is the experience, in that perception, in that observation, there is no division, no conflict. Therefore, when you realize the truth of that, you can logically explain the whole sequence of it.

**JU :** Is that a fact? Is that a truth? How does one know whether this is the truth, when the experience . . . ?

**K :** Let us go slowly. I am angry. At the moment of anger, there is no 'me' at all; there is only that reaction called anger. A second later, I say, 'I have been angry', and I have already separated anger from me.

**PJ :** Yes.

**K :** So, I have separated it a moment later; there is me and there is anger. Then I suppress it; I rationalize it. I have already divided a reaction which is me, into 'me' and 'not-me', and then the whole conflict begins. I waste energy in analysing, in suppressing, in being in conflict with anger. But when I see that anger is me, when I see that I am made up of reactions—anger, fear and so on—the energy is concentrated; there is no waste of energy at all. With that energy which is attention, I hold this reaction called fear. I do not move away from it because I am that. Then, because I have brought all my energy to it, that fact which is called fear disappears.

You wanted to find out in what manner fear can end. I have

shown it. As long as there is a division between you and fear, fear will continue. It is like the Arab and the Jew, the Hindu and the Muslim—as long as this division exists there must be conflict.

**PJ** : But, sir, who observes?

**K** : There is no 'who' that observes. There is only the state of observation.

**PJ** : Does it come about spontaneously?

**K** : Now, you have told me that it is not analysis, that it is not this, that it is not that, and I discard all that. I don't discuss it; I discard it, and my mind is free from all the conceptual, analytical processes of thought. My mind is listening to the fact that the observer is the observed.

**PJ** : You see, sir, when there is the observing of the mind, one sees the extraordinary movement in it. It is beyond anyone's control or capacity to even give a direction to it. It is there. In that state, you say: Bring attention on to fear.

**K** : Which is all your energy . . . .

**PJ** : Which actually means, bring attention to that which is moving. When we question, the response immediately arises in our minds. However, in your mind, responses do not arise; you hold it. Now, what is it that gives you the capacity to hold fear in consciousness? I don't think we have that capacity.

**K** : I don't know; I don't think it is a question of capacity. What is capacity?

**PJ** : I will cut out the word 'capacity'. There is a holding of fear.

**K** : That is all.

**PJ** : That is, this movement which is fluid becomes immovable.

**K** : That is it.

**PJ** : Fear ends. With us that does not happen.

**K :** Can we discuss a fact? Can we hold anything in our minds for a minute or even for a few seconds? Can we hold anything? I love; can I remain with that feeling, that beauty, that clarity which love brings? Can I hold it, just hold it and not say what love is and what it is not? Can I just just hold it like a vessel holding water?

You see, sir, when you have an insight into fear, fear ends. The insight is not analysis, time, remembrance; insight is not all that. It is the immediate perception of something. We do have it. Often we have this sense of clarity about something. Is this all theoretical? You all seem so sceptical . . . .

**JU :** Sir, I find that when you speak of clarity, there is that moment of clarity. I accept that. But it must come as a result of something that happens. It must move from period to period, from level to level. My clarity cannot be the same as your clarity.

**K :** Sir, clarity is clarity; it is not yours or mine. Intelligence is not yours or mine.

**PJ :** Sir, I would like to go into something different. In observing the movement of the mind there is no point at which I say that I have observed totally and that it is over.

**K :** You can never say that.

**PJ :** So, you are talking of an observation which is a state of being; that is, you move in observation; your life is a life of observing.

**K :** Yes, that is right.

**PJ :** Out of that observing, action arises; analysis arises; wisdom comes. Is that observing? Unfortunately, we observe and then enter into the other sphere of non-observing and therefore we always have this dual process going on. None of us know what this observing is. None of us can say that we know what a life of observing is.

**K :** No. I think it is very simple. Can't you observe a person without any prejudice, without any concept?

**PJ :** Yes.

**K :** What is implied in that observation? You observe me, or I observe you. How do you observe? How do you look at me? What is your reaction to that observation?

**PJ :** With all the energy I have, I observe you . . . . No, sir, it becomes very personal; therefore I won't pursue this.

**K :** So I move away from it.

**PJ :** I can't say that I do not know what it is to be in a state of observing without the observer.

**K :** Let's say that I am married. Could we take that as an example? I am married. I have lived with my wife for a number of years. I have all the memories of those five or twenty years. In what manner do I look at her? Tell me. I am married to her; I have lived with her—sexually and all the rest of it. When I see her in the morning, how do I look at her? What is my reaction? Do I see her afresh, as though for the first time, or do I look at her with all the memories that flood my mind?

Do I observe anything for the first time? When I look at that moon, the new moon coming up with the evening star, do I look at it as though I have never seen it before? Do I see the wonder, the beauty, the light? Do I look at anything as though for the first time?

**QUESTIONER (Q) :** Can we die to our yesterdays, can we die to our past?

**K :** Yes, sir. We are always looking with the burden of the past. So, there is no actual looking. This is very important. When I look at my wife, I do not see her as though I am seeing her face for the first time. My brain is caught in memories about her or about this or that. So I am always looking from the past. Is it possible to look at the moon, at the evening star, as though for the first time, that is, without all the associations connected with them? Can I see the sunset which I have seen in America, in England, in Italy and so on, as though I am seeing it for the first time? If I do, it means that my brain is not recording the previous sunsets I know of. Do we see anything as though for the first time?

**Q :** Very rarely . . . . You ask: Can one see the moon and the evening star without the past interfering? Maybe it is the memory of the first time which makes one look.

**K :** I know what you are saying, and that leads us to another question. Is it possible not to record, except what is absolutely necessary? Why should I record the insult or the flattery that I may have received this morning? Both are the same. You flattered me by saying that it was a good talk, and she said that I was an idiot. Why should I record either statement?

**PJ :** You ask the question as if we have the choice of whether to record or not to record.

**K :** There is no choice. I am asking a question in order to investigate. You see, the brain registered the squirrel on the parapet this morning; it registered the kites flying and it registers all that you have said and are saying now in our discussion. Everything is recorded, and it is like a gramophone record playing over and over again. The mind is constantly occupied, isn't it? Now, in that occupation you cannot listen; you cannot see clearly. So one has to inquire why the brain is occupied. I am occupied with God, he is occupied with sex, she with her husband, while somebody else is occupied with power, position, politics, cleverness and so on. Why? Is it that when the brain is not occupied there is the fear of being nothing? Is it because occupation gives me a sense of living, and if I am not occupied I say that I am lost? Is that why we are occupied from morning till night? Or is it a habit, or is it a way for the brain to sharpen itself? This occupation is destroying the brain and making it mechanical. I do not know whether you are following. I have just now stated this. How do you listen to this? Now, does one see that one is occupied actually and, seeing that, remain with it? See what happens then.

When there is occupation, there is no space in the mind. I am the collection of all the experiences of mankind. And, if I knew how to read the book that is me, I would see that the story of all mankind is me. You see, we are so conditioned to this idea that we are all separate individuals, that we all have separate brains, and that the separate brains with their self-centred activity are going to be re-born over and over again. I question this whole concept that I am an individual—which does not mean that I am the collective, for there is a difference. I am not the collective. I am humanity.

*New Delhi*
*5 November 1981*

# The Central Root of Fear

**PUPUL JAYAKAR (PJ)** : You have said, Krishnaji, that intelligence is the greatest security in the facing of fear. The problem is: In a crisis, when fear from the unconscious floods you, where is the place for intelligence? Intelligence demands negation of that which comes in the way. It demands listening, seeing and observation. But when the whole being is flooded by uncontrollable fear, fear which has a cause, but the cause of which is not immediately discernible, in that state where is the place for intelligence? How does one deal with the primeval, archetypal fears which lie at the very base of the human psyche? One of these fears is the destruction of the self, the fear of not being.

**J. KRISHNAMURTI (K)** : What is it we are exploring together?

**PJ** : How does one deal with fear? You have still not answered that. You have talked of intelligence being the greatest security. It is so; but when fear floods you, where is intelligence?

**K** : You are saying that at the moment of a great wave of fear, intelligence is not. And you are asking: How can one deal with that wave of fear at that moment? Is that the question?

Previously published in *Exploration Into Insight*, ed. Pupul Jayakar and Sunanda Patwardhan, Madras: Krishnamurti Foundation India, 1979, pp 102–112.

**SUNANDA PATWARDHAN (SP)** : One sees fear like the branches of a tree. But we deal with these fears one by one and there is no freedom from fear. Is there a quality that sees fear without the branches?

**K** : K asked: Do we see the leaves, the branches, or do we go to the very root of fear?

**SP** : Can we go to the root of each single branch of fear?

**K** : Let us find out.

**PJ** : You may come to see the whole, through one fear.

**K** : I understand. You are saying that there are conscious and unconscious fears and that the unconscious fears become extraordinarily strong at moments and that at those moments intelligence is not in operation. And then you are asking how one can deal with those waves of uncontrollable fear. Isn't that it?

**PJ** : These fears seem to take on a material form; it is a physical thing which overpowers you.

**K** : Yes, it upsets you neurologically, biologically . . . . Let us explore. Fear exists, consciously or at depths, when there is a sense of loneliness, when there is a feeling of complete abandonment by others, a sense of complete isolation, a sense of not being, a sense of utter helplessness. And in those moments, when deep fear arises and there is ungovernable, uninvited fear, obviously intelligence is not.

**PJ** : One may feel that one has faced the fears which are known but unconsciously one is swamped.

**K** : That is what we are saying. Discuss it. One can deal with physical, conscious fears. The outskirts of intelligence can deal with them—the conscious fears, that is.

**PJ** : You can even allow those fears to flower.

**K** : And then in that very flowering there is intelligence. Now how do you deal with the other? Why does the unconscious—we will use that word 'unconscious' for the time being—hold these fears? Or does the unconscious invite these fears? Does it hold them, do they exist in the traditional depths of the unconscious or is it a thing that the unconscious gathers from the environment? Now, why does the unconscious hold fears at all? Are they all an inherent part of the unconscious, of the racial, traditional history of man? Are they in the inherited genes? How do you deal with the problem?

**PJ :** Can we discuss the second one, which is the gathering of fear from the environment?

**K :** First of all, let us deal with the first one. Why does the unconscious hold fears at all? Why do we consider the deeper layers of consciousness as the storehouse, as the residue of fear? Are they imposed by the culture in which we live, by the conscious mind which, not being able to deal with fear, has pushed it down so that it remains at the level of the unconscious? Or is it that the mind with all its content has not resolved its problems and is frightened of not being able to resolve them? I want to find out what the significance of the unconscious is. When you said that these waves of fear come, I said that they are always there, but that, in a crisis, you become aware of them.

**SP :** They exist in consciousness. Why do you say that they are in the unconscious?

**K :** First of all, consciousness is made up of its content. Without its content there is no consciousness. One of its contents is this basic fear and the conscious mind never tackles it; it is there, but it never says, 'I must deal with it'. In moments of crisis that part of consciousness is awakened and is frightened. But fear is always there.

**PJ :** I don't think it is so simple. Is fear not a part of man's cultural inheritance?

**K** : Fear is always there. Is it part of our cultural inheritance? Or is it possible that one can be born in a country, in a culture that does not admit fear?

**PJ** : There is no such culture.

**K** : Of course there is no such culture. And so I am asking myself: Is fear part of culture or is it inherent in man? Fear, as it exists in the animal, as it exists in every living thing, is a sense of not being; it is the sense of being destroyed.

**PJ** : The self-preservative instinct takes the form of fear.

**K** : Is it that the whole structure of cells is frightened of not being? You see, that exists in every living thing. Even the little ant is afraid of not being. We see that fear is there; we see that it is a part of human existence, and one becomes tremendously aware of it in a crisis. How does one deal with it at that moment when the surge of fear comes? Why do we wait for the crisis? I am just asking.

**PJ** : You can't avoid it.

**K** : Just a minute. We say that it is always there, that it is a part of our biological, psychological, structure. The whole human structure—our entire being—is frightened. Fear is a part of the tiniest living thing; it is a part of the minutest cell. Why do we wait for a crisis to come and bring it out? That is a most irrational acceptance of it. I am asking: Why should I have to have a crisis in order to deal with fear?

**PJ** : Otherwise it is non-existent. You see, sir, I can face some fears intelligently. For example, it is possible to face the fear of death with intelligence. Is it possible to face other fears intelligently?

**K** : You say that you can face these fears intelligently, but I question that. I question whether you face even some fears—as you put it—intelligently. I question whether you can have any intelligence at all before you have resolved fear. Intelligence comes only when fear is not. Intelligence is light and you cannot deal with darkness when light is not. Light exists only when darkness is not. I am questioning whether you can deal with fear intelligently when fear exists. I say that you cannot. You may rationalize it, you may see the nature of it, avoid it or go beyond it, but that is not intelligence.

**PJ** : I would say that intelligence lies in an awareness of fear arising, in leaving it alone, in not shaping it, in not turning away from it, and so leading to the dissolution of fear. But you say that where intelligence is, fear does not arise.

**NANDINI MEHTA (NM)** : Will fear not arise?

**K** : We don't allow fear to arise.

**NM** : I think fear arises, but we don't allow it to flower.

**K** : You see, I am questioning, altogether, the whole response to a crisis. Fear is there; why do you need a crisis to awaken it? You say a crisis takes place and you wake up. A word, a gesture, a look, a movement, a thought—those are challenges that you say bring it. I am asking: Why do we wait for the crisis? We are investigating. Do you know what that word 'investigate' means? It means 'to trace out'. Therefore, we are tracing out, we are not saying this, that or the other. We are following it, and I am asking: Why do I wait for a crisis? A gesture, a thought, a word, a look, a whisper—any of these are challenges.

**NM** : I don't look for the crisis. The only thing I am aware of is this, namely, that it arises and I am paralysed.

**K** : You get paralysed, why? Therefore for you, a challenge is necessary. Why don't you contact fear before the challenge? You say that a crisis awakens fear. A crisis includes a thought, a gesture, a word, a whisper, a look, a letter. Is it a challenge which awakens fear? I say to myself: Why should one not awaken to it without a challenge? If fear is there, it must be awake; or is it dormant? And if it is dormant, why is it dormant? Is the conscious mind frightened that fear may awaken? Has it put it to sleep and refused to look at it?

Let us go slowly, we are tracing the path of a rocket. Has the conscious mind been frightened of looking at fear and, therefore, kept fear quiet? Or is fear there, awake, but the conscious mind won't let it flower? Do you admit that fear is part of human life, of existence?

**PJ** : Sir, fear has no independent existence apart from the outer experience, without the stimuli of outer experience.

**K** : Wait, I question it, I don't accept it. You are saying that without the outer stimuli, it is not. If it is true for you, it must be so for me, because I am a human being.

**PJ** : Include in that both the outer and the inner stimuli.

**K** : I don't divide the outer and the inner. It is all one movement.

**PJ** : Fear has no existence apart from the stimuli.

**K** : You are moving away, Pupul.

**PJ** : You are asking: Why don't you look at it, why don't you face it?

**K** : I ask myself: Must I wait for a crisis for this fear to awaken? That's all that I ask. If it is there, who has put it to sleep? Is it because the conscious mind cannot resolve it? The conscious mind is concerned with resolving it, and not being able to do so, it puts it to sleep, squashes it. And the conscious mind is shaken when a crisis takes place and fear arises. So I ask myself: Why should the conscious mind suppress fear?

**SP** : Sir, the instrument of the conscious mind is analysis, the capacity for recognition. With these instruments it is inadequate to deal with fear.

**K** : It can't deal with it. But what is required is real simplicity, not analysis. The conscious mind cannot deal with fear, therefore it says, 'I want to avoid it, I can't look at it. Look what you are doing. You are waiting for a crisis to awaken it, and the conscious mind is all the time avoiding crisis. It is avoiding, reasoning, rationalizing. We are masters at this game. Therefore I say to myself, if fear is there, it is awake. You cannot put to sleep a thing that is part of our inheritance. The conscious mind only thinks that it has put fear to sleep. The conscious mind is shaken when a crisis takes place. Therefore deal with it differently. That is my point. Is this true? The basic fear is of non-existence, a sense of complete fear, of uncertainty, of not being, of dying. Why does the mind not bring that fear out and move with it? Why should it wait for a crisis? Is it that you are lazy and therefore you haven't got the energy to go to the root of it? Is what I am saying irrational?

**PJ :** It is not irrational. I am trying to see if it is valid.

**K :** We say that every living thing is frightened of not being, of not surviving. Fear is part of our blood cells. Our whole being is frightened of not being, frightened of dying, frightened of being killed. So fear of not being is part of our whole psychological, as well as biological structure, and I am asking myself why a crisis is necessary, why challenge should become important. I object to challenge. I want to be ahead of challenge, not behind challenge.

**PJ :** One cannot participate in what you are saying.

**K :** Why can't you? I am going to show it to you. I know I am going to die, but I have intellectualized, rationalized death. Therefore when I say my mind is far ahead of death, it is not. It is only far ahead of thought—which is not being far ahead.

**PJ :** Let us take the actuality of it. One faces death and one feels one is a step ahead and one moves on and suddenly realizes that one is not ahead of it.

**K :** I understand that. It is all the result of a challenge, whether it took place yesterday or a year ago.

**PJ :** So the question is: With what instrument, with what energy, from what dimension does one see; and what does one see?

**K :** I want to be clear. Fear is part of our structure, our inheritance. Biologically, psychologically, the brain cells are frightened of not being. And thought says, 'I am not going to look at this thing' And so when the challenge arises, thought cannot end it.

**PJ :** What do you mean when you say: thought says, 'I don't want to look at it'?

**NM :** Sir, it wants to look at itself also.

**K :** Thought cannot look at the ending of itself. It can only rationalize about it. I am asking you: Why does the mind wait for a challenge? Is it necessary? If you say that it is necessary, then you are waiting for it.

**PJ :** I say: I don't know. I only know that a challenge arises and fear arises.

**K :** No, a challenge awakens fear. Let us stick to that. And I say to you: Why do you wait for a challenge for this to awaken?

**PJ :** Your question is a paradox. Would you say that you don't wait for the challenge but evoke the challenge?

**K :** No, I am opposed to challenge altogether. You are missing my point. My mind will not accept a challenge at any time. A challenge is not necessary in order to awaken one. To say that I am asleep and that a challenge is necessary to awaken me, is a wrong statement.

**PJ :** No, sir, that's not what I am saying.

**K :** So it is awake. Now what sleeps? Is it the conscious mind? Or is it the unconscious mind that is asleep? And are there some parts of the mind that are awake?

**PJ :** When I am awake, I am awake.

**NM :** Do you invite fear?

**K :** If you are awake, no challenge is necessary. So you reject challenge. If, as we said, it is part of our life that we should die, then one is awake all the time.

**PJ :** Not all the time. You are not conscious of fear all the time. It is there all the time under the carpet, but you don't look at it.

**K :** I say: Lift the carpet and look. It is there. That is my point. It is there and awake. So it does not need a challenge to awaken it. I am frightened all the time of not being, of dying, of not achieving. That is the basic fear in our life, in our blood and it is there, always watching, guarding, protecting itself. But it is very much awake. It is never, even for a moment, asleep. Therefore, a challenge is not necessary. What you do about it and how you deal with it comes later.

**PJ :** That is the fact.

**ACHYUT PATWARDHAN (AP) :** Seeing all this, don't you accept the factor of non-attention?

**K :** I said it is awake, I am not talking of attention.

**AP :** Fear is active, operating.

**K :** It is like a snake in the room, it is always there. I may look elsewhere, but it is there. The conscious mind is concerned with how to deal with it, and as it can't deal with it, it moves away. The conscious mind then receives a challenge and tries to face it. Can you face a living thing? That does not need a challenge. But because the conscious mind has blinded itself against fear, the challenge is needed. Right, Pupul?

**NM :** When you think of it, it is just a thought; still that shadow is in the mind.

**K :** Trace it, don't jump to conclusions. You have jumped to conclusions. My mind refuses challenge. The conscious mind will not allow challenges to awaken it. It is awake. But you admit challenge. I don't admit challenge. It is not within my experience. The next step is: When the conscious mind is awake to fear, it cannot invite something that is there. Go step by step. Don't conclude at any second. So, the conscious mind knows it is there, fully awake. Then what are we going to do next?

**PJ :** There lies inadequacy.

**NM :** I am awake.

**K :** You are missing the whole point. It is the conscious mind that is frightened of this. When it is awake, it is not frightened. In itself, it is not frightened. The ant is not frightened. If it is squashed, it is squashed. It is the conscious mind that says, 'I am frightened of this—of not being'. But when I meet with an accident, an aeroplane crashes, there is no fear. At the moment of death I say, 'Yes, I know now what it means to die'. But the conscious mind with all its thoughts says, 'My God, I am going to die, I will not die, I must not die, I will protect myself'; that is the thing that is frightened. Have you never watched an ant? It is never frightened: if somebody kills it, it dies. Now you see something.

**NM :** Sir, have you ever seen an ant? If you put a piece of paper in front of the ant, it dodges it.

**K :** It wants to survive, but it is not thinking about surviving. So we will come back to it. Thought creates fear: it is only thought that says, 'I will die, I am lonely. I am not fulfilled'. See this: that is timeless eternity, that is real eternity. See how extraordinary it is. Why should I be frightened if fear is part of my being? It is only when thought says that life must be different, that there is fear. Can the mind be completely motionless? Can the mind be completely stable? Then that thing comes. When that thing is awake, what then is the central root of fear?

**PJ :** Has it ever happened to you, sir?

**K** : Several times, many times, when the mind is completely stable, without any recoil, neither accepting not denying, nor rationalizing nor escaping, there is no movement of any kind. We have got to the root of it, have we not?

*New Delhi*
*13 November 1972*

# A Dialogue on Death

**J. KRISHNAMURTI (K) :** Mrs Jayakar and I are going to have a very serious discussion, a very serious dialogue—very serious. So if you don't understand or if you get bored, please go out quietly—all right?

**PUPUL JAYAKAR (PJ) :** Krishnaji, one of the questions which I feel is at the very depth of the human mind is 'the coming to be' and 'the ceasing to be'. Life and death. The whole of man's life revolves around the wonder of birth and the fear of death. All his urges, his demands, his desires, his fears, his anxieties, rest between these two poles—birth and death.

At one level we understand birth and death, but I think that that understanding is only at the superficial level. And unless we understand, at depth, the whole problem of existence which is held between the two—the whole problem that lies in the ending of anything—fear, anxiety and the darkness and shadows which surround that one word 'ending' will always be with us.

**K :** Why do you use the word 'problem'? Why do you make that interval between birth and death a problem?

Previously published in the *KFI Bulletin* 1994/1, pp 2–11.

**PJ :** By themselves birth and death are facts, but the mind can never leave them alone. The mind clings to one and rejects the other.

**K :** Why do you use the word 'problem'?

**PJ :** It is a 'problem' because of the shadows that surround that one word 'ending'. There is the joy and splendour of what we see as life and the demand to hold on to it at any cost and to evade that which means an ending. This is a problem. Out of it arises fear, sorrow, all the demands . . . .

**K :** So what is the question?

**PJ :** How do we explore? How can we be free of the darkness that surrounds the word? How can our minds look at death with simplicity and observe it for what it is?

**K :** Are you really considering death or that great period between life and death? That is, are you including the whole process of living with all its complexity, misery, confusion—all that—in your consideration of the ending? Are you concerned to find out what death means and what this long process of struggle, conflict, misery, etc., to which we cling in our avoidance of the other, is? Are you concerned with the whole movement of it?

**PJ :** You see, there is a whole movement of existence in which life and death are. But if you make the scope so wide, I don't think you can get to the anguish and the sorrow of ending. And I want to investigate into the sorrow of ending.

**K :** Are you inquiring into the sorrow of ending or are you inquiring into the whole process of living and of dying, which includes sorrow, fear, and all the rest of it?

**PJ :** In that one sentence what you say is correct—it is the whole movement of living and dying which is existence. You talk of the ending of· sorrow; I talk of that fear, that anguish, which is the sorrow of ending.

**K** : Quite, quite.

**PJ** : The two are slightly different. There is the sorrow, the anguish, of 'something which is' ceasing to be . . . . There is something which is marvellous, something which is beautiful, which fills one's life, and there is always the knowledge that it must end which lurks behind it.

**K** : What is 'ending'?

**PJ** : Ending is that process in which something that exists, that sustains, ceases to be; it is no longer available to our senses.

**K** : I don't quite understand.

**PJ** : Sir, something is and in the very nature of that 'isness' there is the sense of the ending of that; there is the disappearance of that for eternity.

**K** : Why do you use that word 'eternity'?

**PJ** : Because there is an absoluteness in that ending. There is no tomorrow in it.

**K** : Now just a minute—ending what?

**PJ** : Ending that which sustains. There is the sorrow of something so marvellous ending.

**K** : Is it so marvellous?

**PJ** : Let me come to something which is more direct. You are. That you will not be causes great anguish. You are.

**K** : What do you mean, 'You are'?

**PJ** : K is. In that statement—K is—is the anguish of K ceasing to be.

**K** : Death is inevitable. This person—K—is going to end some day. To him it doesn't matter; there is no fear, no anguish. But you look at that person and say, 'Oh my God, he is going to die'. So if I may use that word as you used it, it is your anguish. Now, why?

**PJ** : It is . . . .

**K** : Why?

**PJ** : Why do you ask 'why'?

**K** : Someone dies. I've lived with that person; I've loved that person. He dies, and I'm lost. Why? Why am I in a terrible state— a state of despair, a state of loneliness? Why am I in tears, in anguish? Why am I in sorrow? We are not discussing this intellectually—we are talking much more seriously. I've lost that person. He's been dear to me; he's been my companion. He comes to an end. I think it is really important to understand the ending, because there is something totally new when there is an ending to everything.

**PJ** : That is why I said you cannot ask the 'why' of it.

**K** : 'Why' is merely put as an inquiry.

**PJ** : My sorrow—is it not inevitable? He was the perfume of my existence.

**K** : Yes, I loved him. He was my companion sexually, and because of him I felt fulfilled; I felt rich. And he, that person, comes to an end.

**PJ** : Is not that sorrow?

**K** : It is. My son or my brother dies. It is a tremendous sorrow. I shed tears. I am filled with anxiety. So the mind then says: I must find comfort in the thought that I shall meet him in my next life. I'm asking: Why does man carry the burden of this sorrow? I know that the death of someone is sorrow; I know it is devastating. It is as if the whole of my existence were uprooted. It is like a marvellous tree torn, cut down in an instant.

I'm in sorrow because I've never really understood deeply what ending is. I've lived for forty, fifty, or eighty years and during that entire period I have never realized the meaning of ending—the putting an end to something which I hold dear. I have never totally ended belief, totally ended attachment—ended it, so that it does not continue in another direction.

**PJ** : What makes the mind incapable of ending?

**K** : It's fear, of course. Let's take a very ordinary example, an example that is common to all of us—attachment. Can one end—without any motive or direction—attachment, with all its complexity, and all its implications? Can one have no attachment to anything—to one's experience, knowledge, memory? After all, the ending of knowledge—*that's what is going to happen when death comes*. Knowledge is what one is clinging to. The knowledge of a person whom I've cherished, whom I've looked after, and lived with. There is the memory of the beauty and the conflict that was involved in it. Now, to end totally, absolutely, the memory of all that, is death.

**PJ** : You have often said: 'Living, enter the house of death'.

**K** : Yes. I have done it.

**PJ** : What exactly is meant by that?

**K** : 'To invite death while living' does not mean to commit suicide by taking a pill and, thus, ceasing to exist. I think it is very important to invite death while living. I have done it.

You see, the word 'ending' itself contains a depth of meaning. Let us say that there is something, a memory of an experience that I cherish, that I hold on to because it has given me great delight, a sense of depth and well-being. I cling to that memory. I go to the office, I work, but the memory is so extraordinarily enduring and vital that I hold on to it; therefore I never find out what it means to end. I think there is a great deal in ending, every day, everything that one has psychologically gathered.

**PJ** : You can end attachment.

**K** : That is death.

**PJ** : That is not death.

**K** : What would you call death? The organism coming to an end? Or the image that I've built about you ending?

**PJ** : When you reduce it to that, I'd say that it is the image which you have built about someone; but there is much more to it than that.

**K** : Of course. I've lived with you, cherished you, and the image of you is deeply rooted in me. You die and the image gathers greater strength. Naturally I put flowers at the shrine of that image; I give poetic words to it. But it is the image that is living. I'm talking of the ending of that image. The mind cannot enter into a totally new dimension if there is a shadow of a memory of anything. Because that 'other' is timeless. That other dimension is eternal and if the mind has to enter into that, it must not have any element of time in it. I think this is logical, rational.

**PJ** : But life is not logical; life is not rational.

**K** : Of course not. To understand—without time—that which is everlasting, the mind must be free of all that one has gathered psychologically, which is time. Therefore, there must be ending.

**PJ** : Therefore there is no exploration into ending?

**K** : Oh yes, there is.

**PJ** : What is the exploration into ending?

**K** : What is ending—ending to continuity? The continuity of a particular thought, a particular direction, a particular desire; it is these that give life a continuity. Birth and death—in that great interval there is a deep continuity, like a river. The volume of water makes the river marvellous—like the Ganga, Rhine, Amazon—and we cannot see the beauty of the river. You see, we live on the surface of this vast river of life, and we cannot see the beauty of it because we are always on the surface. And the ending is the ending of the surface.

**PJ** : The ending of it is the ending of the surface.

**K** : Yes, the ending of the surface.

**PJ** : What dies?

**K** : All that I've accumulated, both outwardly and inwardly. I have good taste, and I've built up a good business which brings me a lot of money—nice house, nice wife, nice children, nice garden. And my life has given a continuity to it all. To end that.

**PJ** : Sir, do you mind if I explore a little? You mean to tell me that with the death of the body of K, the consciousness of K will end? Please, I'm putting a lot of weight in this.

**K** : You have said two things: The consciousness of K and the ending of the body. The body will end through accident, disease. That is obvious. What is the consciousness of that person?

**PJ** : Enormous, unending, abounding compassion.

**K** : Yes. I would not call that consciousness.

**PJ** : I'm using the word 'consciousness' because it is associated with the body of K. I cannot think of another word. I could say 'the mind of K'.

**K** : Let's keep to the word 'consciousness', if you don't mind, and let's look at it. The consciousness of a human being is its content. The content is the whole movement of thought. Language, specialization, beliefs, dogmas, rituals, pain, loneliness, desperation, a sense of fear—all that is the movement of thought. If the movement of thought ends, consciousness as we know it is not.

**PJ** : But thought as a movement in consciousness—as we know it—does not exist in the mind of K. Yet there is a state of being which manifests itself when I'm in contact with him. It manifests itself even if you do not reduce it to thought.

**K** : No, no. One must be very careful in pointing out something: Consciousness as we know it is the movement of thought; it is a movement of time.

**PJ** : Yes.

**K** : See that very clearly. Consciousness as we know it is the movement of thought. Therefore, when thought, after investigating, comes to an end—not in the material world but in the psychological world—consciousness as we know it is not.

**PJ** : Sir, you can use any other word but there *is* a state of being which manifests itself as K.

**K** : Yes; you are perfectly right.

**PJ** : What word shall I use?

**K** : I am not asking you to change words but let us say, for example, that through meditation—real meditation and not all the foolish stuff that passes for it—you've come to a point that is absolute. And you say so.

**PJ** : Yes.

**K** : And I see this. I feel it. To me this is a most extraordinary state. Through you, through my contact with you, I feel this immensity. And my whole urge, striving, says that I must capture it. But you have it—of course, it is not *you*, Pupul, having it. It is there. It is not yours or mine; it is there.

**PJ** : But it is there because of you.

**K** : It is there *not* because of me. It is there.

**PJ** : Where?

**K** : It has no place.

**PJ** : I can only accept what you say up to a point.

**K** : All right . . . . First of all, it is not yours or mine.

**PJ** : I only know that it is manifest in the person of K. Therefore when you say that it has no place, I cannot accept it.

**K** : Naturally, because you have identified K with that.

**PJ** : But K *is* that.

**K** : Wait . . . maybe. But K says that it has nothing whatsoever to do with K or anybody else. It is there. Beauty is not yours or mine. It is there. In a tree, in a flower—it's there.

**PJ** : But, sir, the healing and the compassion in K is not out there.

**K** : Of course not. It is not out there.

**PJ** : I'm talking about the healing and compassion of K.

**K** : But that is not K. That is not this. *(Pointing to the body)*

**PJ** : But it will cease to be manifest; that is what I'm saying, inquiring about.

**K** : I get it, I get it. Of course, I understand what you are trying to say. I question that.

**PJ** : What do you mean 'I question that'?

**K** : It may manifest through X. That which is manifested or which is manifesting does not belong to X. It has nothing to do with X. It has nothing to do with K.

**PJ** : I'm prepared to accept that also, namely, that it does not belong to K. But K and 'that' are inseparable.

**K** : All right, but when you identify 'that' with the person, we enter into a very delicate thing.

**PJ** : I want to go into it slowly. Take the Buddha. Whatever the

Buddha-consciousness was, or whatever was manifesting through him, has ceased to be.

**K :** I question it. I doubt it. Let's be very careful. Let us talk about the Buddha. You say that the consciousness of Buddha ceased when he passed away, right? It manifested through him and he was 'that' and when he died you say 'that' disappeared.

**PJ :** I have no knowledge of saying that it disappeared. I only say that it could no longer be contacted.

**K :** Naturally not.

**PJ :** Why do you say 'naturally not'?

**K :** Because he meditated, and all the rest of it. He was illumined, and he came to it. Therefore between him and 'that' there was no division. I, his disciple, say, 'My God, he is dead and with his death the whole thing is over'.

**PJ :** Yes, it is over.

**K :** I say it is not. *That which is good can never be over.* Just as evil (I am using the word 'evil', even though there is too much darkness involved with that word) continues in the world, right? Evil is totally different from that which is good. The good exists and has always existed, but not as the opposite of evil. The evil has in itself continued.

**PJ :** But we are moving away.

**K :** I'm not quite sure, but it doesn't matter; go ahead.

**PJ :** You say that it does not disappear.

**K :** Good can never disappear.

**PJ :** I'm talking of that great illumined compassion. Now I can contact it.

**K :** But you can contact it even if that person is not. That's the whole point. It has nothing to do with a particular person.

**PJ** : Is what you say about being a light to yourself connected with the contacting of 'that' without the person? When you say that 'it' can be contacted without the person . . . .

**K** : Not 'contacted'. It can be perceived, lived; it is there for you to reach out to and hold. For you to reach out and receive it, thought or consciousness as we know it has to come to an end, for *thought is really the enemy of that*. Thought is the enemy of compassion, obviously—right? And to have that flame, it requires, it demands, not a great sacrifice of this and that but an awakened intelligence, an intelligence which sees the movement of thought. And the very awareness of the movement of thought ends it. That's what real meditation is.

**PJ** : What significance then has death?

**K** : None. It has no meaning because you are living with death all the time. It has no significance because you are ending everything all the time. I don't think we see the importance and beauty of ending. We see the continuity with its waves of beauty and all its superficiality.

**PJ** : I drive away tomorrow. Do I cut myself completely from you?

**K** : No, not from me; you cut yourself from 'that'. You cut yourself from that eternity with all its compassion, and so on.

It's simple. I meet the Buddha. I listen to him very carefully. He makes a tremendous impression on me and, then, he goes away. But the truth of what he has said is abiding. He has told me, very carefully, 'Be a light to yourself so that the truth is in you'. It is that seed that is flowering in me. He goes away, but the seed is flowering. And I might say, 'I miss him; I'm sorry I've lost a friend or somebody whom I really loved', but what is important is that the seed of truth will flower. That seed which has been planted by my awareness, alertness, and intense listening, *that* seed will flower. Otherwise what is the point of somebody having it? If X has this extraordinary illumination—I'm using that word as a sense of immense compassion, love, and all that—if only that person has it, and he dies—what then?

**PJ** : May I ask a question, please? What, then, is the reason for his being?

**K** : What is the reason for his being, for his existence? To manifest 'that'; to be the embodiment of 'that'. But why should there be any reason? A flower has no reason. Beauty has no reason; it exists. And if I try to find a reason, the flower is not. I am not trying to mystify all this, or to put it into a fog. As I said, it is there for *anyone* to reach and to hold.

So death, Pupul, like birth, is an extraordinary event. But birth and death are so far apart. The travail of continuity is the misery of man. And if continuity can end each day, you will be living with death. That is total renewal; that is the renewal of something which has no continuity. And that is why it is important to understand the meaning of ending—totally—experience or that which has been experienced and remains in the mind as memory. *(Pause)*

Could we go, if we have time, into the question of whether a human being can live, apart from physical knowledge, without time and knowledge?

**PJ** : Isn't what we said so far, that is living with ending, the very nature of this question? That is, when the mind is capable of living with ending, it is capable of living with the ending of time and knowledge.

**K** : Yes. But all this may be just a lot of words.

**PJ** : No, sir. You see, one of the things is that you can do nothing about it, but you *can* listen and observe—nothing else.

Sir, I am getting to something which is rather different.

**K** : Please go ahead.

**PJ** : Do you think that there can be a learning in the mind to face the ultimate death?

**K** : What is there to learn, Pupul? There is nothing to learn.

**PJ** : The mind must receive without agitation.

**K** : Yes.

**PJ** : The mind must receive a statement like that without agitation. Then, perhaps, when death ultimately comes there will be no agitation.

**K** : Yes, that is right. And that is why death has an extraordinary beauty, an extraordinary vitality.

*Brockwood Park*
*6 June 1981*

# The Nature of God

**PUPUL JAYAKAR (PJ)** : Can we, please, discuss and investigate into the nature of God?

**J. KRISHNAMURTI (K)** : Are you asking what creation is or whether Reality or Truth is God?

**PJ** : Behind that word 'God' lies a millennia of man's quest for something that is absolute, for something that is untouched . . . .

**K** : Yes, for something that is universal.

**PJ** : If we can discuss everything else, why is it not possible to inquire into the nature of 'that'—call it God or creation or the ground of being.

**K** : I think it is possible if one can free the mind of all beliefs and of all the traditional implications and consequences of the word 'God'. Can the brain and mind be totally free to investigate that which the Israelis call the 'nameless' and the Hindus call 'brahman' or the 'highest principle'? The whole world believes in the *word* God. Can we put away all beliefs? For only then will it be possible to investigate.

**PJ** : But, being a word, it is a storehouse of a million years of content. So when the mind says that it is free of belief, what exactly does it mean?

**K** : A person says, 'I believe in God; God is omnipotent and omnipresent. He exists in all things'. That is the traditional acceptance of that word with all its content. Can one be free of the many thousands of years of this tradition? Can one, consciously as well as unconsciously, be free of that word—that word which has played such a tremendous part in the Islamic and Christian world?

**PJ** : At one level it is possible to say that one is free, as, for example, if you were to ask me whether I believed in God, whether I believed in Krishna, Rama or Siva. But that is not the final thing.

**K** : No.

**PJ** : There is a feeling for God that goes much beyond all this. It seems to be integral to the fact of life itself. You see, there is a sense that without 'this' nothing could exist, the sense that 'this' is the ground.

**K** : Shall we discuss that—the ground from which everything originates? How does one find out about that ground? As I said, one can only find out when one is absolutely free. Normally, our unconscious being is loaded, is absolutely crowded with all this . . . .

**PJ** : There is a possibility of a state of being where any movement of the mind as belief is out, and where belief in any particular God is negated.

**K** : Does one negate it verbally or deeply, that is, at the very root of one's being? Can one say, 'I know nothing' and stop there?

**PJ** : I cannot say, 'I know nothing'. But I *can* say that the movement of thought as belief in a particular God does not arise in the mind. Therefore there is nothing outer to negate as belief. But I still do not know the state of I-know-nothing which is a very different state from the outer movement as belief.

**K** : So could we go into that?

**PJ** : How does one proceed?

**K** : Can one negate, completely, the whole movement of knowledge? Not technological knowledge, of course. Can one negate the feeling that one knows? There is deep within one the whole accumulated experience of man which says that there is God. Of course there have been prophets and seers who have said that there is no such thing as God, but their words just add to man's beliefs, to his knowledge. The question is: Can one negate the knowledge of all that one knows?

**PJ** : Let me put it this way. One has comprehended the way of negating the rising movement . . . .

**K** : The rising movement of thought as belief?

**PJ** : Yes, but the depth, the dormancy, the thousands of years that form the matrix of one's being—how does one touch all that?

**K** : That is what one has to do.

**PJ** : Yes, but how does one touch it?

**K** : Could we begin not by inquiring into whether there is God, but by inquiring into why the human mind has worked, has struggled, with becoming—a becoming that is based on knowledge, on constant movement—not only outwardly but also inwardly?

**PJ** : Are the two related?

**K** : Which two?

**PJ** : We started with an investigation into the nature of God and then went on to speak of the matrix and becoming—are they related?

**K** : Aren't they related? I think they are, but I may be wrong. So let us look at it. You see, one's being is essentially based on the feeling that lies deep in one that there is something enormous, something incredibly immense—I am talking about that part of one's being, that knowledge, that tradition, that is the matrix, the ground on which one stands. So long as that is there, one is not actually free. Can one investigate into that?

**QUESTIONER (Q) :** Is there an inherent movement in every human being towards some unknown being? In other words, is there an inherent seeking of something that is beyond what one is taught, beyond what one picks up through one's heritage? Is it genetic?

**K :** In genetics, time is involved.

**PJ :** In genetics is the matrix.

**K :** In it is involved time and the movement of growth, of evolution. Right?

**Q :** Yes, it is a biological movement.

**K :** That is what I want to get at. Even if it is an inherent thing, can one totally empty one's self of all that? Can one empty one's self of the accumulation of a million years? Let us examine it.

Can one empty one's self of that which may be implanted from childhood? Can one empty one's self of the centuries of belief that there is something beyond all this? I think that that is the most deep-rooted belief. It is something that is in the unconscious—deep things always are. And I think that if we want to investigate, that belief must go too.

**PJ :** Can one go to the last movement of the unconscious mind? Sir, is it possible, without the unconscious being exposed, for it to end? How does one experience that which one cannot formulate, that which lies beyond the total particulars of any one person's knowledge?

**K :** I understand.

**PJ :** I can go through the whole of my knowledge, and yet it will not contain it.

**K :** No. But aren't you getting an insight into this, namely, that there must be the total negating of everything man has put together?

**Q :** You are asking us to deny, to negate, everything—even our small insights that bring us to this point, namely, the point where we realize that there is something in what you are saying.

**K :** Pupulji is asking quite a different question, sir. She is asking whether we can investigate, explore into what we call God—the origin, the beginning, of all things.

**Q :** But aren't you saying that even to begin we have to put aside all things, all beliefs; put aside in fact, the very ground on which we stand? I wonder whether our small insights and perceptions are not mixed up with that.

**PJ :** I understand now. Yes, what we consider insights have to go.

**Q :** How then does one begin to investigate? You deny even the basis for perceiving something.

**PJ :** No. But the insight is over. So it is part of the past already—it is as much the past as any other memory. I comprehend the negation of all that arises in the brain. But the layers of the unconscious, the ground on which one stands, can one negate that? Perhaps one is asking the wrong question. Perhaps there can never be a negating of that. How can one negate that?

**K :** Just a minute. Man has tried in several ways to negate everything. He has fasted, he has tortured himself, but he has always remained anchored to something.

**PJ :** Yes.

**K :** Like the great Christian mystics; they were anchored to Jesus, and from there they moved.

**PJ :** May I ask you a question? Do you think we are anchored to you?

**K :** Maybe, but that's irrelevant.

**PJ** : That is not irrelevant.

**Q** : Are we not anchored to our few perceptions?

**K** : If you are, then put them away; weigh the anchor . . . .

**Q** : One can be free of being anchored to most things, but can one cease to be anchored to the question?

**K** : Oh yes, oh yes.

**Q** : In other words, all the answers about God, Reality, etc., are deep in us. That perhaps can be negated, but . . . .

**K** : I wouldn't ask that question: What is God? For then my brain would start spinning a lot of words.

**Q** : It seems to me that we have already put the question and gone beyond the replies. But behind all that remains the inquiry.

**K** : What do you mean 'remains the inquiry'?

**Q** : By the 'inquiry remaining' I mean that the question whether there is something else seems to be innately in us. In other words, the movement towards that question seems to be innately in us.

**K** : If my investigation is a movement towards the understanding of what is called God, that movement itself is a bondage.

**Q** : Why?

**K** : What do you mean 'why'? Obviously movement means a motion *towards* something. And an action, a movement, implies time. Why are you introducing all this?

**Q** : I am trying to get behind what you are saying.

**K** : Don't let us use words that have implications of time, implications of going towards something. Going towards something, trying to find something, implies time—and that must stop.

**Q** : Then how can Pupul ask that question?

**K** : That is the whole point. Our question is whether one can do such a thing in the first place. Is that possible—to be so totally in and with non-movement? For otherwise we will be forever with movement, which is time and thought, and all the rest of it.

First of all, why do we want to find the meaning of God? Why do we want to find the meaning behind all this?

**PJ** : There is a part of us which is still . . . .

**K** : Still seeking, searching, demanding. Is there?

**PJ** : There is a part of us which feels that there is . . . .

**K** : Yes, that's it. We never say, 'I don't know'. I think that that is one of our difficulties. We all want to know. We put God into the realm of knowledge. To say, 'I don't know' is a state of mind that is absolutely motionless.

**PJ** : Look sir, isn't there in the ear listening, the eye seeing, the word said, the whole content of what God is? Is it not necessary to wipe out this matrix?

**K** : Oh yes.

**PJ** : Should not the ear listen to you?

**K** : Can you wipe out the matrix?

**PJ** : I don't know.

**K** : Which is what? When you use the word 'matrix' what do you mean by that?

**PJ** : I only know that beyond the horizons of my mind, behind the obvious beliefs . . . .

**K** : Cut out all that; that is superficial.

**PJ** : . . . there are depths and depths and depths in me. You use a very significant phrase—somewhere or the other—'Play around with the deep'. So you also point to depths which lie below the surface. Is this depth within the matrix?

**K** : No. No, it can't be. My question is: Why do I want to find out whether there is something beyond all this?

**PJ** : Because, Krishnaji, I can do nothing about this matrix.

**K** : I wonder what you call the matrix?

**PJ** : I mean by it this depth which I cannot bring to the surface, into the daylight of consciousness, of perception, of attention. I mean by 'matrix' that which does not come within the purview of my eyes and ears, but is still there. I know it is there. It is 'me'. Even though I am not able to see it, to touch it, I have a feeling that perhaps, *if* there is a right listening to the truth . . . .

**K** : Then why do you use the word 'depth'? For 'depth' is of necessity linked with the measurable.

**PJ** : I am using the word 'depth' to connote something that is beyond my knowledge. You see, if it is within the contours of my horizon, if it is available to my senses, then it is measurable. But if it is not available, I can do nothing about it. I do not have the instruments to reach it.

**K** : How do you know that it is all not imagination? Do you know it as an experience?

**PJ** : Yes.

**K** : Ah! Careful, careful.

**PJ** : The problem is: If you say 'yes' it is a trap, and even if you say 'no' it is a trap.

**K** : I want to be quite clear, Pupul, that we both understand the meaning of the word. I am talking of a *feeling*.

**PJ** : Surely, sir, a word can be uttered lightly, from the surface of the mind, and it can also be uttered with great depth behind it. I am saying that there is this ground that contains the whole history of man. There is life in that utterance; it has great weight and depth. Can't you feel that depth? So, can I not go into it without your asking me whether it is all a matter of imagination? For if it is so, then there is nothing to be done, but to just look and listen. There is no question that one can ask oneself.

**K :** I understand Pupul, but you see that depth—is it the depth of silence? Silence means that the mind, the brain, is utterly still; it is not something that comes and goes.

**PJ :** How can I answer that?

**K :** I think one can if there is no sense of attachment to it, no sense of memory involved in it. Let's begin again.

The whole world believes in God. In Ceylon they were very upset when I said that the word 'God' is put together by thought. Do you remember? Unfortunately I don't know what God is. Let us start with that. I really don't know what God is. Probably I will never find out, and I am not interested in finding out. But what I am concerned with is whether the mind, the brain, can be totally, completely, free from all accumulated knowledge-experience. Because if it is not free, it will function always within its field. It might expand enormously, but it will always be confined to that area. You see, it doesn't matter how much one accumulates, for it will still be within that area and, if the mind moves from that area and says 'I must find out', then it will still be carrying on the movement. I don't know whether I am making myself clear.

My concern is whether the brain, the mind, can be completely free from all taint of knowledge. To me that is tremendously significant, because if it is not, it will never be out of that area. Never.

Any movement of the mind out of that area is still a movement that is anchored in knowledge; it will then only be a seeking of knowledge about God. So my concern is with whether the mind, the brain, is capable of being completely immovable.

When you confront a question of that kind, if you deny both the possibility and the probability of it, then what is left? Do you follow?

Could I have insight, the depth of insight into the movement of knowledge, so that the insight stops the movement? The insight stops the movement, not I or the brain. The stopping of the movement is the ending of knowledge and the beginning of something else. So I am concerned only with that—the ending of knowledge consciously, deeply.

There is this enormous feeling that comes when we realize that we are all one. The feeling that comes from oneness, from a harmonious unity, is extraordinary, and if it is simulated it is worthless, for then you will only be perpetuating yourself. Right?

**Q :** The 'me' that has built all the relationships of the world, that has created all the beauty of the world, all the culture of the world, the art of the world—has that 'me' no connection whatsoever with what we call God?

**Q :** Could we talk a little more about this questioning which seems so complete? Could we discuss having no anchor? Is having no anchor the putting aside of everything?

**K :** Don't you see the importance of it? And, if you do, ask yourself whether it is merely intellectual.

**Q :** Yes, sir, I do see the importance of it; but, apparently that is not enough.

**PJ :** Somehow there is something we are missing.

**K :** Look, Pupul, suppose this person—K—were not here. How would you deal with this problem? How would you deal with the problem of God, with the problem of belief—how would you actually deal with it without any reference to anybody?

Let's move from there. You see, each one of us is totally responsible. We are not referring to past authorities—to saints.

Each one is totally responsible to answer this question. *You* have to answer.

**PJ** : Why should I have to answer?

**K** : I will tell you why. You have to answer because you are part of humanity, and humanity is asking this question. Every saint, every philosopher, every human being somewhere in his depths is asking this question.

**Q** : Sir, is not this question somewhere, in a sense, wrong?

**K** : I said so. But you have to answer it without any reference to what K has said or not said. I come to you with these questions. To me, as a human being, these questions are tremendously important.

**PJ** : May I ask you something? How does one take a question like this and leave it in consciousness?

**K** : Either, Pupul, you have thought about it and gathered tremendous information from books, or you have never thought about this question at all. This may be the first time you're facing this question, so go slowly, go very slowly.

**PJ** : You see, sir, you have a way of taking a question, asking it and, then, remaining with it.

**K** : Yes, that is right.

**PJ** : When we ask such a question, there is a movement of the mind towards it. With you, when such a question is put, there is no movement.

**K** : You're right. Now are you asking 'how' to achieve this state?

**PJ** : I know that I can't.

**K** : No, but you are right to ask that question. Do you understand what Pupul said? I am asking you as a human being, just as human beings have for a million years: What is God? I come and put this question to you. Are you ready to answer it or do you hold the question quietly? Hold it—do you understand? For out of that very holding, that holding where there is no reaction, no response, comes the answer.

**Q** : Could you say something about the nature of that holding?

**K** : I am talking of a holding that is without any wave, without any motive or movement, a holding that is without any trace of trying to find an answer.

**Q** : With most of us, we may not try to find an answer; we may first remain quietly with an unanswered question, but sooner or later an answer comes that may be something from the deep wells of the unconscious, and that answer rises up to fill that space.

**K** : I know. Now, just a minute. I ask you a question: Do you believe in God? Can you say, 'I don't know'? Or do you immediately say, 'I don't believe' or 'I believe' or 'Maybe there is' and so on? Can you look at the question—just look—without saying a single thing? Can you? You see, if you ask a devout Christian that question, he will immediately say, 'Of course I believe in God'. You will also get an immediate reaction if you were to ask a Hindu—it's like pressing a button. But *I* really don't know whether there is God or not.

**PJ** : Then there is nothing the mind can do.

**Q** : Are you saying, sir, that 'holding' is something that takes place outside this area?

**K** : Of course.

**Q** : In holding isn't there an inquiry?

**K** : No, you see, unless you understand this it can lead to a great deal of misunderstanding. Sir, computers can be programmed by ten different professors all of whom have a great deal of knowledge, tremendous information. Now, the computer analyses all their questions and makes a synthesis and replies.

Our brains work that way too. We have been programmed for thousands of years, and the brain replies immediately. If the brain is not programmed, it is watching, looking. Now, can our brains be without a programme?

**Q** : But this activity of looking is not the holding—right? Can you say something about the holding?

**K** : You say it.

**Q** : I have nothing to say.

**K** : Push; you have to push.

**Q** : You have spoken of a cup that holds water, and of the earth that holds the pond. Is there something that holds like the cup and the earth hold?

**K** : No, no, we are going away. Pupulji asked me a question, a question that had great depth. You heard that question, you received that question—what was your response to it?

**Q** : Which question sir?

**K** : She was speaking about the depth, the ground. What was your reaction to that?

**Q** : I was just listening; I was just trying to understand.

**PJ** : You see, sir, when a question is normally put to the mind, it is like a grain of sugar being dropped on the ground—ants from all over come towards it. Similarly, when a question is posed, all the movements, all the responses are awakened, and gravitate towards the question.

Now the question is: Can the question be asked without the movements?

**K** : Without the ants, yes. I am told that when the brain is not operating, it is quiet; it has a movement of its own. We are talking of the brain that is in constant movement, the energy of which is thought. To quieten thought is the problem. How will you deal with this question? Can you question thought completely? Don't answer immediately. Look at it; hold it. This is not an examination. Can you have a mind that is capable of not reacting immediately to a question? Can there be a delaying reaction, perhaps a holding of the question indefinitely?

Let's go back, Pupulji. Can I have no anchors at all—either in knowledge or in belief? Can I see that they have no meaning whatsoever? I think it is absolutely essential not to give meaning to anything.

Is that a state of mind that is out of time? Is that a state of real profound meditation—a meditation in which there is no state of achievement; nothing? The state in which the meditator is not the ground, the origin, of all things.

**PJ** : So are you saying that the meditator is not the ground?

**K** : Obviously, he is not.

**PJ** : Can the ground be without the meditator?

**K** : If the meditator is, the ground is not.

**PJ** : But can there be meditation without the meditator?

**K** : I am speaking of a meditation without the meditator.

**PJ** : Is not meditation a human process?

**K** : No.

**PJ** : Let us investigate this if we may? Meditation cannot be free of the individual being. There can be no meditation without the meditator. You may say that the meditator is not the ground, but . . . .

**K** : No, just a minute. As long as I'm trying to meditate, meditation is not.

**PJ** : Yes.

**K** : Therefore there is only a brain, a mind, that is in a state of meditation.

**PJ** : Yes.

**K** : Now that is the ground. The universe is in a state of meditation. And that is the ground, that is the origin of everything; and that is only possible when the meditator is not.

**PJ** : And that is only possible when there are no anchors . . . .

**K** : Absolutely. That is when there is absolute freedom from sorrow. That state of meditation comes with the complete ending of the self.

You know, Pupul, beginning may be the eternal process, it may be an eternal beginning.

You see, the question really is whether it is at all possible for a brain, for a human being, to be completely, utterly, free of the meditator. This is essential—right? The meditator tries to meditate in order to get somewhere, in order to hide something, in order to put his life in order. Whichever way you put it—you meditate to put your life in order or you put your life in order and then meditate—it is still the meditator in operation. The question is whether it is possible to be free of the meditator. If it is possible to be free of the meditator, then there would be no question of whether there is God or no God for then that meditation is the meditation of the universe.

Is it possible to be so utterly free? I am asking that question. Don't reply; hold it. Do you see what I mean? Let it operate. In the holding of it, energy is being accumulated and that energy will act—not *you*. Do you understand? *(Long pause)*

So, have we understood the nature of God?

*Brockwood Park*
*27 May 1981*

112

# Can the Brain Renew Itself?

**PUPUL JAYAKAR (PJ) :** I was wondering whether we could discuss the nature of birth in the human mind, that is, whether a mind that is jaded, old and incapable of perception can renew itself totally. Can it have a new perception? For you see, sir, the problem with many of us is that as we grow old we find that the quickness of our minds . . . .

**J. KRISHNAMURTI (K) :** Is lost.

**PJ :** Yes, that the capacity to perceive and to take in deeply grows dim.

**K :** Are you asking whether it is possible to keep the mind very young and yet ancient?

**PJ :** Yes. You use the word 'ancient'. In fact, you have used it several times. I would like to know what is meant by the word 'ancient'. Obviously the ancient you speak about is unrelated to time as yesterday. What then is the nature of this ancient?

**K :** Let's go into it. After all, the human brain has its own—as far as one understands and as far as the scientists speak about the quality of the brain and how it works—protective nature; there is a protective chemical reaction when it experiences shock, or pain.

The human brain is very, very ancient, very, very old. It has evolved from the ape to the human. It has evolved through time, through tremendous experience. It has acquired a great deal of knowledge—both outward as well as inward—and so it is really very ancient. And as far as I can understand, it is not a personal brain. It is not 'my' brain or 'your' brain.

**PJ** : But, sir, obviously *your* brain and *my* brain have a different quality of the ancient in them.

**K** : Now wait. I am just exploring; I am just laying the first bricks. Is it granted that the brain is very old, very ancient and that our brains are not individual brains?

**PJ** : Yes.

**K** : Our brains are *not* individual brains. We may have reduced the brain to a personal thing—in fact most of us think of it as 'my' brain and 'your' brain—but the brain cannot have evolved through time as 'my' brain. I mean, such a thing is obviously absurd.

**PJ** : Yes.

**K** : Yes, but unfortunately, most of us think that it is a personal brain. 'My' brain—and it is from this that is born the whole individualistic concept.

**PJ** : Yes.

**K** : Now, are we saying that such an ancient brain has been so conditioned that it has become superficial, rather coarse, rather vulgar and artificial? Has it lost what is imbedded very deep down in the unconscious?

**PJ** : But an ancient mind—as you said just now—is the result of evolution *in* time.

**K** : Of course. Evolution means time.

**PJ** : Now the search which has gone on for centuries . . . .

114

**K** : Since the beginning of time man must have asked . . . .

**PJ** : Yes, man has asked whether it is possible to free the brain of time—time which is built into this aging process. Sir, when you talk of an ancient brain, are you talking of a brain which has also in-built in it . . . .

**K** : The quality of its own deterioration? Yes.

**PJ** : Why is that so?

**K** : It is so because experience and knowledge has limited it, conditioned it, narrowed it down. The more the brain acquires knowledge, the more it limits itself. Right?

**PJ** : You seem to be implying two things, Krishnaji. One is the sense of the ancient as the weight of the past which gives it a sense of being very old, because it is many thousands of years. And all the experiences . . . .

**K** : Have conditioned it, narrowed it down, limited it.

**PJ** : But the ancient you are talking about—are you talking about a brain that has experienced through time?

**K** : No. We will go into that. First let us see how ancient it is in the normal sense of that word, and how it has—in its thousands of years of experience—limited itself. Therefore, in it there is the quality of its own deterioration. And, living in the modern world—with all the noise, with all the terrible shocks and the agonies of war, and so on—has made the brain still more limited, still more enmeshed in conflict. The very limitation brings its own conflict.

**PJ** : Sir, there is a mind which, because of the sense of the thousands of years, gives to it a density and weight.

**K** : Yes, you're quite right.

**PJ** : Then there is a mind which is brittle, which is easily corroded.

**K :** You use the words 'mind' and 'brain'. What are you talking about?

**PJ :** The brain.

**K :** Then keep to the brain. Don't use the word 'mind'.

**PJ :** I'll use the word 'brain'. The brain has a certain weight and density to it.

**K :** Yes. It has a coarseness to it, a heaviness to it.

**PJ :** Now, is that what you mean by the ancient?

**K :** Not quite. Let's go into it slowly. Do we admit that the brain by its own evolution has conditioned itself and, therefore, it has in it the inherent quality of its own destruction?

**PJ :** Yes.

**K :** Now, the question is whether that quality of its in-built deterioration can ever be stopped. Can the brain cells renew themselves in spite of their conditioning? Do you follow what I'm saying?

**PJ :** Yes.

**K :** In spite of the agonies, failures, miseries, and all the other complexities of this modern world in which we live, can the brain renew itself so as to achieve its originality? By 'originality' is meant not a sense of individuality, but the sense of its origin.

**PJ :** Would you say that the brain cells of the baby are original in that sense?

**K :** No, of course not.

**PJ :** So, what is meant by the originality of the brain cells?

**K :** Let's go into it a little bit. The word 'original'—what does it mean? Unique? Special?

**PJ :** The word has a quality of the first time.

**K** : Yes, a pristine quality. 'Original' means untouched, uncontaminated by knowledge.

**PJ** : Yes.

**K** : Can such a brain, which has been conditioned for many thousands of years, wipe away its conditioning and achieve a quality of pristine freshness? But this may be a wrong question altogether.

**PJ** : Scientists say that the brain cells are dying all the time. Therefore the number of brain cells available . . . .

**K** : But the brain also renews itself. Apparently certain cells die and some others are born. The cells are not dying all the time. Otherwise the brain would go to pieces; it would die.

**PJ** : The very fact of aging is that the renewal does not keep pace with the dying of the cells.

**K** : Yes, but that's the whole point. Is it possible for a brain that has been conditioned and which therefore has, as you put it, the in-built quality of its own deterioration, to renew itself? Can that brain renew itself? Can that in-built quality of deterioration end, disappear?

That is, can the brain keep young, fresh, alive, with the quality of its originality?

**PJ** : How would you proceed from there?

**K** : Before we proceed, I think we have to go into the question of what consciousness is, for that is part of our whole being. We have to go not only into the being-conscious-of-things, both outwardly and inwardly, but also into the whole content of consciousness. Because without the content there is no consciousness as we know it. The question is: Can the content which makes up this consciousness end by itself? Can that consciousness end by itself, so that there is a totally different dimension to consciousness?

Now, the content of consciousness is consciousness: pleasure, belief, excitement, sensation, reaction, faith, agony, suffering, affection. The whole of that is consciousness.

**PJ :** Yes.

**K :** And, as long as the content, which is all this, exists, the brain must, because of the conflict within consciousness, wear itself out. And that's why there is no freshness to it. The brain grows old; it ages and dies.

**PJ :** Is the content of consciousness identical with the brain cells?

**K :** Yes, of course.

**PJ :** Because of the very nature of consciousness and its content, the brain wears itself out . . . .

**K :** Through conflict. Be careful.

**PJ :** Yes, I understand that. That very process is wearing out the brain cells.

**K :** That is conflict: the disturbance, the shocks, the pressures.

**PJ :** So the physical and the psychological are really the same. The pain is physical. The content of consciousness is psychological.

**K :** Which is also a process of the physical.

**PJ :** Yes.

**K :** So, it is the psychological as well as the physical which is all this—the reactions which bring about the thought of pain, the thought of agony, the thought of pleasure, the thought of achievement, ambition, belief, faith, and so on.

**PJ :** That creates a disturbance.

**K :** Yes.

118

**PJ** : But it is the nature of the brain cells to continually die. That also is in-built in the brain.

**K** : Of course. It's there, as also its own chemical reactions to protect itself.

**PJ** : Yes. But so is time in-built in the brain cells.

**K** : Of course; after all, the brain is a product of time.

Now, the question really is whether consciousness with its content can totally end. That is, can conflict totally end?

**PJ** : But with conflict totally ending, will time end?

**K** : Yes. After all, that is what the sannyasis, the monks, the real thoughtful people have inquired into. They have all asked the question whether time stops, whether there is an end to time.

**PJ** : Yes; but you are talking of time now as the psychological process of conflict.

**K** : Yes.

**PJ** : Not time as duration—between one sunrise and one sunset.

**K** : No. So what is it that we are trying to find out? What are we trying to investigate together?

**PJ** : What is it that will bring this quality of birth into the brain?

**K** : Let's be clear what we mean by 'birth'. Do we mean by 'birth' a new, fresh element entering the brain?

**PJ** : By using the word 'birth' I am suggesting freshness, purity . . . .

**K** : Wait a minute; be careful. What do you mean by 'birth'? A baby is born but its brain has already the quality and tradition of its father, its mother.

**PJ** : But birth also has the quality of the new. Birth is: It was not, and it is.

**K** : You are using 'birth' in the sense of the old being born. The ancient brain—which is neither yours nor mine, because it is universal—is reborn in a baby.

**PJ** : Yes. But what is born in a brain that is free? Is it the ancient that is reborn?

**K** : Let's be clear, Pupul. First, is it possible to be free of this conditioning of the brain that has brought about its own decay? And, also, is it possible for that consciousness to totally end all its conflicts? For only then will it be possible to have a new birth.

I don't know if you follow what I'm saying. As long as one's brain, that is, one's consciousness, is in conflict, no new element can enter into it. It's obvious. Would you grant that not just verbally but actually? Do you see the fact that as long as I am fighting, fighting, struggling to become something . . . .

**PJ** : Yes, I think one sees that.

**K** : Now, if one actually sees that, inwardly as it were, then the question arises whether it is possible to end it—end suffering, end fear, and so on.

**PJ** : You see, Krishnaji, the danger is that you can end it—end suffering, and all that—without renewal.

**K** : No, wait.

**PJ** : Please, just listen.

**K** : All right.

**PJ** : There is the possibility of ending all these things . . . .

**K** : And yet . . . .

**PJ** : And yet diminishing.

**K** : We mean two different things by 'ending'.

**PJ** : Ending what?

**K :** Ending that 'which is'—which is my consciousness. All the thoughts that I have had, all the complexities that have been accumulated through time—the ending of all that. So we'll have to be clear what we mean by 'ending'. Do you end all 'that which is' by a deliberate act of will, by a deliberate idea, because of a purpose, or some superior goal?

**PJ :** You see, Krishnaji, when an ending actually happens, which is the coming to a stop, the standing still of the mind, it happens without any reason. It is not due to any single cause.

**K :** Yes. Let's go slowly.

**PJ :** So, is it that you throw yourself to chance?

**K :** No. No. Let's be clear first, Pupulji. What do we mean by 'ending'? Does the ending create its own opposite?

**PJ :** No.

**K :** Wait; careful. We generally mean that. I end this in order to get that.

**PJ :** No. I am not talking about that ending.

**K :** I mean by 'ending' the total perception of 'that which is'. In other words, by 'ending' I mean having a total perception of my consciousness, having a whole, a complete perception of that consciousness which is inside. That inside has no motive, no remembrance; it is an immediate perception, and in the ending of it, there is something beyond, which is not touched by thought. That's what I mean by 'ending'.

**PJ :** Is it the million years which you call the 'ancient'?

**K :** That's part of the ancient brain—of course, naturally.

**PJ :** Is it that the totality of that million years sees itself?

**K :** Yes, that's right. That is the real question. Look, Pupul, let's make it a little more simple, a little more definite. Do we see the point that our consciousness has been cultivated through time?

**PJ :** Yes.

**K :** Just a minute. And any reaction to the ending of that is a further series of reactions. Which is, if I desire to end it, then that very desire creates another object to be gained.

**PJ :** Yes.

**K :** Can there be a possibility of perceiving without the movement of the future? Do you understand what I mean? Ending has no future. There is only ending. But the brain says, 'I cannot end that way, because I need a future to survive'.

**PJ :** Yes, because in-built in it is the future.

**K :** Of course. So is there an ending to the psychological demands, conflicts, and so on, *without* the thought of the future? Is there an ending to all this without the thought, 'What will happen if I end?' I don't know if I am conveying anything. You see, we generally give up something if we are guaranteed something else. I'll give up, for example, suffering, if you guarantee me that I'll be happy with the ending of it, or if there is some extraordinary reward awaiting me. This is because my whole brain, my whole consciousness, is based on the notion of reward and punishment. Punishment is the ending and reward is the gaining.

**PJ :** Yes.

**K :** Now, as long as these two elements exist in the brain, the present—modified, of course—will go on, will continue.

**PJ :** Right.

**K :** So, can the two principles of reward and punishment end so that, when suffering ends, the brain is not seeking a future existence in paradise?

**PJ :** But even if it is not seeking a future in paradise, suffering itself corrodes the brain.

**K** : Yes. But you see, Pupulji, it is very important to understand that the brain is constantly seeking security. It must have security. That's why tradition, remembrance, the past, have extraordinary significance. Right? The brain needs security. The baby needs security. Security being food, clothes, shelter and also our faith in God, our faith in some ideal, our faith in a better society in the future.

Now, the brain says, 'I must have deep security; otherwise I can't function'. Right? But just look at it, Pupul: physically there is no security, because you are going to die. And psychologically too there is no security, no actual security at all. Am I going too fast?

**PJ** : No. But I still say that there is one central demand.

**K** : What? To survive?

**PJ** : No, sir.

**K** : What is the central demand?

**PJ** : The central demand is to have a mind, to have a brain, which has the flavour of a new existence.

**K** : Who demands it? Who actually wants such a brain? Not the vast majority of people. They only say, 'Please, let us stay as we are'.

**PJ** : No, but we are not talking about the vast majority. I am discussing with you, or X is discussing with you . . . .

**K** : Let's be clear.

**PJ** : Sir, what I am getting at is that there are many ways of getting security.

**K** : No, no, Pupul, I question whether there is security in the sense we want security.

**PJ** : Sir, the brain will never understand.

**K** : Oh yes, it will. It will.

**PJ** : Because in-built in it . . . .

**K** : But, that is why I am saying perception is important.

**PJ** : Perception of what?

**K** : The perception of what actually 'is'. Move from there. Slowly, slowly.

**PJ** : The perception of 'what is' includes the creative things it has done, the stupid things it has done, what it considers worthwhile, what it does not consider worthwhile. So it is the perception of all this and the ending of all this.

**K** : No, just a minute. Careful, Pupul; let's go slowly, if you don't mind. We are talking about the perception of 'what is' actually going on. Right? What is going on around me physically, outwardly, and what is going on or happening psychologically, inwardly— that is 'what is'.

**PJ** : Yes.

**K** : Now the question is: Can 'what is' be transformed? 'What is' is my consciousness which is part of the brain.

**PJ** : But in the emptying of that consciousness . . . .

**K** : That's the whole point. We are asking the question: Is that possible? Is it possible to empty or to wipe away the whole of my past? The past is time. The whole of the content of my consciousness is the past, which may project the future, but the future still has its roots in the past. Do you understand?

**PJ** : Yes.

**K** : Now, is it possible to empty out everything? This is really a tremendous question. It is not an ideological or intellectual question. Is it psychologically possible not to have the burden of a thousand yesterdays?

The ending of that is the beginning of the new. The ending of that *is* the new.

**PJ :** You asked just now, 'Is it possible, psychologically, not to have the burden of a thousand yesterdays?'

**K :** Yes.

**PJ :** Is the problem in the burden or in the thousand yesterdays?

**K :** *The thousand yesterdays is the burden.* You cannot separate the two.

**PJ :** The thousand yesterdays is a fact. The burden is because I have given a special content to many of the experiences I have had.

**K :** Just a minute. Would there be the thousand yesterdays if there was no remembrance of the sorrows held in those thousand days? Can I separate the yesterdays by the calendar?

**PJ :** Yes. You can separate the thousand yesterdays from the burden.

**K :** Show me how.

**PJ :** Let us take one's own life. You can cut away the thousand yesterdays from the pain, from the sorrow, which is the burden.

**K :** What do you mean by 'cut away'? Also, can *you* cut away? You see, cutting away implies two parts.

**PJ :** It is possible to understand what one has to do with the superficial memories of the yesterdays.

**K :** Do you know what that means? Have I really wiped out or ended the thousand yesterdays with all their superficialities, their pettiness, their narrowness, brutality, cruelty, ambitions, and so on? Can I wipe all that away? Can all that end? You say, 'I can cut away', but who holds the knife? What is the knife, and who or what is the entity that is cutting?

**PJ :** Why do you draw a distinction between the *ending* of 'what is' and the *cutting* away?

125

**K** : 'Ending' to me implies that there is no continuation of something that has been. 'Cutting away' implies two parts of the same thing.

Now I'm asking, is it first of all possible to completely end the whole content of human consciousness which has grown through millennia? And that content is this confusion, vulgarity, coarseness, pettiness and the triviality of our stupid lives.

**PJ** : But it is also the goodness . . . .

**K** : Now, wait a minute. I must be very careful. Goodness is something entirely different. Goodness has no opposite. Goodness is not the outcome of that which is not good. The ending of that which is not good is goodness. Now, is it possible to end all conflict?

**PJ** : Yes, there is an ending to conflict.

**K** : Is there, Pupul, really an ending? Or is there merely a forgetfulness of that which has been and which has caused conflict?

**PJ** : You mean to say, sir, that the very fact of the ending of conflict is the birth of the new?

**K** : Yes. Do you see the implications of conflict? Do you see the depth of it, not just the superficiality? The superficiality is merely to say that I'm no longer British or French or that I don't belong to this country or that country or this religion or that religion. I am not speaking of the ending of superficial things. I am talking of what is deeply imbedded.

**PJ** : You're talking of conflict as separation from another.

**K** : Yes, as separateness, as isolation which inevitably breeds conflict. That is the real thing. What does that mean? When there is no conflict, can all problems end? And when a problem arises, can one end it immediately? Problems mean conflict.

**PJ** : Why do problems arise?

**K** : A problem is something thrown at you, something which is a challenge. A problem is something you have to face.

**PJ** : Yes.

**K** : We resolve a problem intellectually or physically—which creates still further problems.

**PJ** : You mean to say, sir, for the birth of the new . . . .

**K** : Yes, you're getting it . . . . It must be so. And, therefore, the birth of the new is the most ancient.

**PJ** : Can we go into that a little? Would you, please, say a little about it?

**K** : For, after all, that is the ground beyond which there is no other ground. That's the origin beyond which there is no other origin. *(Long pause)*

See, Pupul, this is really a question of whether the brain can ever be free from its own bondage. After all, ending something is not total freedom. Right? I can end, for example, my hurts. I can end them, very simply. But the images that I have created about myself, those images get hurt.

**PJ** : Yes.

**K** : And the maker of the images is the problem. So the thing is to live a life without a single image. Then there will be no hurt, no fear, and if there is no fear, there will be no sense of safety or comfort—God, and all the rest of it.

Would you say that the origin of all life is the ancient of ancients, beyond all thought of old or new? Would you say that that is the origin of all life and, also, that when the mind—which includes the brain—reaches that point, it is the ground which is totally original, new, uncontaminated? My question is whether it is possible for the mind to reach that.

Meditation has been one of the means to reach it. The silencing of the mind has been one of the ways through which man hopes to bring it about. We are all making efforts to come to it. What I'm saying is that it requires no effort. The very word 'effort' means conflict. That which has no conflict, cannot be approached through conflict.

**PJ** : In a sense, sir, does it really mean that there is no partial approach at all in your teaching?

**K** : Impossible. How can there be? If I were to approach it through the various paths which the Hindus have discovered—*karma, yoga*, and the rest, all of which are partial—I would never be able to come near it; I would never be able to approach it.

**PJ** : Then what does one do? I am an ordinary human being—what do I do?

**K** : That is the real problem. You cannot do anything. You can only do physical activities. Psychologically you cannot do anything.

**PJ** : What do you mean by 'physical' activity?

**K** : Creating a garden, building a house . . . .

**PJ** : The physical movement is going on. So what does one do?

**K** : But, if there is no psychological fear, there will be no division of countries, and so on. There will be no division—period.

**PJ** : Yes, but the fact is that there is psychological fear.

**K** : That's just it. Therefore, you will never get there. A mind, a brain, which has lived in psychological isolation and all its attendant conflicts, can never possibly come to that ground—that ground which is the origin of all life. Obviously not. How can my petty mind, worrying about my beastly little self . . . ?

**PJ** : Then the whole of life is so futile, sir. If after doing everything I haven't even taken the first step, then where am I?

**K** : What is the first step? Just a minute; go into it. What is the first step?

**PJ** : I would say that the first step is seeing 'whatever is'.

**K** : Seeing 'what is'. Right. Wait. How do you see it? How do you approach it? For on that depends the totality of 'what is'. Do you only see 'what is' partially? If you see the totality of 'what is', it is finished.

**PJ** : You see, sir, it doesn't just work like that.

**K** : Of course not. Because our minds, our thoughts, are fragmented; therefore you approach life, or 'what is' actually with your fragmented mind, fragmented brain . . . .

**PJ** : *(Interrupting)* But again, I'll say, with time the fragmented gets less. Don't jump on me but, with time, it does get less, and it *is* possible when we listen to you, for the mind to be still, for the mind not to make any movement, not to make any effort. But that's still not the first step.

**K** : The first step is to observe or to perceive 'what is'.

**PJ** : Yes.

**K** : *That* is where I would begin—by seeing if I lead a life of fragmentation. *(Pause)*

You see, Pupul, if I were to perceive 'what is' partially, that would lead to further complications. Right? Partial perception creates problems. Now, is it possible to see the whole complex of 'what is'? Is it possible to see the whole, and not the fragment? Because if I approach life—which is my consciousness, the way of thought, feeling, actions—fragmentarily, then I am lost. That's what is happening in the world. We are totally lost. So is it possible to look at life as a whole without fragmentation? Pupul, that is the crux.

**PJ** : Why doesn't the ancient mind see this?

**K** : It won't. It can't. How can it see this? How can total, complete, order . . . .

**PJ** : But you just said that the ancient . . . .

**K** : Just a minute, *that is the ancient*. The original ground is the most ancient.

**PJ** : Now that's there.

**K** : No.

**PJ** : What do you mean, 'No'?

**K** : It is there as an idea. And that is what all people have maintained—an idea. There is God—that's just an idea, a concept, a projection of our own desire to be comforted, to be happy. *(Long pause)*

You see, Pupul, the question is whether a human being can live a life in which there is no fragmentary action. If somebody were to ask, 'Where am I to begin?' I would say, 'Begin there; find out for yourself if you lead a fragmentary life'. Do you know what a fragmentary life is? It is saying one thing and doing another. A fragmented way of living is isolation; therefore you have no relationship with your husband or wife; you have no relationship with the rest of humanity. So, begin there.

Do you know what that means? Do you know what a tremendous inquiry you have to make to find out?

**PJ** : What is inquiry?

**K** : Observation. Inquiry is to observe very clearly without any bias, without any direction, without any motive, how my life is fragmented. It is just to observe it, and not to say, 'I must not be fragmented and, therefore, I must be whole'. The idea of becoming whole is another fragmentation.

**PJ** : So the birth of the new . . . .

**K** : Is not possible unless you see this.

*Brockwood Park*
*22 June 1982*

# The Ending of Fear

**PUPUL JAYAKAR (PJ)** : Sir, I would like to approach this dialogue as if I were asking you a question for the first time. I am in sorrow and, being caught in sorrow, I ask for a way out. You have been talking of the way of self-knowing as the starting point of investigation, so my question is: How does one start? What is the starting point of investigation?

**J. KRISHNAMURTI (K)** : First of all, it is necessary for us to understand that all problems are interrelated. There is no one separate problem, independent of other problems. They are all closely related and, so, if we could solve or understand one problem—directly, deeply—we really would have solved all problems.

**PJ** : Sir, I am a simple person; I do not know what it is to go deep enough to solve one problem.

**K** : Take, for example, the question of fear, for fear is common to all mankind. Whether you live in the West or in the Middle East or in the Far East or here in India, you will find that fear is one of the basic problems with which man is confronted. And he has not been able to solve it at all; for millennia he has borne the

---

This is an edited version of a television broadcast from the Doordarshan Kendra, Madras.

burden of it. To understand the problem of fear—which really does cripple one's mind, one's heart, one's behaviour—we must first be clear as to how we approach the problem.

**PJ** : What do you mean by 'approach'?

**K** : The word 'approach' means 'to come close to', 'to come in contact with', 'to be very, very, very, near' . . . .

**PJ** : How does one come near a problem like fear? Fear having arisen, the instinct is to run away from it, to move away from it, to suppress it, to do everything to avoid it. But you say, 'Come close to it'.

**K** : Yes, come close to it.

**PJ** : What does the closeness imply?

**K** : First of all, it is utterly futile to run away from it. You may run away through worship, through prayer, through every form of entertainment—so-called religious as well as other forms—but, when all the entertainment is over, when all the prayers and so on are over, you will be exactly where you were. There will still be fear there. Basically, you will not have resolved it. So it's no good escaping from it. That's the first fact.

**PJ** : Sir, if you do not escape from it, you have to see how you are escaping.

**K** : Of course, one must be aware of how one is escaping.

**PJ** : Now, to see how one is escaping, one must observe it.

**K** : Yes, first one must observe fear.

**PJ** : Now, how does one observe fear, and where does one observe it?

**K** : Is that fear separate from you—something out there, totally unrelated to you—or are you that fear? You see, Pupul, fear is not different from you; you are fear.

**PJ :** Sir, fear is not outside us; it is, to us, something inside.

**K :** That's it.

**PJ :** We see ourselves as separate from that which arises within us.

**K :** That is really the problem, namely, that we always treat our reactions as though they were different from us—the observers.

**PJ :** Sir, if I may say so, you are taking it so far away that I have lost contact with you.

**K :** All right; let us go slowly, step by step.

**PJ :** Yes, sir.

**K :** Let's go into it. I have, for example, fear.

**PJ :** Yes, fear of so many kinds.

**K :** No, Pupul, you see the *objects* of fear may vary, but fear is . . . .

**PJ :** Fear is a tremendous movement of shrinking inside you. Now you say, 'Observe that; look', but I cannot look when I am in a state of fear.

**K :** Oh yes, you can. When fear arises, look at it; understand it; find out, investigate, what the cause is.

**PJ :** Can you investigate when fear is upon you?

**K :** Oh yes. That requires attention, a certain awareness. Look, I am aware of the environment; I am aware of the size of this room.

**PJ :** Yes.

**K :** I may say that it's ugly and that it's not in proportion, or this or that, but I'm aware of it.

**PJ :** Yes.

**K :** Similarly, I can be aware of my fear. I am afraid that I might die. I am afraid of losing a job. I am afraid of something that has happened now or in the past. I am afraid of something that is going to happen in the future.

**PJ :** Now, when you say that I can be aware of it, I can be aware of it as a statement.

**K :** No, no, no. Pupul that's . . . .

**PJ :** Yes, sir; I can also be aware of it as a state of being within myself.

**K :** It's part of me!

**PJ :** When you say that it's part of me, I don't understand that. But I can grow aware of those intimations of fear which are within me. So, I have an awareness of the outside, and of these intimations of fear within me. Now, how does one proceed from there?

Sir, we were talking about 'awareness', about 'coming close' to fear. Can one come close to fear and be aware of the within—the within where fear manifests itself? If so, the question arises as to who the person is who observes fear, and so on.

**K :** Yes. Pupul, suppose you have a headache; that headache is part of you.

**PJ :** Yes.

**K :** If you're angry, it's part of you; if you're envious, it's part of you.

**PJ :** Yes.

**K :** If you are afraid, it's part of you; you are not separate from fear.

**PJ :** No, sir, when I have a headache, I can observe myself with a headache, but when there is fear—when I am afraid—I cannot observe myself in a state of fear.

**K** : Look, I am aware that I have a headache; I am aware that I am hungry.

**PJ** : Yes.

**K** : I am also aware that I am greedy. That awareness indicates to me that that greed is part of me; it indicates that it's not something outside of me.

**PJ** : No, it's not.

**K** : So fear is me.

**PJ** : Yes.

**K** : Now, we're asking: Is it possible to observe that fear?

**PJ** : Yes, that's really the question.

**K** : That's the real question, yes.

**PJ** : Is it possible to observe that fear?

**K** : Yes.

**PJ** : Sir, when you say 'observe' fear, do you mean: to *actually see* it?

**K** : After all, you know all the symptoms of fear.

**PJ** : Yes, I know the symptoms of fear . . . .

**K** : Wait; you know all the symptoms and, perhaps, also the cause of it.

**PJ** : Yes.

**K** : You also know, perhaps, the reaction to the cause, and the naming of that reaction as 'fear'—which is part of you.

**PJ** : Yes.

**K** : But unfortunately, because of tradition, education and so on, you say, 'Fear is not me. I am the observer; fear is something different from me'.

**PJ :** Our whole education has been to deal *with* something.

**K :** Yes.

**PJ :** We attempt to deal with problems. So we deal with fear.

**K :** Yes, you deal with fear as though it was a problem outside of yourself.

**PJ :** No, sir, even with regard to a problem inside myself . . . . You see, I deal *with* it—which means that there is a division, which means that I see myself as separate from that problem.

**K :** That's it; we're trained that way. Our tradition, our whole habitual thinking is: I can 'operate' on fear—which means that you separate yourself from fear.

**PJ :** Yes, tradition, education, makes me think that I am separate from fear.

**K :** But we've just now acknowledged that we are fear. I *am* fear.

**PJ :** No, sir, fear is a manifestation of one of the aspects of the 'me'.

**K :** Of the 'I', yes. Fear, violence, agony, loneliness, desperation, depression, insecurity, all the many beliefs, disbeliefs—all that is part of me.

**PJ :** Yes, and you are saying, 'Observe that'.

**K :** Observe it, without the remembrance of past fears. Observe it as though for the first time. That is the difficulty.

**PJ :** Sir, to observe as though for the first time—that is not possible. That is not possible because my observation carries all the memories of all the observations, all the experiences, I have had before.

**K :** That's right.

**PJ :** You see, sir, it is with those memories that I observe.

**K** : That's what I'm saying. Those memories of the past a. observer. And you observe fear as though fear was somet. separate from you. We said that fear, greed, envy, belief, loneliness, sorrow—all that—is me. I am not separate from all that. That constitutes me.

**PJ** : Yes. But it remains at the level of a concept.

**K** : That is the difficulty. You see, again, we are trained not to observe purely, but to make what we observe into an idea, an abstraction; and with that abstraction we look at the fact.

**PJ** : Now, would you tell me 'how' to look?

**K** : How do you look at a tree—which is the most astonishing thing on the earth? How do you look at a tree?

**PJ** : Well, my eye falls on the tree . . . .

**K** : Yes.

**PJ** : And it either passes by, or it dwells on the tree.

**K** : It—the tree—doesn't pass us by; *we* pass it by.

**PJ** : Yes, my eyes pass over it if I am not interested or, if I am, my eyes dwell on the tree and I start inquiring into its various . . . .

**K** : You look at it. First, you look at it casually, and name it a 'tree'; you then say that it belongs to a certain species, a certain category, and so on. But you see, Pupul, with the very naming, you have already stopped looking at it.

**PJ** : Therefore, you are saying . . . .

**K** : I am saying that the word interferes with the observation.

**PJ** : How does one observe without the word interfering with the observation?

**K** : For that we have to investigate how we are caught in words;

we have to investigate how our minds, our brains, function with words.

**PJ** : Now, if I may ask you, is the ground of observation the mind?

**K** : It all depends on what you mean by 'observation'. Observation can be very superficial. If it is really meaningful observation—observation that has depth—then there is no word.

**PJ** : Sir, but first of all let me start with the word, because . . . .

**K** : Of course.

**PJ** : That which has to be observed is the ground of the mind.

**K** : We are talking about fear.

**PJ** : As it moves on the ground of the mind.

**K** : No, it's part of the mind.

**PJ** : So, the observation is . . . .

**K** : It is the observation of the mind which has all the characteristics, all the other qualities . . . .

**PJ** : Yes. So, as fear disappears, anger arises or want arises . . . .

**K** : And so on, and so on. As we said, they're all interrelated.

**PJ** : They're interrelated, but the act of observing . . . .

**K** : The act of observing is not interrelated.

**PJ** : Therefore, the observing of the ground of the mind . . . .

**K** : No, if I may point out, I wouldn't use the word 'ground'; it is to observe the nature of my mind, which is fear and all the rest of it.

**PJ** : I wouldn't even categorize it.

**K** : That's better.

**PJ** : So, there is an observing of the mind.

**K** : There is the observing of the activities of the mind.

**PJ** : Yes, there is an observing of the activities of the mind. And I have found, in that observing, that there is a slowing down of the mind.

**K** : Naturally.

**PJ** : Now, when desire arises and there is an observing of it, there is also an ending of it; but some other thing arises.

**K** : Yes, one thing after another.

**PJ** : Now, does one go back to the desire which has just ended, or does one look at the next thing that has appeared?

**K** : Let us go slowly. Let us suppose that I am observing desire—right? But—as I observe—my mind, my brain, is not wholly attentive to desire; it goes after another thought which arises. You see, thoughts continually arise.

**PJ** : Yes.

**K** : So my mind goes after another feeling, and so on; it's a movement.

**PJ** : Yes.

**K** : Now, I want to understand fear.

**PJ** : Yes.

**K** : All the reactions with regard to fear arise—suppression, analysis, escape.

**PJ** : Yes.

**K** : Now, it is very difficult to be completely attentive to one factor of fear, and not to move away from it.

**PJ** : Yes.

**K** : That means the observer—the observer being the past—is absent in the observation.

**PJ** : Yes, but sir, I would like to pause for an instant here, because this is where the difficulty arises. I awake to fear within my mind, but by the time I look at it, it has changed its nature and a new thought arises. My question is: Should awareness turn back to what was—in this instance, fear—or should it remain with what has arisen?

**K** : Remain with what has arisen.

**PJ** : Therefore attention—I won't use the word 'mind' here—constantly moves from one thing to another.

**K** : Yes, it moves from one thing to another—which are all interrelated.

**PJ** : It moves from one thing to another because awareness is like a light . . . .

**K** : Yes, yes.

**PJ** : And whatever arises, you look at. The difficulty, sir, is that since 'fear' is the object which has to be inquired into, if some other thing arises, we feel that we should move back to that state of fear.

**K** : You see, one of our difficulties is that we want a quick answer. 'I am afraid; so, please, tell me how to get rid of it quickly.' That's all. We are so impatient. Where impatience is concerned, there is time. Where patience is, there is no time.

Now, I want to understand the nature of fear. In looking at fear, another thought arises and I pursue the other thought, not fear.

**PJ** : Yes.

**K** : I pursue the other thought; I inquire into what gave rise to it, and so on. So I pursue each thought as it arises.

**PJ** : Yes.

**K** : But ultimately I come back to this point—this point of fear.

**PJ** : Because, the arising of these various manifestations are related.

**K** : Therefore you are back.

**PJ** : Yes, but you don't deliberately come back.

**K** : No, of course not.

**PJ** : But as these manifestations—manifestations of different things—arise, spring up in the mind . . . .

**K** : Yes, and as you pursue them, as you observe them . . . .

**PJ** : There is an ending.

**K** : Yes, that's right; they calm down. You see, it is like a tide ebbing and rising.

**PJ** : So this is the whole field of observation.

**K** : Yes. The point is to observe without any resistance. Thoughts arising, one after another, is a form of resistance to fear.

**PJ** : Yes.

**K** : Can you observe without resistance? And when you have observed, when you have examined the various thoughts as they arise, they dissipate and then, you are back; therefore there is no resistance or avoidance or escape from the fact of fear.

**PJ** : Now, I'll proceed to another subject—a subject that is closely interrelated, namely 'recognition', 'naming'. Sir, that which comes in the way of observation is the immediate recognition and 'naming' of 'what is' or what arises.

**K** : Yes, that is the real problem. Just hold a minute there, please.

That is the real problem. The recognizing process is the remembrance of the past incidents of fear that have been recorded in the brain.

**PJ :** Yes.

**K :** That is, when a new reaction—a reaction which we have, in this case, termed 'fear'—arises, the brain immediately says, 'Yes, I've had this feeling before'. You see, there is a recognizing process immediately.

Now, the point is to see, to observe, the fact in front of us—the fact which *is* us—very closely, without any remembrance of past incidents at all. That is, when the remembrance of past incidents of fear is in abeyance, you look at fear as though you're looking at it for the very first time.

**PJ :** Is there a quenching of fear with the abeyance of the past in that observation?

**K :** Yes. We are saying that when there is the observation without the observer—for the observer is the result of a thousand memories; he is, in fact, the conglomeration of the past—when there is pure observation, then that observation really, deeply, profoundly, puts out the fire of fear.

**PJ :** You see, you speak of this enormous thing of observing without the observer as if it were a very simple affair.

**K :** It sounds very simple, yes.

**PJ :** In reality it is not.

**K :** Of course not.

**PJ :** Because in the very act of observation the past is like a flood which overtakes us.

**K :** Because we are used to it. It's our habit; it's our tradition; it's our education.

**PJ :** Sir, you spoke of 'approaching' fear, so I'm asking you whether there is a way of approaching . . . .

**K :** That's it; that's just it. There is a way of approaching fear. You see, what is important is not fear but how you approach fear.

**PJ :** Which is the observing without the observer.

**K :** Wait, wait; I haven't come to that yet. Let us go slowly. How do I approach a problem? Generally, I want to resolve it. I want to put it away as it disturbs me. I want to run away from it. I want to suppress it through various forms of activities. You see, my approach to a problem is never free from any kind of desire, opinion, and so on. If there is freedom from all that, the problem is not. The problem exists because of my confusion.

**PJ :** So therefore there seems to be only one way, and that is to observe and listen . . . .

**K :** To oneself.

**PJ :** To the sounds of oneself.

**K :** Yes. That is, to recognize that you are the past, the present and the future—to recognize that you are the time-maker, and that you are a slave to time, which is the past. It is to see the great complexity of all that, and to remain with that complexity and not try to avoid it, to escape from it or try and act on it. It is to just remain with the fact—the fact that you are a slave to time.

Time is a part of fear. You see, I am afraid of the future, I am afraid of the past; I am not actually afraid of the present. I am afraid of something that might happen in the future, or of something that has happened in the past. At the very second which is the present there is no fear at all.

**PJ :** So this is an act of—if I may use this phrase—catching the mind before it gets caught in the tomorrow or the yesterday.

**K** : No, not 'catching', because then you would have the problem of the catcher and the caught.

The point is to understand this real, this deep, fact that you are, essentially, the time-maker. You are the future; the future is not separate from you.

You see, we are so used to time. Evolution is time. Progress is time. Learning a language takes time. To learn or to gain any skill takes time. So time has become extraordinarily important. But we fail to see that time is also fear, and that to grasp the nature of fear, one has to look at it very closely, without impatience, without any desire to escape from it and so on. We have to live with it, and to live with it changes its character.

**PJ** : Thank you very much, sir.

*Madras*
*7 January 1982*

# The Book of Mankind

**PUPUL JAYAKAR (PJ)** : Sir, yesterday you spoke of reading the book of the self, which is the book of mankind. And you asked a question: With what instrument will I look?

Now, this book is never complete. As you are reading it, you are creating it. In the very observing of something, the future is also being created. In this state of flux, there are one or two questions which have to be clarified. We have talked about the story of 'what is' from the first time we met you. But what is the nature of this 'what is'? What is the nature of what is seen? Because unless we are clear on the nature of what is seen, the instrument that sees can never be clear. So, can we please go into the nature of 'what is'?

**J. KRISHNAMURTI (K)** : The whole history of man for forty thousand years or more is part of our consciousness; it is part of our story. We as human beings are the whole history of man. If we grant that, then the only instrument with which we can read this vast complex history is thought. In fact, thought is the only instrument we have. Thought has built the past, and the human mind is the residue, the storehouse, of the entire accumulation of the past: past experience, all the superstitions, all the beliefs, the various Gods, the various rituals, and so on. The whole movement of man-in-time is in the background of every human being. If once we see the fact of this, then we can start from here. Unless we are clear about this, how can we read this immense and complicated book of knowledge?

**PJ** : Obviously human heritage is *my* heritage. The two are not separate.

**K** : But very few are willing to accept that.

**PJ** : No, Krishnaji, at one level I am sure most people would accept it.

**K** : I doubt it.

**PJ** : Human heritage does not belong to a single person. All that has taken place, the ideas that have formed the brain, in fact, the whole development of the human race is common to all of mankind.

**K** : Wait, Pupul. Most people would not have thought about this. If they have, I doubt whether they would see the fact of this. I want to establish that first. If a few of us see the truth that we carry—all the time—this vast human heritage, then we can proceed. We should see the truth of it, not merely the argument of it or the verbal structure of it.

**ACHYUT PATWARDHAN (AP)** : Sir, would you not concede that although all this may have been accumulated through thought . . . .

**K** : Time and thought . . . .

**AP** : Yes, time. and thought. You see, sir, when I say that I am the inheritor of the heritage of man, it is not the result of a sequential thought process. When I say that I am the inheritor of it all, it is not as verbalized thought.

**K** : Do you as a human being, a human being who has studied the history of the world, see the truth that you are the result of the whole of human heritage? Do you see that you are this vast and complex book of the story of man? Do you see it not as a matter of argument but as a fact? Either it is an argumentative concept or it is so—in your blood, in your heart, in your thoughts, in your life.

**AP** : If it is in my blood, in my whole being, then it is not a sequential thought process; it is a totality.

**K** : Please, let us not introduce the word 'totality'. It is so. If we three, at least, see the truth of it, we can proceed from here.

**PJ** : It is as much a truth as the fact that the human body has evolved. Let me put it this way: it is a universal phenomenon. To that extent, I accept that I am human heritage.

**K** : Right. From there proceed. In me abides the whole story of man: his sorrows, his anxieties, his loneliness, his miseries, his happiness, and so on. This vast story is me. Now, to go back to the question that we raised the other day: What is the instrument with which we read that book?

**PJ** : Before we go to the instrument with which we read the book, what is it that we read?

**K** : As you are reading it, it is changing. As I am reading it, it is moving.

**PJ** : Yes. As I read, the future comes into existence; the future is projected.

**K** : Wait a minute. Let us be clear by what we mean by the word 'future'. The future is the past modifying itself in the present and going on to the future. So the past becomes the future.

**PJ** : The very thought that arises now, contains in it the germ of the future.

**K** : It contains in it the germ of the future, *if* there is no alteration.

**PJ** : So we have to be clear about the nature of this 'what is' which we have talked about for years.

147

**K** : No, you are going into something else, Pupul. Let us begin here. I am the totality of mankind, I am the storehouse of all human endeavour—I don't want to use that word 'totality'. I am not aware it. I do not know the nature of it, the content of it, but I want to study it. I want to learn if it is possible to explore the nature of consciousness. I want to explore not my consciousness but the consciousness of man.

**PJ** : The moment you say that I am reading the consciousness of man . . . .

**K** : Which is the book of man. You see, there is no 'my' consciousness.

**PJ** : Yes, of course. The moment you say that I am reading the consciousness of man and not my consciousness, the attitude to that reading has undergone a total change.

**K** : That's right. If you are under the illusion that this consciousness is *yours*—separate from every other consciousness—then we will be moving in two different directions. Unfortunately, most people— including many psychologists—believe that consciousness is separate, that it is individual.

**PJ** : There is a trap there.

**K** : Yes, there is a trap.

**PJ** : We say that we are the history of mankind, but when we start investigating consciousness . . . .

**K** : Which is the story of man . . . .

**PJ** : But if we are objectively looking at the history of man . . . .

**K** : Which is the consciousness of man.

**PJ** : But if we are objectively looking at the history of man, we would read it one way. We would read that history in encyclopaedias. But the moment 'we see that the history arises within us, within our consciousness, our response will, immediately, be of a totally different nature.

**K :** That's what I was coming to. Naturally, if one actually sees—after logical examination and investigation—that one's consciousness is universal, if one can see that the consciousness that exists within the individual is the consciousness of all human beings, then one's whole activity of perception changes. Right? Now, do I regard this consciousness as 'mine'? We must be clear on this point. Do I regard this consciousness as my private ground? You see, it is in the discovery that all human beings are lonely and that all people suffer that I discover something tremendous. To discover the consciousness of the whole of mankind is a tremendous perception.

**PJ :** I would say that the consciousness of mankind is revealed on my private ground.

**K :** Just a minute. You are saying that by understanding 'my' consciousness I recognize that it is the consciousness of man. I go along with that, but at no point must I insist that it is mine.

**PJ :** I cannot say that what is revealed to me in my consciousness is unique to me. It is part of the total consciousness of man, but it is revealed on my ground and, therefore, my relationship to it is very different.

**K :** Are you saying that in the investigation into my consciousness there is the discovery that it is not my private ground?—That in the investigation into what I have called 'my' consciousness as separate from everyone else's, there is the discovery that what I have called my consciousness is nothing but the consciousness of the rest of man.

**PJ :** But this is not quite so. You see, the observing of that which arises has no place in it for this other state, namely, that it is the consciousness of mankind.

**K :** I don't quite follow.

**PJ :** Let us take, for example, an instance of observing loneliness or sorrow arise. This observation—namely, the arising of loneliness in my consciousness—does not bring to the forefront the factor that it is the loneliness of all mankind. At that point, it is just loneliness.

**K :** It is in the investigation of my loneliness or my sorrow, which I have so far been scrupulously confining to my courtyard and my private ground, that I discover this fact. It is in the discovery that all men are lonely and that all men suffer, that I discover something tremendous. The discovery that it is the whole of mankind that suffers is an enormous perception.

**PJ :** What brings this perception about? Let us see it as though through a microscope. Loneliness arises, or sorrow arises. Then there is an observing of that thing which we call sorrow. What brings in the other element, namely, that I am observing not my petty sorrow, but the sorrow of mankind?

**K :** No, I don't observe. Look, Pupulji. I have seen—as must you all have—that wherever you go, loneliness and sorrow live together. This is so in Europe, in America, in India. This factor is shared by all of us. To realize or to admit to oneself—even as a logical conclusion—that this thing is shared by all of us, is a great beginning. You see, change has already taken place.

**PJ :** Yes. But I would like to go back. What is it that has to be observed?

**K :** I observe sorrow. Loneliness and sorrow are synonymous.

**PJ :** Which are emotional responses to a situation. I feel suddenly a sense of shrinking . . . .

**K :** A feeling of great loss.

**PJ :** And I look.

**K** : No, no, no; you don't look. Let's be clear. Suppose you have lost a great friend or a wife whom you really loved. What has actually taken place here? There is the ending of that person, and with that ending there is the ending of your entire relationship with that person. And suddenly there is the realization of how utterly lonely you are, because that has been the only relationship that meant something. So when, suddenly, that is gone, there is a sense of great loss.

Now, just hold it for a minute. Remain with it; don't let thought or any other feeling interfere with that state. If you don't escape from it, suppress it or analyse it, you will have suddenly discovered this extraordinary phenomenon, namely, that with the loss of some person or some conclusion that you have held most dear, you are shattered and that a certain state of mind has come to an end. Right? You can invent a future, but that future will remain an invention. The ending here is an ending without any future. Can the mind remain with this fact? Can it remain with this fact not as an observer observing the fact? For the observer is the fact. The observer is that state and, therefore, there is no difference between the observer and the thing that he is observing. He is the suffering; he is that ending. It is like a jewel you are holding. The moment you want to part with it, you have entered a different state of consciousness altogether.

**PJ** : I understand.

**K** : Now, the history of mankind is my history. Right?

**PJ** : Yes.

**K** : I want to read this book. It must be an extraordinary book. It has not been written. There are no chapters. There are no paragraphs. It is just one tremendous movement.

**PJ** : Can any mind contain the enormity of it?

**K** : We must begin here. What is the mind and what is the brain? Can I go on with this? Question me as we go along. The brain has infinite capacity. Look what it has done in the technological world—something incredible! But psychologically it has been conditioned through evolution—evolution being time.

**PJ :** Through the concept of time.

**K :** No. Please go slowly into this; be careful. See that the brain has extraordinary capacity in the technological world and that in the other direction, namely in the psychological world, it has not moved at all. Because it has not moved, it has not flowered. It is conditioned; it is limited. But the mind is not limited.

**PJ :** When you speak of the mind, what is it you speak of?

**K :** The mind of the universe, the mind of nature; everything that has been created and is in the process of creation is the movement of the mind. And therefore there is no limit to creation.

**AP :** Are you suggesting that when I say that I am the entire heritage of man, it is not the brain that can take in this factor?

**K :** It is the brain that takes in this factor, because I have communicated through thought and through words, and you are looking at it through thought, through words. So the communication is verbal and through thought. Sir, please, let us not go back to that . . . .

**AP :** At present, whatever I understand, I understand through the brain.

**K :** No, no.

**PJ :** We have moved to another dimension altogether which, if we understand, is this: The brain has done tremendous things in the field of technology, but in the realm of the psyche it is still static. We were talking about the reading of the book of mankind, and my question was: Can a single brain contain it? And Krishnaji came to the brain and the mind. He said that the brain being limited and not having moved, can only move . . . .

**K** : Within its own circuit.

**PJ** : The mind being the very source of creation has no limit and therefore this whole history of man is within it, if I may use that expression. I don't want to put it that way but . . . .

**K** : Go ahead, put it that way.

**PJ** : When you talk of the mind, it is all that is created and is in the process of creation.

**K** : Pupul, let us be very clear and very careful when we speak of creation. Thought has created, in the physical world, not only the churches, the temples and the mosques but also all the things that are in them. Thought has created wars. Thought has created the conflict between man and man. Thought is responsible for all this and, because thought in itself is limited, thought cannot perceive a mind that is immeasurable. But, obviously, thought tries to understand it because that is its function. The function of thought is to reduce everything to its limited, mechanical, fragmentary activity. Right? And we are saying that as long as the brain is conditioned, it can never understand the immensity of the nature of the mind. If you see this, you will also see 'your' responsibility—unfortunately, we have to use words—to uncondition the brain, to uncondition the limitation which thought has imposed on it. Yes, I've got it. That's it.

**PJ** : Is the responsibility to uncondition the brain which is conditioned and, so, cannot move out of its grooves, or to end this movement of the brain?

**K** : Which is the same thing.

**PJ** : No.

**K** : I don't quite understand.

**PJ** : Is what it finds itself unable to do the deconditioning of the brain?

153

**K** : No.

**PJ** : Or is it to hold the brain in abeyance so that the perception which is the mind can operate?

**K** : You are putting in modern language what the old tradition says, namely, that there is, in me, God. There is in me God or some element which is not contaminated, and which then operates on that . . . .

**PJ** : You have drawn the distinction between the brain and the mind. You have drawn the distinction between the conditioned and the non-conditioned state. You have drawn the distinction between that which has an ending . . . .

**K** : I have not talked about an ending.

**PJ** : Everything that is in the brain as it functions is fragmented.

**K** : Yes. I have said that we must differentiate between the two meanings of the words. I say that the brain which is limited cannot understand what the mind is. It can only apprehend, grow aware of it when there is no conditioning.

**PJ** : But you went further.

**K** : That I shouldn't have spoken. *(Laughs)*

**PJ** : But you have spoken.

**K** : That was unfortunate. Dr Bohm and a few others discussed the same matter. You see Pupul, it is really very interesting. Let's leave the mind alone for the moment. See what an extraordinary capacity the brain has in the technological, scientific, world. See the surgery and all the biological experiments that are taking place. They have transplanted a man-made heart! The incredible scientific world is the activity of thought. But thought is limited because knowledge is limited. The question is whether it can ever be free from its limitation. It can't. It can never be free of its limitation because it is born of limitation. I don't know whether you see this.

**PJ :** May I ask a question? What is the distinction between thought and the brain?

**K :** Thought is the activity of the brain.

**PJ :** Is there anything in the brain apart from thought?

**K :** *(Laughs)* I won't fall into the trap. You are now going back to the old . . . .

**PJ :** I'm not. If you accept that the brain has tremendous capacity and that it is using only a very small part of it, and also if you could do with the psyche what you have done with technology . . . .

**K :** Then the universe is open to you. That's what I am saying. The brain has been able to do such extraordinary things technologically. Now, if the brain can free itself from the limitations of the psyche, it will be incredible what it can do. I say that then the brain is the mind; then it is totally free. Then there is no sense of division. There is a sense of completeness, wholeness . . . I don't want to enter into it, you understand, Pupul.

**PJ :** If the brain has had the energy, the drive, the insight to pursue technology, why is it . . . .

**K :** Why are you not willing to turn the other way?

**PJ :** You see, man is prepared to go into space and die. So it's not a question of death or disappearance . . . .

**K :** But there's a great deal behind that—national pride, praise, fame, being a hero. It's not as if man is really prepared to die. He has been conditioned, through immense propaganda, to die for his country. Look what man has done. In the name of God, in the name of the country, he has burnt people, tortured people.

**PJ :** What is that element that gives human beings the curiosity to drive in the direction of technology?

**K :** I think our education is responsible for that. Because every culture has emphasized, except for some few dead cultures, that you have to earn a livelihood, that you have to work, work, work, that you have to study, memorize, repeat, repeat. That is all that they say. This morning I met some of the students here at Rishi Valley. Unfortunately, they are the same. They haven't thought about anything apart from mathematics, history, geography—memorize, repeat, good marks, good job, and so on. If you were to ask them to move a little away from this, they would be lost. You see, they have not given even a thought to the other.

**AP :** You see, sir, scientists who go to the impossible question are very few. Only a few of them are willing to move in a new direction. So also, today, there are a few who see the present crisis of the survival of humanity. There are a few people today who have sufficient motivation to say that this is the most intolerable predicament for man and that the brain must be explored.

**PJ :** They are exploring the brain but not the psyche.

**K :** Sir, they are exploring the brain; its functions. Just look at it. The brain has extraordinary capacity—I don't like to use the word 'capacity' because it is based on experience, and capacity based on experience is not capacity at all. There is a different kind of movement which is not based on experience, knowledge. Sir, the brain has done extraordinary things in the technological world, but psychologically it has not moved an inch after all these thousands and thousands of years.

Now if there is a breakthrough, there will be no division between the mind and the energy of the brain. Do you understand? The energy of the brain has done technological work . . . .

**PJ :** Yes, but it has never been released for this.

**K :** For the other.

**AP :** It is the energy of attention.

**K :** Don't use the word 'attention'; just stick to the word 'energy', sir. Psychologically my energy is practically nil. And I'm saying that when that limitation has been broken down or broken through, there is a totally different energy. So far it is only channelled through technology, which is merely the activity of thought and, therefore, that energy is limited. The breaking down of the psyche is not the energy of thought. Technology is the energy of thought, and the energy of thought is limited.

**AP :** Agreed.

**K :** No, no.

**PJ :** We have to probe some more into the instruments that man has. Let us examine those instruments. One is thought, and the others are the senses.

**K :** Sensory responses; the sensitivity of the senses.

**PJ :** Yes.

**K :** Hold, hold, hold—the sensitivity of the senses and thought which are both the same.

**AP :** How, sir?

**PJ :** This is what we must discuss. The sensitivity of the senses and thought—are they both the same?

**K :** I will show it to you. I have just caught something, but don't just accept what I say. *(Laughs)* The sensitivity of the senses. Our senses are controlled by thought—right?

**PJ :** No.

**K :** Just a minute; don't take a stand. Wait; I may drop it. If you take a stand, we are lost.

**PJ :** No, I'm not going to take a stand.

**K :** My senses are now shaped, are controlled by thought. Take, for example, my sense of taste—anything that is bitter, I don't

157

like, and anything that is sweet, I do. So thought has come in. The question is whether there is a movement of all the senses, total senses, without the interference of thought. Look at the question first.

Have you ever looked at the vast movement of the sea, at the movement of the tides, and at the enormous power of the waves, with all your senses operating? If you do that, there is no interference of thought. Now when thought interferes with the senses, it must inevitably be to limit them or control them. I am going to stick to this.

**PJ** : What you have said is so. There is a challenge and my senses respond according to the conditioning of thought. But there is a response of the senses . . . .

**K** : Always partial—because thought is always watching, always controlling the senses. I must, I must not.

**PJ** : At some instant there can be water reflected in water.

**K** : What is this?

**PJ** : It can be like water being reflected in water. There can be a state where there is nothing contained in those senses.

**K** : Right.

**PJ** : So, I want to push further—if you don't jump down my throat.

**K** : *(Laughs)* I won't.

**PJ** : That is, there is some connection between the senses—I am not very clear about it. You see, sir, when you think of your brain, you think of it as there *(Touches head)* somewhere in the head. But when the senses do not operate from thought, do not contain thought, the place of operation changes.

**K** : That's right. That's all I am saying. It's simple enough. When the senses are observing completely, there is no centre. When you look completely at the movement of the sea, or at the extraordinary sights of the Himalayas when there is not a cloud in the sky, there is no centre; there is no thought. The moment thought comes in, there is a centre. Right?

**PJ** : We have discussed thought, we have discussed the senses. Is there a third movement?

**K** : Yes. That is the whole point.

**AP** : What is that? Would you please repeat it?

**PJ** : We have talked of thought, we have talked of the senses. I am asking whether there is any other movement.

**K** : Ah! This is difficult. Is there an instrument—no, not an instrument but a movement, an action, a state that is not static, but which is yet not a movement of thought? That is your question, isn't it?

**PJ** : Not a movement of thought, not a movement of the senses . . . .

**K** : Wait, let's look at those two things carefully—'not thought' and 'not the movement of the senses'. When you observe the sea with all your senses, there is no sensory movement. Right? Of course. The senses are not aware that they are heightened. I wonder whether I have made myself clear. Anything that is excellent is not aware of its own excellence. Goodness in the highest sense of the word has no sense of being good.

**PJ** : You are talking of the essence of all thought, of the essence of all the senses. Then it is essence itself that is the instrument.

**K** : No; leave it for the moment. When there is a heightened excellence of the senses, the senses are not aware. We only realize that the senses are fully awake when thought comes in. The heightened state has already gone.

Now when thought is aware of its own tremendous limitation, then it is broken through. But to realize that, is not to verbalize

159

it; it is to actually see that thought has no place in the movement
. . . . Wait a minute, I must go into this carefully. Pupul, what are
we trying to get at?

**PJ :** We are reading the story of mankind and we are asking what
the instrument with which we probe is.

**K :** I will tell you. The story of mankind is an endless movement.
It has no beginning and no end. If you once grant that it has no
ending . . . . But my brain being limited, is looking for an ending.
Right? So I am approaching the book to find out what the end of
all this is.

**PJ :** The search is for the end.

**K :** Of course, of course. But to realize that there is no end—do
you realize what it means?

To realize that there is no end is to enter into something called
love. Love has no end. I may love my wife—she dies or I die, but
the thing called love goes on; it has no end. But as I have
identified myself with my wife, I either say that my love has gone
or I begin to love someone else. And all that is no more than
pleasure. I don't want to go into it now.

So, how do you read the book? You don't read it at all. Right?
There is no book to read. And when you come to this really deep
point, namely, that this book has no end and no beginning, you
realize that you are the book. This does not mean that you become
eternal, but that life as this movement has no end. It is then the
universe. It is then the cosmos. It is then the whole thing.

Do you think that I have been talking nonsense? If someone heard
all this—someone who was serious, of course—would it all sound
so extraordinarily wild? But what I am saying is not wild. It is
logical and very clear and can be stated in Sorbonne, Harvard or
in Delhi. It will hold water.

*Rishi Valley*
*19 December 1982*

# Uncovering the Source

**J. KRISHNAMURTI (K)** : Can we have a dialogue on something that not only appeals to the Western mind but also to the Indian mind that has, perhaps, thought about these things much longer than the Western world? Considering both the West and the East, what do you think would be of the greatest significance? What do you think would be something that is enduring, something that is worthwhile?

**PUPUL JAYAKAR (PJ)** : Sir, most of our lives are so futile.

**K** : Yes.

**PJ** : And unless one discovers within oneself the capacity to leap out of the futility, one will never be able to have a creative spring. You see, sir, when the mind has a creative spring, whatever be the circumstances, one seems to go beyond them. And that happens when the mind is not dependent on anything, and when it has some space, some perception.

I have been wondering for the last few months—what is the ground of the creative?

**K** : I wonder what you mean by 'creative'? An artist says he is creative. But would you call the activity of a poet, of a thinker, or even of a scientist who makes a new discovery creative activity?

**PJ** : Perhaps.

**K** : But it is limited.

**PJ** : Sir, why do you bring in the word 'limited'?

**K** : All right; let us not use the word 'limited'. Instead let's use the word partial.

**PJ** : But, sir, I can't bring in the word 'partial', because I don't know the other.

**K** : It's partial because it is not related to daily life. A scientist may discover extraordinary things and, so, call his life creative. But the greatest scientist may lead a very mediocre life.

**PJ** : But you see, that's why I did not speak of a creative action . . . .

**K** : But of a creative mind?

**PJ** : But of a ground, a mind, a perception, which rests in the creative.

**K** : I think you should make the question a little more clear.

**PJ** : You have never answered any questions on the ground of manifestation. Let's take it at the simplest level. This 'coming to be' of anything.

**K** : Of birth—that of a baby or a mango-tree or a bird? Are you asking what the source of all life—both the manifest and the non-manifest—is?

**PJ** : Yes. If it is possible, I would like to probe into what you have said just now: the manifest, the unmanifest and the pre-manifest . . . I won't even use the word unmanifest.

**K** : Are we discussing this subject in a technological, scientific sense or are we probing into something which you and I don't know? Just a minute, I want to make it clear. Because, after all, we know about the birth of a baby. We know how it comes into being.

**PJ** : One may know how it comes into being, but one still does not know . . . .

**K** : What?

**PJ** : The quality of life which pervades it. You see, sir, the actuality of birth is very different from the description of birth.

**K** : Yes.

**PJ** : It is the same with everything.

**K** : The description is not the thing. The explanation is not the actual.

**PJ** : But you cannot live through life without going into this 'coming into existence'.

**K** : I don't quite follow what you are trying to convey. I am not simply putting obstructions; I really don't quite follow. Can we talk about what the origin, the beginning, of all life or of all existence is, without having to move further and further back infinitely but by trying to discover or come upon something which is the beginning of all things? Do you follow what I mean? You see, various religious people say, 'God is the origin of everything'. But 'God' is just a word, and a word doesn't convey . . . . Do you follow what I am saying?

**PJ** : Yes.

**K** : We are concerned right now about the origin of all life. Are we delving really deeply—without any belief, without any dogma, and so on—or are we just having a theoretical dialogue, where we are moving between the actual and the non-actual, and trying to probe into something with thought? I don't know if you understand what I am saying.

**PJ** : I understand what you are saying. You see, sir, we have narrowed the word 'creative' to mean, as you said, painting, or writing a book, or discovering something in science.

**K :** That's right.

**PJ :** But basically, the whole meaning of a tree, a human being, the earth, the sky . . . .

**K :** Man has asked this question . . . .

**PJ :** Of course he's asked this question.

**K :** He has asked what the meaning and the origin of all this is.

**PJ :** Yes. Where does it arise?

**K :** That's it. That's what you are asking, isn't it? What is the ground from which all this arises?

**PJ :** Yes.

**K :** What is the source of all existence, all life, all action? Now, how does one inquire into that? What is our approach to it? How do we come to investigate into something that demands an extraordinary freedom (and the very word freedom means love) and an absolutely non-conditioned mind, if I can use that word? It requires that quality of mind which is both practical and sensitive and which has the quality of great compassion.

**PJ :** I can't start with that.

**K :** No. So how do we come to that point and move on from there?

**PJ :** Sir, if you put it that way, I am stuck; I can't move.

**K :** No, I am just asking; I don't say it must be that. Isn't that the process of inquiry?

**PJ :** I say that this question arises in my mind and I would like to move with this question.

**K :** Right.

**PJ :** If I say that the mind can question only when it is free and, therefore, love, what do I do?

**K :** You can't do anything. But how do you inquire into something, a question, that man has asked for millions of years? How do you inquire into something that he gave a name to and then was satisfied with? We are not doing that. We are asking, how does a mind inquire into something that must be extraordinary, that must have a quality of not only the universal, the cosmic—if one can use that word—but something that is of supreme order? How does one's inquiry begin? Where does it begin? If you inquire with thought, that doesn't lead very far.

**PJ :** No. You asked: How does the inquiry begin?

**K :** Yes, what is the manner, what is the approach of a mind that wants to inquire into something that it doesn't know and which demands an extraordinary quality of subtlety, of order, and so on? Where do I begin?

**PJ :** Obviously by being aware of the disorder within oneself.

**K :** You see, Pupul, I am after all the manifest. I have been born. I am a human being.

**PJ :** Yes, but obviously, sir, there can be no other starting point.

**K :** The world outside, the world inside. What is the criterion which measures the outer and the inner? What is the measurement? I am not using the word 'judgement'; I am using, purposely, the word 'measurement'.

**PJ :** But is it necessary to measure?

**K :** If I inquire into myself in a monastery, I can deceive myself enormously. But if I have a measure—just let me use that word for the moment—of what actually is happening in the world outside of me, if I can observe all that without any bias, and if I can see and relate what is happening outside to what is happening inside, then I will see that it is one movement and not two separate movements.

**PJ** : Sir, I am not in a monastery. I am in the midst of life.

**K** : That's right.

**PJ** : And being in the midst of life, I see action at various levels—action that is both connected with me and disconnected with me. I also see the responses within me to actions. I see the capacity which I may have gathered over the years. I have even been able to remain without reacting to it. I see all that. And I move into that. I move with it.

**K** : You *are* it. Don't say, 'I move with it'.

**PJ** : Yes, I am it.

**K** : You are that.

**PJ** : But you see it is easier to say, 'I am it' with regard to the interior movement. To see that with regard to an exterior movement is much more difficult. If you tell me that I am all the wars which are taking place in the world, that's very difficult for me to see.

**K** : No. Pupul, we are responsible—in the deepest sense of that word—for all the wars that are taking place.

**PJ** : Yes, but that's a distant thing to me. You must understand that that responsibility is a distant responsibility. Perhaps I might say 'Yes, I am responsible', if I take 'responsibility' to the very end, to the ultimate meaning of it all, but I can't link it in the same way to what is within me.

**K** : Quite.

**PJ** : Naturally, a response within me is a living response.

**K** : I hope my next question won't deviate from what we are discussing. You see, I want to know why you don't feel total

166

responsibility for the wars, the brutality, the terrible things that are happening in the world? Why don't you feel totally responsible?

**PJ** : How is one totally responsible? By being born?

**K** : No; but my entire way of living, my entire way of thinking and of acting—as a nationalist, this or that—has contributed to the present state of the world.

**PJ** : You are making it so difficult. A man commits a sadistic murder. I can't say that I am responsible for that sadistic murder.

**K** : Of course not.

**PJ** : Sir, you know, when you take it to that extent, it is impossible for me to feel the reality of it.

**K** : Let's leave that for a moment. I have asked the question. Leave it.

**PJ** : Yes, I think it's better to leave that. But let's probe into the ground of existence which is the 'isness' of life.

**K** : 'Isness'—the verb 'is'.

**PJ** : The only way to probe is to move into oneself, whatever that means.

**K** : All right. Let's take for the moment those words—to go, to move or to enter into the whole complex of oneself. Now, I can't enter into it as an observer from the outside, for I am all that.

**PJ** : Yes, it's not even that I state what I am.

**K** : Yes.

**PJ** : I don't state; I discover, I uncover.

**K** : Uncover, yes. 'Uncover' rather than 'discover'.

**PJ** : I uncover what I am. And in uncovering what I am, I comprehend that one is uncovering the whole existence of man.

**K :** Yes.

**PJ :** That's possible to see.

**K :** Yes, that's very simple.

**PJ :** So in this journey of uncovering, the superficial things are swept clean.

**K :** That's fairly simple.

**PJ :** But once the superficial is over, the room has been swept.

**K :** Isn't that important too? Who sweeps the room? What does it mean—to have swept the room? Do you follow what I am asking? Is the sweeping, or cleansing, or uncovering, a complete moving away from all the superficial reactions, superficial conditionings, and a trying to enter into the nature of the movement that conditions the mind?

**PJ :** Obviously, sir, you can't say that you have swept the room and it is over . . . .

**K :** Yes.

**PJ :** The dust gathers again.

**K :** Yes.

**PJ :** Sweeping is a movement which is part of living. The grosser elements can certainly be eliminated. You see, sir, it is possible to sweep away the more obvious things, but the subtler things survive in corners which you have not been able to get to.

**K :** Yes, that's right. But, let's go a little more into the obvious things . . . .

**PJ :** You know for instance, Krishnaji, ambition . . . .

**K :** Yes.

**PJ :** Or envy . . . .

**K :** Yes, and hatred. But you know, Pupul, can one really be free of hatred? Can one really wipe it away? Let's go into it a little bit. To be free of hatred must mean something extraordinary. Can one be free of all sense of aggression, all sense of the enemy? There is no enemy. The enemy is you.

**PJ :** But hatred is a different thing.

**K :** That's why I want to discuss it.

**PJ :** It is different from the quality of aggression. Let's go into it a little, sir.

**K :** Aggression is related to hatred, because it's part of the same movement. An aggressive nation or an aggressive person inevitably hurts another, and that hurt breeds hatred.

**PJ :** Yes, that's why I say that there are the grosser things and there are the subtler things. Hatred—anyone who has known hatred—knows that hatred is a very powerful and a very destructive thing. But aggression may, to some extent, be part of one's nature.

**K :** Yes, of course, it's part . . . .

**PJ :** It may be that it is part of your make up as a human being.

**K :** Yes, to survive, and all the rest.

**PJ :** You may be more assertive than another, that is aggression. To be assertive is not hatred. That's why I made the distinction between the grosser things which can be swept clean and the . . . .

**K :** But how does one know what is gross and what is subtle? What is the mind that says that this is . . . Pupul, move. Let's move.

**PJ :** That's why I think the only way to move into this is to see that nothing is trivial.

**K :** That nothing, that no reaction . . . .

**PJ** : Is trivial.

**K** : Yes, that nothing is trivial and that all things, all reactions, have their source in one's conditioning.

**PJ** : You know, sir, I recently saw the casting of a tremendous metal cauldron—a cauldron that was about seven feet in diameter. The slightest flaw—it didn't matter how slight it was—would have cracked the cauldron. And it's exactly like that. It doesn't matter how slight, how subtle it is, it still cracks the investigation.

**K** : I understand that. Aren't you saying to me that it needs great training, great discipline, great attention, a sense of tremendous control, energy and very, very subtle hands—like that of the potter who moulds some marvellous thing?

**PJ** : Doesn't it?

**K** : Oh yes, it does.

**PJ** : And this is where I think that one takes the word that you use, the word 'free', and interprets it to mean a certain flabbiness of the spirit.

**K** : Oh no, no, no.

**PJ** : Please let us pursue this . . . .

**K** : Yes.

**PJ** : As it is very important.

**K** : It's not flabbiness of spirit. Good Lord!

**PJ** : No, but sir, it may mean for me the non-acceptance of any authority, not just that of authority in the realm of the psyche, in the realm of the spirit. I may take it to mean licence and, therefore, think it unnecessary to do certain things.

**K** : Oh, no, no, no.

**PJ** : I may think that I can live a futile life, a trivial life. I may think that it just doesn't matter; I may think that nothing matters.

**K :** No, no. You see, Pupul, the very word 'freedom', as far as I understand, means affection, love . . . .

**PJ :** And a tremendous discipline. Might we use the word 'discipline'?

**K :** I know you are using the word discipline, but I am not sure . . . .

**PJ :** I am speaking of 'discipline' as a demand for such watchfulness that the trivial does not, at any time, creep in.

**K :** No, you see, the point is this: Does watchfulness, which is awareness, need training? Does it need discipline? We have to understand the meaning of that word 'discipline'.

**PJ :** Sir, we commonly mean by discipline some kind of regimentation. For example, if I were to sit cross-legged and look, unblinkingly, at the wall every morning, forcing myself, at the same time, not to have a single thought, that would be considered discipline. But I mean by 'discipline' the mind awakening to the fact that it must be aware of every movement within itself. Sir, that also is a discipline.

**K :** No, Pupul, 'discipline' in the general sense is connected with training, with conformity, imitation, restraint.

**PJ :** No, but if there is diligence . . . . Sir, without diligence nothing is possible. So may we discard the word 'discipline', and put in the word 'diligence'?

**K :** Wait, wait. Go slowly. 'To be diligent' means to be aware of what you are doing, to be aware of what you are thinking, to be aware of your reactions.

**PJ :** Yes.

**K :** And from those reactions, to observe the actions taking place. Now, the question is: In that observation, in that awareness, is the action controlled, is the action put into a certain framework?

**PJ** : No, obviously not.

**K** : What I am objecting to altogether—and, of course, this is subject to discussion—is the word 'discipline'.

**PJ** : But, sir, you have become, if I may say so, allergic to that word.

**K** : No, I am not allergic; I have got an allergy but I am not allergic to that word. *(Laughs)*

**PJ** : No, sir, you are restricting the use of that word to mean merely the putting of something into a framework.

**K** : Yes, but I also hold that the very act of learning is its own discipline.

**PJ** : Yes. But how does the act of learning come to be? Can we, please sir, take it one step back? From where does the need for observation arise? Why should I observe?

**K** : For a very simple reason, namely, to see whether it's possible for a human mind to change something, to change itself, to change the world which is entering into such a catastrophic area.

**PJ** : Yes, but sir, if I start with that premise . . . .

**K** : No, no, it is not a premise; it is so.

**PJ** : All right. If I start there, or if I start with sorrow—which is very often the real ground from which one starts . . . .

**K** : Yes.

**PJ** : The ground is really sorrow. But I think we have moved away.

**K** : Yes, I was coming to that.

**PJ** : So, let's go back to the question.

**K** : Now, what we started out with was an inquiry into the origin, the ground, of all life.

**PJ** : Yes.

**K** : To inquire into that, you have to inquire into yourself, because you are the expression of that.

**PJ** : Yes.

**K** : You are life.

**PJ** : Yes.

**K** : Now we are trying to discuss the origin of that, and I can only do that by understanding myself.

**PJ** : Yes.

**K** : Now, the 'myself' is so terribly complex. The self is a living complex; it is a messy, disordered entity. How do we approach a problem that is complex, a problem that is not to be easily diagnosed? Do we say, 'This is right', 'This is wrong', 'It should be', 'It should not be'?

**PJ** : But is it not because one starts with an attention which is looking for an ordered entity, that one finds disorder?

**K** : I am not looking for disorder or order. We are missing something. I said the world is in disorder. I observe it; I see that it is so. I begin with that.

**PJ** : Yes.

**K** : There is disorder outside and disorder inside. I am in disorder. Let's leave it there for the moment. Now, how do I comprehend or become aware of the origin of disorder? If I can begin to understand the origin of disorder, I can move more and more deeply into something which may be total chaos but which is total order. Do you follow what I mean?

**PJ** : Isn't it by being as simple as possible?

**K** : Yes, that's what I am trying to say.

**PJ** : And I have certain instruments of inquiry: eyes, ears, the other senses.

**K** : Yes, but you don't inquire with your ears or with your eyes.

**PJ** : Don't you?

**K** : A little bit, yes. I inquire when I look around at the world outside, or when I read something. The question is: Do I look into myself with my eyes? I can see myself in a mirror with my optic eyes. But I can't see the complexity of myself with my eyes. I must be aware, sensitively, without any choice, of this condition.

**PJ** : Why do you say, sir, that you cannot be aware with your eyes?

**K** : What do you mean 'with your eyes'? Do you mean the inward eye?

**PJ** : No. You see, there is a way of looking out and there is a way of looking in, a way of listening in.

**K** : You must be a little careful here, because it's misleading.

**PJ** : Let's go into it. Is there any other way?

**K** : Yes, I think there is.

**PJ** : Let's go into the other way, sir. Is the eye, the ear, not part of the other way?

**K** : Breathing? Hearing? Seeing? Feeling? Those are actually sensory responses, right? I see that colour. I hear that noise. I taste something, and so on. All those are sensory responses.

**PJ** : Yes. But is there not a seeing of anger—a reaction of anger—a listening to a reaction of anger?

**K :** Do you listen with your ears or do you observe anger?

**PJ :** How do you observe anger?

**K :** When you are angry, you look at the cause and the effect of anger.

**PJ :** When you are angry, you can't . . . .

**K :** Yes, you can't at that moment. So, later on . . . .

**PJ :** You see the nature of the mind which has been in a state of anger. But you see, sir, the word you use is 'see'. You say that you *see* the nature of the mind . . . .

**K :** I understand what you are asking. You are asking: The very act of listening, the very act of feeling, inwardly—are those acts performed by the eyes? That is, do we see, do we hear—inwardly—with our eyes, and with our sensory ears?

**PJ :** You see, sir, if you put it that way, then you never get to the point, because the sensory ear is so used to listening to the outer that it can never comprehend what it is to listen to the within.

**K :** But would it help if we talked about perception?

**PJ :** No, sir; I say it would help if you talked about seeing, about listening with the eye and the ear—because there is a seeing and listening with the eye and the ear.

**K :** Wait a minute. I hear you make that statement. I've understood the words and see the meaning of what you are saying. Right?

**PJ :** Yes.

**K :** The verbal communication has taken place.

**PJ :** Yes.

**K :** But the deeper significance . . . .

**PJ :** But that has also taken place, sir. While I am listening to you and seeing you, I am also listening and seeing my own mind, the ground of the mind.

**K** : No.

**PJ** : Then what is taking place?

**K** : Who is listening?

**PJ** : There is listening. I am not saying *who* is listening.

**K** : But, just a minute, Pupul, we must be clear on this point. Let's go into it a little more carefully.

**PJ** : Take an act where you are totally attentive. What is the state of the mind in that act of being totally attentive?

**K** : What is the state of action that's born out of complete attention? I'll answer it. But to answer that question, one must first understand what we mean by complete attention. Attention is not concentration. I think that's clear.

**PJ** : No, sir, it's not.

**K** : No, you see, Pupul, it's not a case for mere agreement. I want to be clear on that.

**PJ** : Of course, sir, attention is not concentration.

**K** : Attention means that there is no centre from which you are attending.

**PJ** : No, of course not.

**K** : Don't just say, 'Of course not'; please see what's implied in it.

**PJ** : You see, sir, I would like to ask you one thing. Are we still dusting the periphery?

**K** : No, no; I don't want to dust the periphery.

**PJ** : If you are not dusting the periphery, then, when you ask that question, I cannot understand.

**K :** I want to be clear, that's all.

**PJ :** Unless I understand what attention is, I can't even take the first step.

**K :** No, that's why I want to be clear. What does attention—to attend completely—mean?

**PJ :** You see, 'to attend completely' is for the 'I' not to be there.

**K :** Yes, that is the real thing. When there is attention, there is no 'I'. It isn't a state of *I* am attending, but only a state of mind which is wholly attentive.

**PJ :** With all the senses . . . .

**K :** With all the senses and the whole body.

**PJ :** The whole being is awake, if I may say so.

**K :** Yes, you can use that word.

**PJ :** And if you are in that state when your being is awake, then you can listen, you can observe; you can proceed from there.

**K :** You appear to be going off again. I want to inquire into myself. Right? That's what we are saying. Because I myself am life and if I am to inquire into what I am, my inquiry has to be correct, accurate, not distorted. It is only then that I may come upon the ground, the beginning of all life. It is only then that the origin may be discovered, may be uncovered.

**PJ :** If we start from there, we will find that the 'I' is there in the first step.

**K :** Yes. The first step is to see clearly, to hear clearly.

**PJ :** But the 'I' is there . . . .

**K :** Yes, of course.

**PJ :** There's the observer . . . .

**K :** And the observed. Now, wait a minute, Pupul, do not move away from that. I know that there is the observer and the observed. Now, I am inquiring whether that is actually so. So far I have taken it for granted.

**PJ :** Obviously, sir, when I first start inquiring, I start with the observer.

**K :** Yes, I start with the observer.

**PJ :** Now you have placed that thought, that doubt, in my mind and I ask, 'Is there the observer?'

**K :** Is there an observer separate from the observed?

**PJ :** Having that statement within me, I look for the observer.

**K :** Yes. Who is the observer? Let's look into this slowly. Because if I understand the observer, then perhaps the observer may see the falseness of the division between the observer and the observed.

**PJ :** Who will see?

**K :** The point is not who will see, but the perception of what is true. You see, what is of importance is perception, not who sees.

**PJ :** So, the seeing of what the truth of the observer is will end the state of division.

**K :** Yes, that is what I have said a thousand times.

**PJ :** Yes, for this instant it is so.

**K :** Go ahead. What are you trying to say?

**PJ :** What I am saying is that diligence or discipline is needed so that the inquiry is alive within one.

**K :** That does not need training.

**PJ :** I am not talking of training. I am using the word 'discipline'

178

without bringing in the word 'training'. I say that I cannot expect to have an understanding of what you say unless the mind is awake and is diligent about being awake.

**K :** Go ahead.

**PJ :** You cannot deny this.

**K :** No. It has to be diligent; it has to be watchful; it has to be attentive, subtle, hesitant. It has to be all that. I can only inquire into myself through my reactions—the way I think, the way I act, the way I respond to the environment, the way I observe my relationship to another.

**PJ :** I find that as I first observe myself, the responses and reactions are rapid, confused, continuous.

**K :** I know; they are contradictory, and so on.

**PJ :** In the very observing, some space comes into being.

**K :** Yes, some space, some order.

**PJ :** That's just the beginning, sir.

**K :** I know. Why do we stay 'at the beginning'? Pupul, I would like to ask a question. Is it necessary to go through all this? Is it necessary to watch my actions, to watch my reactions, my responses? Is it necessary to observe, diligently, my relationship with another? Must I go through all this? Or . . . ?

**PJ :** The fact is, sir, one has gone through all this.

**K :** You may have gone through it because you have accepted that pattern.

**PJ :** No.

**K :** Just wait a minute. You see that is what we have all done— the thinkers, the sannyasis, the monks, and . . . .

**PJ :** And Krishnamurti.

**K :** I'm not sure. Wait, just a minute. I want to discuss this point seriously.

**PJ :** Either you have, in the past thirty years, taken a jump or . . . .

**K :** Wait a minute. Let's look at it. We have accepted this pattern of examination, analysis and investigation. We have accepted these reactions, we have paid attention to them. We have watched the 'self' and so on. Now, there is something in it which rings a false note—at least to me.

**PJ :** You mean to say that a person caught in the whole confusion of existence . . . .

**K :** Pupul, he won't even listen to all this.

**PJ :** There has to be space in order to listen.

**K :** Yes.

**PJ :** How does that space arise?

**K :** You suffer. Now, you can either say, 'I must find out' or you merely say, 'God exists, and I am comforted by that'.

**PJ :** No sir. You ask: Is it necessary to go through all this?

**K :** Yes, that is what I am asking, for I think that it may not be necessary.

**PJ :** Then show me how.

**K :** Wait, I'll show it to you. Let's go into it. We shall call, for the moment, your diligent watching of your reactions, the analytical process of inquiry. Now, this analytical, self-investigative process, this constant watching, man has done for thousands of years.

**PJ :** He has not. He has done something quite different.

**K :** What has he done that's different?

**PJ** : He has looked at his mind and tried to suppress . . . .

**K** : Ah, you see, that's part of the pattern. Suppress, escape, substitute, transcend—all that is within that framework.

**PJ** : It's not the same thing as to observe without doing anything about the observation.

**K** : No, Pupul, if I may point out—perhaps I may be wrong—you are not answering my question: Must I go through all this?

**PJ** : You see the word 'must' is a very . . . .

**K** : All right, I won't use the word 'must', but the question remains. Is it necessary, is it imperative, is it essential, that I go through all this?

**PJ** : No, but are you trying to say that out of the middle of chaos you can leap to a state of total non-chaos?

**K** : No, I won't put it that way.

**PJ** : Then what are you saying?

**K** : No, wait a minute. I am saying, very clearly, that humanity has gone through this process. It has been the pattern of our existence—of course, some have gone through the process more diligently, sacrificing everything, inquiring, analysing, searching, and so on. You do this too, and at the end of it all you may be just a dead entity.

**PJ** : No, it may not be so.

**K** : *May* not be. You see, Pupul, very few—very, very, few—have got out of it.

**PJ** : Yes, but that is why I say that it may not be. But, sir, you are saying that it—this whole process—is not necessary.

**K** : I know. So your point is, if it is not necessary, then show me the other.

**PJ** : Yes, show me the other. ·

**K** : I'll show it to you. But first step out of this.

**PJ** : You see, sir . . . .

**K** : Wait, wait, wait. I'll show it to you.

**PJ** : But look what you are asking.

**K** : I know.

**PJ** : If I step out of the other, it's already there.

**K** : Of course. Step out. That's what I am saying. Don't take time to go through all this.

**PJ** : No, but what is meant by 'step out of it'?

**K** : I'll tell you what I mean. Let me talk a little. I recognize or I perceive—whatever be the word you use—that man has tried this process of introspective observation, diligence and so on, for a million years in different ways, and somehow the mind is not clear at the end of it. I see this very clearly. I see that somehow this movement is very, very shallow. Now, can you listen to that statement—that the whole process is shallow—and actually see the truth of it? If you do, it means that your disordered mind is now quiet; it is listening to find out. Your confused, traditional mind now not only says that you are accustomed to this diligent observation of all your activities but also that the entire process is really very superficial. Once you see the truth of this, you are out of it. It's like putting away something utterly meaningless.

Wait; let me put it another way. My mind is disorderly. My life is disorderly. You come along and say, 'Be diligent; be watchful of your actions, of your thoughts, of your relationship'. You say, 'Be watchful all the time'. And I say that that's impossible because my mind won't allow me to be diligent all the time. It is not diligent; it is negligent, and I struggle between these two.

**PJ :** But do you mean to say, Krishnaji, that a mind which is not capable of observing . . . .

**K :** No. I am saying that a mind that's willing to listen . . . .

**PJ :** But, please listen to me, sir. Do you think a mind can be in that state of listening?

**K :** That's very simple.

**PJ :** Is it?

**K :** Yes. I say just listen to a story that I am telling you. You are interested. Your mind is quiet; you are eager to see what the story is about and so on.

**PJ :** I'm sorry, sir, it doesn't happen that way.

**K :** No?

**PJ :** No.

**K :** Just a minute. Don't say no. I ask you, Pupul, to listen to what I am saying.

**PJ :** I listen.

**K :** No. Wait, wait. Listen. I am going to explain what I mean by listening.

**PJ :** Yes.

**K :** I mean by 'listening' not only the listening with the sensory ear, but the listening with the ear that has no movement. *That* is really listening.

Listening is not translating; listening is not comparing; listening is not trying to find out. Listening is something that is complete. Now, when you listen, completely, without any movement, to a man who comes along and says, 'Don't go through all this diligent process, because it is false, because it is superficial', what takes place? If you hear the truth of his statement, what takes place?

What actually takes place when you see something really true?

Now, this diligent process is time-consuming. Right? I have no time. My life is so short. I've got so many problems, and you are adding another; be diligent. And I say, 'Please, I am withered; I am worn out by problems, and you have introduced another problem'. So the man says, 'I know you have got many problems which are all interrelated. Forget your problems for the moment and listen to me. That's all'.

**PJ** : No, you are talking of a mind which is already mature. Such a mind, while listening to a statement like this . . . .

**K** : You see, Pupul, we have made our minds so immature that we are incapable of listening to anything.

**PJ** : But you see, Krishnaji, you start by making things impossible.

**K** : Of course. See the truth. See something impossible that you have found. It has a tremendous . . . .

**PJ** : Can I find the energy which is needed?

**K** : Yes.

**PJ** : Can I find the energy to deal with an impossible thing?

**K** : That's what it is. This diligent affair has been possible. I say it is something so trivial.

**PJ** : I ask you, what is the mind which can deal with an impossible statement like that? What is that mind?

**K** : It's very simple. That which is utterly impossible is non-existent. We think everything is possible. I am getting it.

**PJ** : See what you are getting at, sir. You are saying that it is non-existent. So with a non-existent mind . . . .

**K** : No, no. Look, Pupulji, just a minute. Can we both, you and I, agree—even temporarily—that this diligent process has really led nowhere? Can we see that this process has led to various activities—some of which may be beneficial—but that this process, this inquiry which says 'I must go to the very source of things' is not the way?

**PJ :** Yes, obviously. I would accept that.

**K :** That's all. If you accept that it's not through a diligent awareness . . . .

**PJ :** But, sir, even to come to a point when I say that it is so . . . .

**K :** What has happened to a mind that says that this is too trivial, too superficial? What is the quality of your mind?

**PJ :** I know what you are trying to say, sir.

**K :** No, you answer my question. What is the quality of a mind which has been caught in the process of diligent inquiry when it sees that the process which it has been caught in has no deep, fundamental value? This diligent process will not lead or help to comprehend or come upon or uncover the origin. This process is time-consuming. The other may have no time at all.

**PJ :** But, look at the danger of what you are saying. The danger is that I will not be concerned with sweeping the room.

**K :** No. I am inquiring into myself. That very inquiry demands that the mind and the heart—my whole existence—is orderly.

**PJ :** You start with the impossible.

**K :** *(With great energy)* Of course, I start with the impossible, Pupul, otherwise . . . Pupul, what is possible? You have done all that's possible.

**PJ :** No, sir.

**K :** No, no. Man has done everything that's possible. Man has fasted, sacrificed; man has done everything to find the origin of

185

things. Man has done all that has been possible, and that has led nowhere. That's what I am saying—possibility has led nowhere. It has led to certain benefits—social, and so on. It has also led to a great deal of misery for mankind. So, the man tells me that this diligent process is time-consuming and, therefore, time-binding. He tells me that as long as I am doing this, I am just scratching the surface. The surface may be the most extraordinary, pleasant and ennobling thing—but it's just the surface. If you grant—no not merely grant but actually see, actually feel—in your blood, as it were—that this is false, you will have already stepped out of something that is the ordinary into something that is extraordinary.

And we are not willing to do that. We want to go through all this. We treat it like learning a language. To learn a language, discipline, diligence, attention and so on are necessary. We carry the same mentality into the other. That's what I object to.       .

**PJ** : I put aside the other.

**K** : Aha. It is not a game that we are playing.

**PJ** : No, I am not playing a game. One puts aside the other.

**K** : Which means, careful Pupul . . . .

**PJ** : That even this seeing, this listening, is at an end—if I may put it this way.

**K** : Which means—what? That the movement of diligence has stopped—right? Of course. If that is false, it has gone. So what has happened to the mind—the mind that has been caught in diligent inquiry and so on, all of which is time-bound, and has been seen by me to be utterly superficial? What is the state of my mind? Right? It is a fresh mind. It is a totally new mind. And such a mind is necessary to inquire into, to uncover the origin.

If I talked like this to a very disciplined, 'religious' man, he wouldn't even bother to listen. He would say, 'All this is nonsense'.

But you, in our dialogue, say, 'Let's go into it' and, so, you put yourself into a position of listening. Find out.

Now, such a mind has no bondage to time. You see, the diligent process is to become something; it is to clarify, to understand, to go beyond. This mind has no beyond—it is not *becoming* something.

Could you, would you, go as far as that?

**PJ** : You see, the moment movement ends . . . .

**K** : No, I ask you, would you go so far as to see the fact that such a mind cannot have any kind of dependence, any kind of attachment?

**PJ** : Yes, that I see. Sir, all that which you have talked about is the movement of becoming.

**K** : That's right. All that is the perpetuation of the self in a different form, in a different network of words. You see, if you tell me this, I will want to find the source. And when I start out to uncover the source—which is, for me, a passion—I will want to find out, I will want to uncover the origin of all life. When there is that uncovering of origins, then my life, my actions—everything—is different.

That's why I see that the understanding of the diligent process is a time-consuming fact which is destructive. It may be necessary in order to learn a technique, but this is not a technique to be learnt. *(Long pause)*

**PJ** : Sir, you have an antique mind—a mind of great antiquity.

**K** : What?

**PJ** : You have an antique mind—'antique' in the sense that it contains the whole of human . . . .

**K** : You see, Pupul, that's why it's important to understand that I am the world.

**PJ** : No one else would make that kind of statement but you.

**K** : And one must make it. Otherwise, when you see all the destruction, the brutality, the killing, the wars—every form of violence that has never stopped—where are you? A man who loved wouldn't be British or Israeli or Arab. A man who loved couldn't kill another. I see this process has been going on for thousands and thousands of years—everybody trying to *become* something. And all the diligent, religious workers are helping man to become something—to achieve illumination, to achieve enlightenment. It's so absurd.

**PJ** : With you, sir, the whole movement of the dormant has ended.

**K** : That is, *(Laughs)* 'diligence' has ended. Becoming has ended. Pupul, let us not make this into some elitist understanding. Any person who pays attention, who wants to hear, who is passionate and not just casual about it and who, really, says, 'I must find the source of life', will listen. He will listen—not to me; he will just listen. It's in the air.

*Brockwood Park*
*21 June 1982*

# Brain, Mind, Emptiness

**PUPUL JAYAKAR (PJ) :** Sir, recently I read a short report in one of the newspapers that a spaceship had been released which would travel to the outer spaces of the universe. It would be part of the universe, and there would be no ending to it because there would be no friction, no time.

**J. KRISHNAMURTI (K) :** Yes.

**PJ :** My question is: Is there a within of the self, of the human brain, the human mind—call it what you will—is there a within of things, whether of man, of the tree, of nature, which is a space without ending, and is it a mirror image of that vastness which exists?

**K :** Are you asking, if I may repeat what you've said, whether there is or there can be a space without end, an eternity outside time within the human brain? I'd like to distinguish between the brain and the mind. You see, we can speculate a great deal—like philosophers have done—but that speculation is not actuality.

**PJ :** No, but if you do not posit a thing, then you cannot even . . . .

**K :** No. I want to be clear on this point. Are we now, in our conversation, speculating and theorizing, or are we really trying to find out, in ourselves, whether there is something that is immense, whether there is, in actuality, a movement which is not of time but which is eternal?

**PJ :** How do you start inquiring? Do you start by examination or by posing the question? If you don't pose the question . . . .

**K :** We've posed the question.

**PJ :** Now, what comes out of it—speculation or examination—depends on how you approach it; but the question has to be posed.

**K :** We have put the question: Can the brain realize the truth as to whether there is eternity or not? That's the question, right?

**PJ :** Yes.

**K :** Now, you ask: How do you begin to inquire into it? How do you begin to feel, gently, hesitantly, your way into this really fundamental question? Whether man is bound to time forever or whether the brain can realize itself—not imaginatively, not romantically, but actually—in a state of eternity, is a question that has been asked for thousands of years. And that is the question we're asking too.

**PJ :** You started by drawing a distinction between the brain and the mind.

**K :** Yes.

**PJ :** Would you, please, elaborate?

**K :** First, we are saying that the brain or at least some part of it is conditioned. That conditioning is brought about through experience. That conditioning is knowledge and memory. And as experience, knowledge and memory are limited, thought is limited.

**PJ :** Yes.

**K :** Now, we have been functioning within the area of thought.

**PJ** : Yes.

**K** : And to discover something new, there has to be, at least temporarily, a period when thought is not in movement, when thought is in abeyance.

**PJ** : The brain is a material thing.

**K** : Yes.

**PJ** : It has its own activity.

**K** : Yes, it has its own activity which is not imposed by thought.

**PJ** : But for centuries the operation of the brain has been the operation of thought.

**K** : That's all. That is what we are saying, namely that the whole movement of the brain—at least that part of the brain which has been used—is conditioned by thought, and thought is always limited and therefore it is conditioned to conflict. That which is limited must create division.

**PJ** : What is the mind then?

**K** : The mind is a wholly different dimension which has no contact with thought. Let me explain. The brain—that part of the brain which has been functioning as an instrument of thought—has been conditioned, and as long as that part of the brain remains in that state there is no communication—entire communication—with the mind. So, when that conditioning is not, then that mind which is totally on a different dimension, communicates with the brain and acts—using thought.

**PJ** : But you've already posited . . . .

**K** : Oh, definitely.

**PJ** : A state which is outside the realm of thought.

**K** : That's right—outside. And, therefore outside the realm of . . . .

191

**PJ** : Time.

**K** : Yes, time.

**PJ** : As time seems to be the essential core of this problem . . . .

**K** : Time and thought.

**PJ** : Thought is a product of time. I mean, in a sense, thought is time.

**K** : That's it, that's the real point. Where do you start, you mean?

**PJ** : No, no. Perhaps if we could go into this whole business of the flow of time, and at what instant interception is possible . . . .

**K** : What do you mean 'interception'? I don't quite understand the usage of that word. Who intercepts?

**PJ** : I'm not talking of an interceptor, but of the flow . . . .

**K** : The ending of it.

**PJ** : I was going to use another word, but you could use the word 'ending'.

**K** : Let's use simpler words.

**PJ** : Time is from a past immemorial.

**K** : Yes—which is thought.

**PJ** : Thought is also from a past immemorial, projecting into a future, which is also eternal.

**K** : In terms of thought.

**PJ** : Eternal.

**K** : No. *(Emphatic)* The future is conditioned by the past—as a human psyche.

**PJ** : Yes. So, unless human civilization, human culture ends, unless the human being ceases to be . . . .

192

**K** : Ceases to be conditioned, right?

**PJ** : Yes, but you will still use thought.

**K** : No.

**PJ** : The content will undergo a change, but the mechanism of thought will continue.

**K** : Now, let's put it this way. Thought is the chief instrument we have. Right?

**PJ** : Yes.

**K** : Thousands of years of various efforts and actions have not only made that instrument dull, but that instrument has also reached the end of its tether. Thought-time is limited, conditioned, divided, and in a perpetual state of turmoil. Now, can that end? That's the question.

**PJ** : Now, this movement of the past as thought, as the yesterday . . . .

**K** : As today.

**PJ** : What is the 'today'?

**K** : The 'today' is the movement of the past modified—memory. We are a bundle of memories.

**PJ** : That is true, but the contact with time . . . .

**K** : What do you mean 'contact with time'? *Time is thought.*

**PJ** : No, but the contact with time, as a psychological process, is in the present, isn't it?

**K** : Pupul, let's be very careful. Time is thought. Don't separate time as if it were something different from thought. It is time-thought.

**PJ** : Yes. I'm using the past, present and future . . . .

**K :** Are you asking: What is the 'now'?

**PJ :** It's 'interception' that I'm talking about. Let me use my word till I get it wiped away.

**K :** All right, all right; 'interception', but I don't quite understand.

**PJ :** Interception is 'contact with'—contact with the fact.

**K :** Contact with the fact that the whole movement of thought . . . .

**PJ :** Not even that. Just contact with 'what is'.

**K :** Which is the 'now'.

**PJ :** Which is whatever is. Your statement just now, and my listening to it, is the contact with 'what is'.

**K :** May I put it in the way that I understand it? The past, the present and the future is a movement of time-thought. How do you realize it? How do you come to see the truth of it, the fact of it?

**PJ :** No, sir, there is such a thing as tactile touch.

**K :** Yes, touch. How do you touch this thing? How do you—to use your words—come into contact with this fact that I am a whole series of memories which is time-thought?

**PJ :** No, let us be more concrete. That I am going away this afternoon, and that I may be leaving you, is a thought.

**K :** It's not a thought; it's an actuality.

**PJ :** Actuality, yes; but out of that there is a certain pain of leaving you, in which the emotional, psychological elements come to cover up the fact.

**K :** Yes, which is—what?

**PJ :** So, what is to be contacted? Not the fact that I'm going away . . . .

**K** : But what?

**PJ** : But this pain.

**K** : The pain? I understand. Are you asking: The pain of a thousand years and centuries—the pain of loneliness, sorrow, grief; the agony, the anxiety and all that—is that separate from the 'me' who feels it?

**PJ** : It may not be separate.

**K** : It is me. *(Emphatic)*

**PJ** : How do I touch it?

**K** : I don't quite understand your usage of 'How do *I* touch it?'

**PJ** : Sir, it's only in the present . . . .

**K** : I see what you mean.

**PJ** : It is only in the present that the whole of this edifice rests.

**K** : That's what I said. The 'now' contains the past, the future and the present.

**PJ** : Yes.

**K** : Wait, let's understand this. The present is the whole past and the future.

**PJ** : Yes.

**K** : *This is the present.* The present is me with all the memories of a thousand years, and those thousand years are being modified all the time. All that is the 'now'—the present.

**PJ** : But the present is also something which is not static. It's over before . . . .

**K** : Of course, of course. The moment you've said it, it's gone.

**PJ** : It's gone. So what is it that you actually see, what is it that you actually observe?

**K :** You actually observe the fact . . . .

**PJ :** What fact?

**K :** The fact—just a minute—that the present is the whole movement of time and thought. You, actually, see the truth of that. You have—let's not use the word 'see'—an insight, a perception, into the fact that the 'now' is all time and thought.

**PJ :** Does that perception emanate from the brain?

**K :** Either it comes by perceiving with the eyes and so on, or that perception is an insight which has nothing to do with time and thought.

**PJ :** But it arises within the brain?

**K :** Or does it arise outside the brain? That is your question, right?

**PJ :** Yes, it's very important.

**K :** I know—that's why I want to be clear. Is it within the sphere of the brain or is it that insight comes when there is freedom from conditioning, which is the operation of the mind?—That is supreme intelligence, you follow?

**PJ :** No, I don't follow.

**K :** Let's be clear. The brain is conditioned by time and thought, time-thought. As long as that conditioning remains, insight is not possible. You may have occasional insight into something, but not pure insight, which means the comprehension of the totality of things—I use the word 'totality' and not 'wholeness', because that word is now being used so much. That insight is not of time-thought, and it is the perception of completeness. Therefore that insight is part of that brain which is in a different dimension.

**PJ :** Without sight there cannot be insight.

**K :** That's all I'm saying.

**PJ** : Sir, perceiving, listening—which is contained in perceiving—seems to me the essential essence of insight.

**K** : Would you repeat that again, please, slowly?

**PJ** : Let us take the word 'insight'. It means 'seeing into'.

**K** : Seeing into.

**PJ** : Seeing into seeing?

**K** : No, just a minute; let's look at that word 'seeing'. Insight into or the comprehension of the totality, of the vastness of something, is possible only when there is the cessation of thought and time. Thought and time are limited; therefore such limitation cannot have insight.

**PJ** : To understand what you are saying, I have to have an open ear and eyes that see. Out of that sound, out of that form, out of that whole . . . .

**K** : Yes, out of the whole meaning of the words, and so on . . . .

**PJ** : Arises a seeing which goes beyond. I'm trying to get at something.

**K** : What are you trying to get at? I don't quite . . . .

**PJ** : You talk of insight. Now, insight cannot arise without attention.

**K** : No, wait; don't introduce the word 'attention'.

**PJ** : Or sight, seeing.

**K** : No, stick to the same thing. That is, insight cannot exist as long as time-thought plays a part.

**PJ** : You see, it's like: Which comes first?

**K** : What do you mean, 'Which comes first?'

**PJ** : I mean in my consciousness, in my approach to this, I can't start with insight.

**K :** No.

**PJ :** I can only start with observation.

**K :** You can only start by realizing the truth of time. Psychological time and thought are always limited. That's a fact. *(Emphatic)*

**PJ :** That, Krishnaji, is a fact . . . .

**K :** No, wait, *start from that*. Start from the realization that time-thought is always limited and, therefore, whatever it does will always be limited and therefore contradictory, divisive and giving rise to endless conflict. That's all I'm saying. You can see the fact of that.

**PJ :** You can see the fact of that outside of yourself.

**K :** Wait, wait. You can see it politically, religiously. All through the world it is a fact that time and thought, in their activity, have wrought havoc in the world. That's a fact.

**PJ :** Yes, yes.

**K :** So, now the question is: Can that limitation ever end or is man condemned, forever, to live within the time-thought area?

**PJ :** What is the relationship of the brain cells and the action of the senses—I'm not using the word 'thought' at the moment—on a statement like this? Do you see the fact that time-thought is limited? And what exactly does it mean? How does one see that? It's like telling me that I am an illusion.

**K :** What?

**PJ :** It is exactly like telling me that 'Pupul is an illusion'.

**K :** No, I didn't say that.

**PJ :** But *I'm* saying that.

**K :** No, *you are not an illusion*.

**PJ** : No sir, it's exactly like that . . . .

**K** : No. *(Emphatic)*

**PJ** : Because the moment you say, 'After all Pupul is a psychological bundle of the past, a psychological movement of time and thought which is the psyche, and that psyche is limited' . . . .

**K** : Yes, it is limited, and whatever it does is limited.

**PJ** : Then, I would ask: What's wrong with it being limited?

**K** : There is nothing wrong if you want to live in perpetual conflict.

**PJ** : A move further. To end it is not only to say, to feel, that it is limited, but there must be an actual ending to it.

**K** : I say that there is.

**PJ** : What is the nature of this ending?

**K** : What do you mean by 'the ending'? Let's take the word 'ending'. I must be clear about what you and I are saying. I must be clear that we both understand the same thing when we use the words—'to end something'. To end attachment. Not to do this or that. Not to smoke. To put an end to it. The ending.

**PJ** : The flow ceases to flow.

**K** : Yes, if you like; yes. The movement of thought and time ceases—psychologically. What is your difficulty? You are making a simple thing terribly complex.

**PJ** : No, sir, there is a point of perception which is a point of insight.

**K** : Yes.

**PJ** : What is that point of insight?

**K** : What do you mean 'point of insight'?

**PJ** : In what time-space do I see it?

**K** : Look, Pupul, let's be simple. Time-thought has divided the world: politically, geographically, religiously. That's a fact. Can't you see the fact?

**PJ** : No, sir, I look at the outside and I see . . . .

**K** : No, wait, wait. Don't look outside. This is . . . .

**PJ** : No, I don't see the fact.

**K** : What do you mean 'I don't see the fact'?

**PJ** : Because if I saw the fact, if I really saw the fact . . . .

**K** : You would stop that kind of thing.

**PJ** : It would be all over.

**K** : That's all I'm saying.

**PJ** : Why is it, if it is such a simple thing—which I don't think it is, because it has such devious ways . . . .

**K** : No. *(Emphatic)* That's the whole point. If you have an insight that the movement of thought-time is divisive—at whatever level, in whatever realm, in whatever area—that it is a movement of endless conflict . . . .

**PJ** : Yes, but you can see it when it's a matter outside you.

**K** : Now, can you see this movement outside, can you see what it does in the world, what misery it has caused in the world? Inwardly the movement is the psyche which is time-thought; the psyche is a movement of time-thought. *This* inward movement has created that. *(Pointing outside)* **Simple**. The divisive psychological movement has created the external fact. I am a Hindu. I am a German. I feel secure in the word. I feel secure in the feeling that I belong to something.

**PJ :** You see, Krishnaji, I would say that all these—being a Hindu or being greedy—one has seen as a product of this movement of time-thought.

**K :** That's all I'm saying.

**PJ :** But it's not quite . . . .

**K :** What is your difficulty?

**PJ :** There is, within it all, a sense of 'I exist'.

**K :** That's the whole point. *(With emphasis)* You don't realize that the psyche is *that.*

**PJ :** Yes, that's essentially the nature of the problem.

**K :** Why don't you? Because—it's simple enough, why do you make it complex? You think that the psyche is something other than a conditioned state. You think that there is something in you—in the brain or somewhere—which is timeless, which is God, which is this, which is that, and that if only you can reach *that,* everything will be all right. That's part of your conditioning. Because you are uncertain, because you are confused, God or the highest principle or some kind of conviction gives you safety, protection, certainty. That's all.

**PJ :** What is the nature of the ground from which insight springs?

**K :** I've told you. Insight can only take place when there is freedom from time and thought.

**PJ :** Time and thought. You see, it's so sort of unending.

**K :** No. It is not. You are complicating a very simple fact, as most of us do. To live in peace is to flower; it is to understand the extraordinary world of peace. Peace cannot be brought about by thought.

**PJ :** You see—please understand, Krishnaji—it is the brain itself which listens to that statement.

**K :** Yes, it listens, and then what happens? Just a minute. What happens? If it listens, it's quiet.

**PJ :** It's quiet.

**K :** It isn't ruminating. It's not going on, if you see what I mean. It's not rattling. It's quiet.

**PJ :** Yes, it's quiet.

**K :** Wait, wait. When it really, *actually,* listens, and there is quietness that is not induced, then there is insight. I don't have to explain in ten different ways the limitation of thought. *It is so.*

**PJ :** I see what you are saying. Is there anything further than that?

**K :** Oh yes, there is. Oh God, there is a great deal more. Which is: Is listening only possible when it is connected to a sound—a sound within an area, or is there also a listening to something, let's say, for example, to what you are saying, without the verbal sound? I say that if there is a verbal sound, I'm not listening, but only understanding the words. But you want to convey to me something much more than the words. If the words are making a sound in my hearing, I cannot deeply understand the depth of what you are saying. So, I want to find out something much more— which is what we started with, namely, the present.

**PJ :** Yes.

**K :** The present is the 'now'. The 'now' is the whole movement of time-thought.

**PJ :** Yes.

**K :** It is the whole structure. If the structure of time and thought ends, the 'now' has a totally different meaning. The 'now' then is nothing. And nothing contains all. I mean, zero contains all the figures. Right?

**PJ :** Yes.

**K :** But we are afraid to be nothing.

**PJ** : When you say, 'Contains the all', do you mean that it is the essence of all humanity, the environment, nature and . . . .

**K** : Yes, yes.

**PJ** : The cosmos as such?

**K** : No. *There is nothing.* The psyche is a bundle of memories, and those memories are dead. They operate, function in us, but they are the outcome of past experiences, which have gone. I am a movement of memories. Now, if I have an insight that I am nothing . . . that there is nothing *(Correcting himself quickly),* then 'I' don't exist.

**PJ** : You said something about sound and listening.

**K** : Yes, listening without sound. You see the beauty of it?

**PJ** : Yes, it is possible when the mind itself is totally still.

**K** : No, don't bring in the mind for the moment. When the brain is absolutely quiet, there is no sound made by the word. *That is real listening.* The word has given me what you want to convey. You want to tell me, 'I'm going this afternoon'. I listen to that . . . .

**PJ** : But the brain has not been active in listening.

**K** : Yes. The brain, when it is active, is noise. Let's come back to this business of sound, because it's very interesting. What is sound? Sound—pure sound—can only exist when there is space and silence. Otherwise it's just noise. *(Pause)*

I'd like to come back to the fact that all one's education, all one's past experience and knowledge, is a movement in becoming—both inwardly and outwardly. Becoming is the accumulation of memory—more and more and more memories which constitute knowledge. Now, as long as that movement exists, there is fear of being nothing. But when one has an insight that there is nothing, when one really sees the fallacy, the illusion of becoming—which is endless time-thought and conflict—then there is an ending of that. That is, the ending of the movement which is the psyche, which is time-thought. The ending of that is to be nothing. Nothing then contains the whole universe—not my petty little fears, petty little anxieties and problems, and my sorrow with regard to, you know, a dozen things. After all, Pupulji, 'nothing' means the entire world of compassion. Compassion is nothing. And, therefore, that nothingness is supreme intelligence. That's all there is. I don't know if I'm conveying this.

**PJ :** Yes.

**K :** So, why are human beings—just ordinary, intelligent human beings—frightened of being nothing, frightened to see that they really are verbal illusions, that they are nothing but dead memories? *That's a fact.* I don't *like* to think I'm just nothing but memories, but the truth is that I *am* memories. If I have no memory, either I'm in a state of amnesia or I understand the whole movement of memory, which is time-thought, and see the fact that as long as there is this movement, there must be endless conflict, struggle, pain. And when there is an insight into that, nothing means something entirely different. That 'nothing' is the present, and it's not a 'varying' present.

**PJ :** Not a varying present.

**K :** It isn't that one day it's this, and the next day it is different. That nothing is no time. Therefore it's not ending one day, and being another day. You see, if one goes into this problem, not theoretically—as the astrophysicists are doing, namely trying to understand the universe in terms of gases—but actually—here, as part of the human being, and not out there—there must be no shadow of time and thought. You see, Pupul, *that* after all is real meditation. That's what *śūnya* means in Sanskrit. But we've interpreted it in a hundred different ways; we have commentaries about this and that. But the actual fact is that we are 'nothing' except words and options and judgements. I mean, all that is a petty affair, and we've made our lives petty.

So, we have to grasp, to understand, that the zero contains all the numbers, and that in nothing is all the world contained—not the pain and the anxiety which are all so small. Of course I know that when I'm suffering, that's the only thing I have, or when there is fear, that's the only thing. But unfortunately, you see, I don't realize that it is such a petty little thing.

So, having listened to all this, what is your comprehension? What is it you realize? If you could put it into words, Pupul, it would be rather good. What is it that you, and those who are going to listen to all this—it may be rubbish, it may be true—what do you capture, realize? Do you see the immensity of all this?

**PJ** : It's really an ending, an ending of the psychological nature of the self . . . .

**K** : Yes.

**PJ** : Because that is becoming.

**K** : No. Wait a minute, Pupulji. Because it's going to be very helpful to all of us, I've asked the question: As you listen to all this, what's your response, what's your reaction, what have you realized? Do you say, 'By Jove, I've got it. I've got the perfume of it'?

**PJ** : Sir, don't ask me that question.

**K** : Why?

**PJ** : Because anything I say would sound . . . . Because as you were speaking there was immensity.

**K** : Yes. Now wait a minute. There was that. I could feel it, you could. There was the tension of that, but is it temporary—for the moment, for a second—and it's gone, and then is there once again the whole business of remembering it, capturing it, inviting it?

**PJ** : No, no. I say that one has moved from there at least. Another thing one realizes is that the most difficult thing in the world is to be totally simple.

205

**K** : Yes. To be simple—that's right. If one is really simple, one can understand the enormous complexity of things. But we start with all the complexities and never see the simplicity. That's our training. We have trained our brains to see the complexity, and then try to find an answer to the complexity. But we don't see the extraordinary simplicity of life, of *facts* rather.

**PJ** : May I move away a little?

**K** : Yes please do; I'm glad.

**PJ** : In the Indian tradition, out of sound were born all the elements, all the *pañca-mahābhūtas*. There is the sound which reverberates, and is yet not heard.

**K** : That's it. But after all, Pupul, especially in the Indian tradition, from the Buddha, from Nagarjuna, and the ancient Hindus, there is that state of nothingness, in which, they said, you must deny the whole thing. Nagarjuna came to that point. As far as I've been told and understand—I may be mistaken—he denied everything, every movement of the psyche.

**PJ** : Yes, every movement of the brain cell as we . . . .

**K** : Yes, it is there in the books; it is there in tradition. Now, why haven't they pursued that? You see, even the most intelligent of them, even the most religious devotee has pursued some structure, and not the feeling of religion, the feeling of the divine, the sense of something sacred. Why haven't they pursued denying, not the world—you can't deny the world—but the 'me'? They have not denied, they have not totally negated, the 'me'. What they have done is to deny the world—which one cannot—and they have ended up only making a mess of their own lives.

**PJ** : Sir, really, you know, renunciation—let me use that word . . . .

**K** : I know renunciation.

**PJ** : It is the negation of the 'me'.

**K** : But it's not negation. The 'me' exists still. I may renounce my house, but . . . .

**PJ** : Sir, basically, renunciation is never in the outer.

**K** : Yes, never outside but inside—which means what? Don't be attached—even to a highest principle. Don't be attached to your ideal—the loin-cloth. I think what is happening is that we are really caught in a net of words, in theories, and not in actuality. I suffer. I must find a way to end that, and not escape into some kind of silly illusion. Why have human beings not faced the fact, but changed the fact? Do you follow my question? Is it because we are living in illusions, with ideas and conclusions and all those unrealities? All this is so obvious.

**PJ** : We are living with the history of mankind. That is the history of mankind.

**K** : Yes, and mankind is me, and 'me' is this endless misery. So, if you want to end misery, end the 'me'. The ending of 'me' is not an action of will. The ending of 'me' doesn't come about through fasting, and all that childish business that human beings, who've been called 'saints', have gone through.

**PJ** : It's really the ending of time, isn't it, sir?

**K** : Yes, isn't it? The ending of time-thought. That means to listen without the sound. Listen to the universe without a sound. We were talking the other day, in New York, to a doctor who is, I believe, very well known. He said, 'All these questions are all right, sir, but the fundamental issue is whether the brain cells— which have been conditioned for centuries—can really bring about a mutation in themselves. Then the whole thing would be simple'. Do you understand?

**PJ** : Yes.

**K** : I said, 'It's possible only through insight', and then we went into it as we've gone into it now. You see, *nobody* is willing to listen to this in its entirety. They listen partially. They agree, in the sense, they go together up to a certain point and stop there. If man really says, 'There must be peace in the world, therefore, I must live peacefully', then there will be peace in the world. But he—man—doesn't want to live in peace. He does everything that is the opposite of that. He continues with his ambition, his arrogance, his silly, petty fears and all that. So, we have reduced the vastness of all this to petty little reactions. Do you realize that, Pupul? And so we live such petty lives. This applies to everyone—from the highest to the lowest.

**PJ :** What is sound to you, sir?

**K :** Sound is the tree. Wait a minute. Take music. Pure Indian chanting, Rig Vedic chanting or the Gregorian chants—they are extraordinarily close together. And one listens to all the songs of praise, which are . . . *(Shrinks back)* I won't go into all that. Then, you listen to the sound of the waves, the sound of strong wind among the trees, the sound of the person whom you have lived with for many years; you get used to all this. But if you don't get used to all this, then sound has an extraordinary meaning. Then you hear everything afresh.

Say, for instance, you tell me that time-thought is the whole movement of man's life; therefore limited. Now, you have communicated to me a simple fact, and I listen to it. I listen to it without the sound of the word. I've captured the significance, the depth of that statement, and I can't lose it. It isn't that I've heard it now, and it's gone when I go outside. I've listened to it in it's entirety. That means, the sound has conveyed the fact that it is so. And what is so is absolute—always. I believe that in the Hebraic tradition one can only say of Jehova—or whatever the nameless one is—'I am'. *Tat tvam asi* and so on, in Sanskrit.

*Brockwood Park*
*25 June 1983*

# What is Culture?

**PUPUL JAYAKAR (PJ)** : Krishnaji, there is a strange phenomenon in the world today, where the East reaches out to the West to find sustenance, and the West reaches out to the East for, in inverted commas, 'wisdom' to fill some vacuum. My question is: Is there an Indian mind which may contain the same elements of sorrow, greed, anger, etc., as the Western mind but where the ground from which these spring is different?

**J. KRISHNAMURTI (K)** : Are you asking whether Eastern thought, Eastern culture, the Eastern way of life, is different from that of the West?

**PJ** : Well, obviously the Indian way of life is different from that of the West . . . .

**K** : It is.

**PJ** : Yes, because the conditioning of the two are different. But, in a sense, they complement each other.

**K** : In what way?

**PJ** : In the sense that the East, or India, more specifically, lacks

---

Previously published in the *KFI Bulletin 1989/2*, pp 2–24.

perhaps that precision of carrying an abstraction to concrete action.

**K :** Are you saying that in India they live more in abstraction?

**PJ :** Yes. They are not so concerned about action in the environment or with action as such.

**K :** What would you say they are concerned with?

**PJ :** Today, of course, there is a great change taking place. It's very difficult to say what the Indian mind is, because the Indian mind today is looking—at one level—for the same material comforts.

**K :** It is looking for progress in the technological world, and applying it in daily life, and so on.

**PJ :** Yes, progress in the technological world and consumerism have percolated very deeply into the Indian spirit.

**K :** So, what ultimately is the difference between Indian culture and Western culture?

**PJ :** Perhaps, in spite of this material overtone, there still is, in India, a certain insight into things because of a certain edge to the whole delving process itself. In India the delving process or inquiry goes into the field of the self, the within. For centuries the Indian mind has been nurtured in this feeling. Whereas, in the West, right from the time of the Greeks, there has always been a movement away—a movement towards the outer, the environment.

**K :** I understand. The other day I heard on the television a very well-known Indian being interviewed. He said that the technological world now in India is humanizing the Indian mind. I wonder what he meant by that. Did he mean that instead of living in abstractions and theories with all the complexity of ideation and so on, the technological world is bringing the Indians down to earth?

**PJ :** And perhaps it is necessary to some extent.

**K :** Obviously it's necessary.

**PJ :** So, if these two minds have a different essence . . . .

**K :** I question that very much. I question whether thought is ever Eastern or Western. You see, there is only thought. It is not Eastern thought or Western thought. The expression of thought may be different in India and in the West, but it is still a process of thought.

**PJ :** But is it also not true that what the brain cells contain in the West, and what the centuries of knowledge and so-called wisdom have given to the brain cells in the East make them perceive differently?

**K :** I would like to question what you are saying, if I may. I find that when I go to India there is much more materialism now than there used to be. There is more concern with money, position, power and all that. And of course there is over-population, and all the complexities of modern civilization. Are you saying that the Indian mind has a tendency to an inward search much more so than the mind of the West?

**PJ :** I would say so. I would say that there is the inner environment and the outer environment, and that the outer environment is the concern of the West while the inner environment has been the concern of the East.

**K :** Has been the concern, yes; *but it has been the concern of very, very few people.*

**PJ :** But it is only those few who create culture.

**K :** Yes. Well, the Western world is much more concerned, as far as I can see—I may be mistaken—with worldly affairs.

**PJ :** But what turned it in that direction?

**K :** Politics, economics, geographical location and climate.

**PJ :** No, you see, if it was only the climate, then India, Mexico and Equatorial Africa would have had the same mind. But they don't. So, that's not the answer.

**K :** No, of course not. It's not only the climate. You see, it is the whole so-called religious way of life in the West which is very, very different from that of the East.

**PJ :** That's it. That's what I'm saying. That somewhere along the line, they are people of one racial stock seemingly divided.

**K :** Divided, yes.

**PJ :** In the West there was a discovery and a dialogue with nature. But the direction in which the West turned led to technology and all the great scientific truths. India also had a dialogue with nature and with the self, but the dialogues were in themselves of a different kind.

**K :** So, are you trying to say that the Eastern mind, the Indian mind, is more concerned with religious matters than the Western mind?

**PJ :** I am, yes.

**K :** Here, in the West, it's all rather superficial—though they think it's rather deep—and there, in India, the tradition, literature and everything says, 'The world is not so important as the understanding of the self, the understanding of the universe, the understanding of the cosmos, the highest principle—*brahman*'.

**PJ :** Yes. The swiftness with which the mind can start the inquiry is perhaps different in the West, where the inquiring and the great insights have been in a different direction.

**K :** In the West, you see, in religious matters, doubt, scepticism, questioning is absolutely denied. Faith is all important in the West. But in Indian religions, in Buddhism and so on, doubt, questioning and inquiry become all important.

**PJ :** Today both the cultures are in a crisis.

**K :** Yes, of course, both cultures are in a crisis. Pupul, would you say that it is not merely the cultures but the whole of human consciousness that is in a crisis?

**PJ :** Yes. Well, would you distinguish human consciousness from culture?

**K :** No.

**PJ :** In a sense they are the same.

**K :** Yes, basically they are the same; they are not different.

**PJ :** So, the crisis, at the very root, has made them search somewhere away from themselves. They feel an inadequacy and so they turn to the other culture. It's happening in both countries.

**K :** Yes, but you see Pupul, in their search from their materialistic outlook, if I may use that word, the people of the West are being caught not only in all kinds of superstitious, romantic, occult ideas but also by these gurus who come over here (to the West, that is). What I want to find out is whether human consciousness—which is in a crisis—can not only resolve that crisis without war, without destroying humanity, but also whether human beings can ever go beyond their own limitation. I don't know whether I am making myself clear.

**PJ :** Sir, the outer and inner are like two mirror images of the directions in which man has moved. The problem really is that if man has to survive, the two have to be . . . .

**K :** The two have to live together.

**PJ :** No, not just live together, but a human culture, which would contain both, must come into being.

**K :** Yes, that's it. Now, what do you mean by the word 'culture'? What do you mean by 'culture'?

**PJ :** Isn't culture everything that the brain contains?

**K :** That is, would you say that culture is the training of the brain, the refinement of the brain and the expression of that refinement in action, in behaviour, in relationship, and also that it is a process of inquiry that leads to something totally untouched by thought? I would say that that is culture.

**PJ :** Would you include inquiry in the field of culture?

**K :** Of course.

**PJ :** Isn't culture a closed circuit?

**K :** You can make culture a closed circuit or you can break it and go beyond.

**PJ :** But today culture, as it exists, is a closed circuit.

**K :** That's why I want to understand what you mean by the word 'culture'.

**PJ :** Culture, as we understand it today Krishnaji, is the sum of our perceptions, the way we look at things, our thoughts, our feelings, our attitudes, the operation of our senses.

**K :** Go on.

**PJ :** You can keep on adding to this.

**K :** That is, religion, faith, belief, superstition.

**PJ :** All the outer and the inner . . . .

**K :** Yes.

**PJ :** Which keep on growing—but growing within that contour. It remains a contour. And when you talk of a search, which is in no way connected with this, would you include it in the field of culture?

**K :** Of course. Would you say—I'm just trying to clarify the matter—that the whole movement of culture is like a tide going out and coming in, and that human endeavour is this process of going out and coming in, without ever inquiring whether that process can ever stop? Do you understand? What I mean is that we act and react.

**PJ :** Yes.

**K :** That's human nature—like the ebb and flow of the tide. I react, and out of the reaction act, and from that action react. It's back and forth.

**PJ :** Yes.

**K :** Now, I'm asking whether this reaction of reward and punishment can stop and take a totally different turn. Our lives, our functions, our reactions are based on reward and punishment— both physically and psychologically. Right?

**PJ :** Yes.

**K :** And that's all we know—deeply. There is this reaction of reward and the avoidance of punishment and so on—like the tide. Now, I'm asking whether there is another sense of action which is not based on this action-reaction. Do you understand what I am talking about?

**PJ :** As this action-reaction is an impulse of the brain cells . . . .

**K :** It's our conditioning.

**PJ :** And it's an impulse of the brain cells.

**K :** Yes, of course, of course.

**PJ :** It's the way the brain cells respond and the way they receive through the senses.

**K :** Our question really is: What is culture?

**PJ :** And we went into it.

**K :** A little bit.

**PJ** : Yes, a little bit. It can be expanded much further, but still it remains within the same . . . .

**K** : Yes, it's in the same field.

**PJ** : Would you say then that culture is that which is contained in the brain cells?

**K** : Of course.

**PJ** : Anything else?

**K** : All our past memories.

**PJ** : Yes. So if you take all that, is there anything else?

**K** : I understand now. This is a different question, because—we must be careful, very careful—if there is something else—*if*—then that something else can operate on the brain cells which are conditioned. Right? *If* there is something in the brain, the activity of that something else can bring about a freedom from this narrow, limited culture. But is there something else within the brain?

**PJ** : But even physiologically they are saying, Krishnaji, that the operation of the brain cells today is a very, very minute portion of it's capacity.

**K** : I know that. Why?

**PJ** : Because conditioning limits it, and it has never been free of those processes which . . . .

**K** : Limit it. Which means, thought is limited.

**PJ** : Yes, it's put all its eggs in one basket.

**K** : One basket; that's how I want to put it. Thought is limited, and we are all functioning within that limitation. Right? Experience, knowledge, memory and thought are limited forever.

**PJ** : What place have the senses and the perceptive processes in this?

**K :** That brings another question, which is: Can the senses operate without the interference of thought? Do you understand my question?

**PJ :** As they operate today, Krishnaji, they seem to have one root—thought. The movement of the senses, as they operate, is the movement of thought.

**K :** That's all. Therefore it's limited. I'm inquiring, with a lot of hesitation and a certain amount of scepticism, whether the brain cells—which have evolved through thousands of years, experienced untold sorrow, loneliness, despair, and tried to escape from its own fears through every form of 'religious' endeavour, and all the rest of it—can ever, by themselves, change and bring about a mutation in themselves.

**PJ :** But if they don't bring about a mutation in themselves . . . .

**K :** What would?

**PJ :** . . . and there is nothing else . . . ?

**K :** Yes, I understand your question.

**PJ :** You see, this is the paradox. Really, sir, it is a paradox.

**K :** This is also the everlasting question; the Hindus raised it long ago—many, many centuries ago.

**PJ :** Yes, yes.

**K :** They raised this question: Is there an outside agency—God, the highest principle, and so on, and so on . . . .

**PJ :** The higher self.

**K :** 'The higher self'—that's a wrong way of . . . *(Smiles)* but we'll use it for the moment. Is there a 'higher self' that can operate on the conditioned brain?

**PJ :** Or is it rather, sir, whether it can awaken within the brain? These are two separate things. One, an outside . . . .

**K :** . . . agency operating.

**PJ :** Agency or energy operating, or two, an action from within the brain cells—the untapped portion of the brain cells—an action that awakens, which transforms.

**K :** Yes, I understand your question. Let's inquire into it; let's discuss it. Is there an outside agency—outside energy, let's call it for the moment—that will bring about a mutation in the brain cells which are conditioned? Right?

**PJ :** May I say something?

**K :** Yes of course, please.

**PJ :** The problem is that energy really never touches the brain cells. There are so many obstacles that one has built, that the flow of energy never seems to touch and create . . . .

**K :** What are we discussing?

**PJ :** We are discussing the possibility of a human culture.

**K :** A culture which is not . . . .

**PJ :** Either of India or of the West.

**K :** Yes.

**PJ :** A culture which contains all mankind, if I may say so.

**K :** Yes, all humanity.

**PJ :** A culture in which the division between the outer and inner ends, and where insight is insight, and not insight into the outer or insight into the inner.

**K :** That I understand. So what's the question?

**PJ :** So, for that the instrument is the brain cell.

**K :** Yes.

**PJ :** The tool which operates is the brain cell.

**K :** Is the brain.

**PJ :** Is the brain. Now, something has to happen in the brain.

**K :** Yes. I say it can happen—without the idea that there is an outside agency that will somehow cleanse the brain that has been conditioned, or by inventing an outside agency, as most religions have done. Right?

The question is: Can the conditioned brain awaken to it's own conditioning and so perceive its own limitation, and stay there for a moment? I don't know if I'm making my point clear.

You see, we are all the time—are we not?—trying to do something. Which is, the 'doer' is different from that which is being done. Right? For example, suppose I realize that my brain is conditioned, and so all my activities, feelings and relationships with others are limited. I realize that. And then I say, 'That limitation must be broken down'. So, I'm operating on the limitation. But the 'I' is also limited. The 'I' is not separate from the other. So, can we bridge that? The 'I' is not separate from the limitation which it is trying to break down. Both—the limitation of the self, and the limitation of the conditioning—are similar; they are not separate. The 'I' is not separate from its own qualities.

**PJ :** Nor is it separate from what it observes. When you say that we are all the time trying to do something . . . .

**K :** Operate on the other. Our whole life is that, apart from the technological world. 'I am this and I must change that', and the brain is now conditioned in this division: The actor is different from the action.

**PJ :** That of course, yes.

**K :** And so that condition goes on. But when one realizes that the actor *is* the action, then the whole outlook changes altogether. Now, let's come back for the moment. We are asking, Pupulji, are we not, what brings about a change in the human brain?

**PJ** : That's really the crucial . . . .

**K** : . . . point, yes.

**PJ** : What is it that makes it end?

**K** : Yes. Let's go into it a little bit more. Man has lived on this earth for a million years, more or less, and we are, psychologically, as primitive as we were before. We have not, basically, changed very much. We are killing each other, seeking power, position. We are corrupt in everything that we do in the world today—psychologically. What will make human beings—humanity—change all that?

**PJ** : A great insight.

**K** : Insight. Now, is so-called culture preventing this? Do you understand my question? Take Indian culture. A few people, like the great thinkers, have gone into this question. And the majority of the people just repeat, repeat, repeat, repeat. It's just tradition—a dead thing. And they live with a dead thing. Right? Now, here too, in the West, tradition is a tremendous power.

So, looking at all this, I ask: What will make human beings bring about a radical mutation in themselves? Culture has tried to bring about certain changes in human behaviour. Right?

**PJ** : Yes.

**K** : And religions have said, 'Behave this way', 'Don't do this', 'Don't kill'. But we go on killing. 'Be brotherly', and we are not brotherly. 'Love one another', and we don't. You follow? There are the edicts, the sanctions, and we are doing everything quite the opposite. Right?

**PJ** : Both cultures have collapsed, really.

**K** : That's what I want to find out. Have they collapsed and, therefore, have no value at all any more? And is that why man is now at a loss? If you go to America, for example, they have no tradition.

Right? Each one is doing what he likes. Each one is doing 'his thing'. And they are doing the same thing here—in a different way. So, what will bring about a mutation in the brain cells which then . . . ? *(Gestures expansively)*

**PJ** : So, what you're saying really is that it doesn't matter whether the Indian matrix is different or the Western matrix is different . . . .

**K** : Or not different.

**PJ** : You are saying that the problem is identical, namely, the mutation in the human brain.

**K** : Yes, that's it; let's stick to that. I mean, after all, Indians— even the poorest—suffer as they suffer here in the West. Loneliness, despair, misery; all that is just the same as it is here. So, let's forget the East and the West and see what prevents this mutation from taking place.

**PJ** : Sir, is there any other way of perceiving the actual?

**K** : The actual. That's what we've maintained for sixty years. That the 'what is', the actual, is more important than the idea of the actual. The ideal, the various concepts and conclusions have no value at all because one is distanced from the facts, from what is going on and, because we are caught up with ideas, apparently to see it is tremendously difficult.

**PJ** : But in perceiving the actual there is no movement of the brain.

**K** : That's all I'm saying. Facts, if one observes very carefully, in themselves bring about a change. I don't know if I'm making myself clear.

**PJ** : Yes.

**K** : Take sorrow. It's human sorrow. It's not Western sorrow or Eastern sorrow. Sorrow is not yours or mine. And we are always trying to move away from sorrow. Now, could we understand the depth and the meaning of sorrow—not understand intellectually, but actually delve into the nature of sorrow? What is impeding or blocking the human brain from inquiring deeply within itself?

**PJ** : Sir, if I may, I want to ask one thing. You use the words 'delving' and 'inquiring' into oneself. Both are words connected with movement.

**K** : Movement, yes.

**PJ** : Yet you speak of 'the ending of movement'.

**K** : Yes, of course, of course. Movement is time, movement is thought. The ending of movement: Can that really end or do we *think* it can end? Do you understand my question?

**PJ** : Yes, sir.

**K** : After all, the people who have somewhat gone into this kind of thing, both in the past and in the present, have always divided: the entity that inquires and that which is to be inquired into. That's my objection. I think that is the major block.

**PJ** : So, when you use the word 'inquiry', you use it as perception.

**K** : Perceiving, observing, watching. We'll go into that in a minute, if we have time, but I want to come back to this, if I may. What will make human beings alter the way they behave? There is this appalling brutality. What will change all this? Who will change it?—Not the politicians, not the priests, not the people who are talking about the environment, the ecologists, and so on. They've not changed the human being. If man himself will not change, who will? The Church has tried to change man—right?— and it hasn't succeeded. Religions have tried throughout the world to humanize man, to make him more intelligent, more considerate and affectionate. So far they have not succeeded. Culture has not succeeded.

**PJ** : You say all this Krishnaji, but that in itself does not bring man to that perception of fact.

**K** : So what will make him? Say, for instance, you and another, have this perception. I may not have it. So what affect has your perception on me? Again, if you have perception and power, position, I either worship you or I kill you. Right? So I'm asking a much deeper question. I want to really find out why human beings, after so many millennia, are like this: One group against another, one tribe against another, one nation against another. The horror that's going on! A new culture: Will that bring about a change? Does man *want* to change? Or does he say, 'Things are all right, let's go on. We'll evolve to a certain stage eventually'.

**PJ** : Most people feel that.

**K** : Yes, that's what's so appalling about it. *Eventually*. 'Give another thousand years and we'll all be marvellous human beings'; which is so absurd. In the meantime we are destroying each other.

**PJ** : Sir, may I ask you something? What is the actual moment of facing the fact? What is the actuality of it?

**K** : What is a fact, Pupul? We were discussing the other day, with a group of people here, that a fact is that which has been done, remembered, and that which is being done now, and that which has happened yesterday and is remembered.

**PJ** : Or even a rising wave of fear, horror, anything.

**K** : Yes, yes.

**PJ** : Now, how does one actually . . . ?

**K** : Wait a minute, let us be clear when we say what a fact is. The fact of last week's incident is gone, but I remember it. Right? There is the remembrance of something pleasant or unpleasant as it happened—which was a fact—and which is stored in the brain, and what is being done now—also a fact—coloured by the past, controlled by the past, shaped by the past. So, can I see this whole movement as a fact? The whole movement—the future, the present and the past.

**PJ** : The seeing-it-as-a-fact is seeing it without a cliché.

**K** : Without a cliché, without any prejudice, without any bias.

**PJ** : Without anything surrounding it.

**K** : That's right. Which means what?

**PJ** : Negating, first of all, all the responses which arise surrounding the remembrances.

**K** : Negating the remembrances. Just keep to that for the moment.

**PJ** : The remembrances which arise . . . .

**K** : Out of the fact of last week's pleasure or pain, reward or punishment. Now, is that possible?

**PJ** : Yes, that is possible.

**K** : That is possible. Why?

**PJ** : Because, the very attention itself . . . .

**K** : Dissipates memory, remembrance. Now, an incident happened last week. Can the brain be so attentive that it does not carry on remembering? My son is dead, and I've suffered. But the memory of that son has such strength in my brain, that I constantly remember it. It rises and disappears; but it's there. So, can the brain say, 'Yes, my son is dead; that's the end of it'?

**PJ** : Does one say that or when there is an arising . . . ?

**K** : There is then an ending? Which means an endless arising and ending.

**PJ** : No, but there is an arising . . . .

**K** : Which is a remembrance. Let's keep to the word.

**PJ** : Yes, which is a remembrance. Out of that, there is the movement of pain. The negation of that pain ends not only the pain but also the arising.

**K** : Which means what? Go into it a little bit more. What does that mean? My son is dead. I remember all the things that he did, etc., etc. There is the photograph of him on the piano or on the mantelpiece, and there is this constant remembrance—flowing in and flowing out. That's a fact.

**PJ** : But the negating of that pain and the dissolving of this— doesn't it have a direct action on the brain?

**K** : That's what I'm coming to. Which means what? My son is dead; that's a fact. I can't change a fact. He's gone. It may sound cruel to say it—but he's gone. Yet I'm carrying him all the time. The brain is carrying him as memory, and the reminder is always there. I never say, 'He's gone. *That's a fact'*. I live on memory— which is a dead thing. Memories are not actual. Now, the ending of the fact—'My son is gone'—doesn't mean that I have lost love or anything. My son is gone; that's a fact.

**PJ** : But what remains when a fact is perceived?

**K** : May I say something without being shocking? Nothing. My son is gone; my brother or my wife—whoever it is—is gone. This is not an assertion of cruelty or a denial of my affection, my love. Not the love of *my* son, but the *identification* of love with my son. I don't know if I'm . . . .

**PJ** : You're drawing a distinction between 'love of my son' . . . .

**K** : And love.

**PJ** : . . . and 'love'.

**K** : Then, if I love my son in the deeper sense of the word, I love man; I love humanity. It is not only that 'I love my son' but that I love the whole human world; I love the earth, the trees, the stars, the whole universe. But that's a different matter. We were asking a really good question, namely: What takes place when there is pure perception, the perception of a fact—without any bias, without any kind of escape and so on? And, to see the fact completely—is that possible? When I'm in sorrow of my son's death, I'm lost. It's a great shock; it's something terrible that has taken place. At that moment you can't say anything to me. As I come out of this confusion and loneliness and despair and sorrow, then perhaps I'll be sensitive enough to perceive this fact.

**PJ** : You can't tell a person who has just lost a . . . .

**K** : No. No, that will be cruel. But a man who says, 'My son is dead; what is it all about? Death is common to all humanity. Why do we exist?' is sensitive, asking, inquiring. He's awake. He wants to find an answer to all this.

**PJ** : Sir, at one level it seems so simple . . . .

**K** : I know, and I think we must keep it simple and not bring about a lot of intellectual theories and ideas into it.

**PJ** : Is the mind afraid of the simple?

**K** : No, I think it's because we are so highly intellectual; it's been a part of our education, part of our culture. Ideas are tremendously important; concepts are essential.

**PJ** : Sir, in the whole field of Indian culture, the highest is the dissolution of the self. And you talk of the dissolution of the fact—which is essentially the dissolution of the self—as so simple.

**K** : Yes, but the dissolution of the self has become a concept, and we are worshipping a concept—as they are all doing all over the world. Concepts are invented by thought, through analysis and so on. You come to a concept, and hold that concept as the most extraordinarily important thing. So, come back to the point: What will make human beings throughout the world behave?—Not behave my way or your way, but *behave*. Don't kill. Don't be afraid. Love. Have great affection and so on. What would bring it about? Nothing has succeeded. Do you understand? Knowledge hasn't helped.

**PJ** : Isn't it because fear is his shadow?

**K** : Fear, and also we want to know what the future is.

**PJ** : Which is part of fear.

**K** : Yes. We want to know, because we have—this is simple enough—sought security in so many things, and they have all failed. And now we say, 'There must be security somewhere'. And I question whether there is any security anywhere at all—even in God, for that's a projection of our own fears.

**PJ** : What's the action of this dissolution on the brain cells, on the brain itself?

**K** : I would use the word 'insight'. Insight is not a matter of memory, not a matter of knowledge and time—which are all thought. I would say that insight is the absence—total absence—of the whole movement of thought as time and remembrance; so there is direct perception. It's like: I've been going north for the last ten thousand years; my brain is accustomed to going north, and somebody comes along and says, 'That leads you nowhere. Go east'. When I turn around and go east, the brain cells change. I'll put it differently. The whole movement of thought is limited. Yet thought, throughout the world, is the most important thing. We are driven by thought. But thought will not solve any of our problems—except technological problems. If I see that, I've stopped going north. And I think that at the ending of a certain direction—the ending of a movement that has been going on for thousands of years—at that moment there is an insight which brings about a change, a mutation in the brain cells.

One sees this very clearly and one asks: What will make others—make humanity—change? What will make my son, my daughter, change? They hear all this, they read something about all this from biologists, psychologists and so on, and yet they continue on their own way. Is the past—tradition—so strong? I have thought about myself for the last thousand years and I still am thinking about myself: 'I must fulfil myself.' 'I must be great.' 'I must become something.' This is my condition; this is my tradition. And the past is incarnating all the time. Is it part of our culture to continue in our condition?

**PJ :** I would say that it is part of our culture.

**K :** Culture may be part of our hindrance. Religious concepts may be our hindrance. So, what is the brain to do? They are saying that one part of the brain is old, and another part of the brain is something totally new, and that if you can open the door to the new there might be change. For, according to these specialists, we are only using a very, very small part of our brain.

**PJ :** Obviously when there is attention . . . .

**K :** The whole brain . . . .

**PJ :** . . . the fragment has ended.

**K :** That's it. We can talk about that, we can describe what attention is, we can go into it and so on. But at the end of it, a listener says, 'All right, I understand all this but I am what I am. I understand this intellectually, verbally, but it hasn't touched the depth of my being'.

**PJ :** But isn't it a question of that first contact with thought in the mind?

**K :** I'm sorry, I haven't quite got it.

**PJ :** I have a feeling, sir, that we talk about observing thought, which is an entirely different thing to the actual state of attention.

**K :** That is, thought being aware of itself. Now, I'm afraid we are going away from this. It's a very central issue. The world is becoming more and more superficial. More and more money-minded. Money, power, position, fulfilment, identification—me, me, me. All this is being encouraged by everything around you. Now, you who have travelled, who have seen all this too, what do you make of all this business? There are these extraordinary, intelligent people—clever people—and the most stupid people, the neurotic, the people who have come to a conclusion and never move from that conclusion—like the Communists.

**PJ** : You can only touch the people who are not committed.

**K** : So, are there people who are not committed?

**PJ** : I would say that today that is the one sign of health: there are people who are not committed.

**K** : Are they young people?

**PJ** : Today, as never before in the last twenty or thirty years, there are people who are not committed to anything.

**K** : I question that.

**PJ** : No, really sir, I would say so. On the one hand you see this tremendous deterioration of everything, and on the other, somewhere, there is this movement away from a commitment. They may not know where to turn, they may not have a direction, but they don't belong to anything.

**K** : There are people like that, I know. But they become, you see, rather vague. They become rather confused.

**PJ** : Yes, because they turn these into concepts.

**K** : Yes.

**PJ** : It's so easy to turn what you say into a concept, and to have axioms which contain what you say.

**K** : Of course, of course.

**PJ** : If there is a human culture, which perhaps may be the culture of the mind, in such a state—if I may ask—what happens to all the civilizations which the world has seen and known?

**K :** Gone. Take for instance the Egyptian civilization.

**PJ :** No, they may have gone, but they are still contained in the human race. But when you wipe out . . . .

**K :** Which means Pupul, actually: What is freedom? Are we aware that we are prisoners of our own fantasies, imaginations, conclusions, ideas? Are we aware of all that?

**PJ :** I think we are.

**K :** Pupul, if we are aware, if we are attentive to all that, the thing is burnt out.

**PJ :** But, it doesn't end, sir. *This* is of course gone, but at some point where we can't . . . because you don't admit of an in-between state.

**K :** That's impossible.

**PJ :** See, this is the whole problem.

**K :** 'In-between'—it's like a man who is violent and trying to be non-violent; in the 'in-between' state he is violent.

**PJ :** No, not necessarily. You see, isn't it also a question of this whole movement of time?

**K :** Time and thought and so on. Which is what? Limitation. If we could just acknowledge or see the fact that thought—in any direction, in any field: surgery, technology, computers and also inquiring into itself—is limited, we will see that one's inquiry will also be very, very, very limited.

**PJ :** Yes, but the difference is, sir, I might see that, but the attention necessary for it to remain alive in my waking day is not there.

**K :** I know.

**PJ :** Is it that the quantum, the capacity, the strength of that attention which . . . ?

**K** : How do you have that passion, how do you have that sustained movement of energy that is not dissipated by thought, not dissipated by any kind of activity? I think that only comes when you understand sorrow and the ending of sorrow. *Then* comes compassion and love and that intelligence which is the energy which has no depression—that state which is not touched by any of the human qualities.

**PJ** : You mean it neither rises nor falls.

**K** : No. To rise and fall, you must be aware that it's rising and falling. And who is it who's aware and so on?

**PJ** : Is it possible, throughout the day, to hold that passion?

**K** : It is there. You don't hold it. It is like a perfume that's there. That's why I think that one has to understand the whole conditioning of our consciousness. I think *that* is the real study, real inquiry, real exploration: to go into our consciousness, which is the common ground of all humanity. We never inquire into it and study it—not that we should inquire as a professor or psychologist inquires and studies. We never say, 'Look, I am going to study this consciousness which is me. I am going to look into it'.

**PJ** : I can't say one doesn't; one *says* that . . . .

**K** : But doesn't do it.

**PJ** : One *does* it.

**K** : Partially.

**PJ** : I won't accept that, sir. One does it, one attends, one inquires.

**K** : And then what?

**PJ** : And then suddenly . . . .

**K** : And have you come to the end of it?

**PJ** : No, suddenly one finds that one has been inattentive.

**K** : No, I don't think inattention matters. You may be tired. Your brain has inquired enough and you may say, 'Enough for today'. Well, there's nothing wrong with that. You see, I object to this question of attention and inattention.

**PJ** : But that is the basic question in most of our minds.

**K** : No, I would not put it that way. I would only say that where there is this ending of something—totally—there is a new beginning which has its own momentum. It has nothing to do with one. That means, one must be completely free of the self. And to be free of the self is one of the most difficult things, because it hides under different rocks, different trees, different activities.

*Brockwood Park*
*24 June 1983*

# Where do I Begin?

**PUPUL JAYAKAR (PJ)** : If you remember, Krishnaji, three days ago we started discussing the ground of a mind from which a new mind emerges. While discussing it, you said that from a ground which is conflict, fear, anger, the new can never emerge; you said that something entirely new is necessary. You also spoke about the senses operating at their highest, simultaneously. I want to start with a question: I'm a newcomer to your talks; I hear this. Where do I begin?

**J. KRISHNAMURTI (K)** : Probably at first you won't make head or tail of it. You won't know what K is talking about. So we will have to establish the linguistic, the semantic, meaning, and also be aware of our relationship to nature. Yes, I would begin with that.

I would question why there are no wild animals here at all. I would go into that because if we lost touch with nature of which we are a part, we would lose touch with humanity, with our fellow beings. I would begin there—with my relationship to nature, with my relationship to the beauty of all that.

Pupul, how do you look at nature? How do you look at those hills which are supposed to be amongst the most ancient hills in the world? How do you look at those rocks, those boulders, those trees, those dry rivers and streams? How do you look at those poor village children who walk twelve miles a day to a school? How do you look at those poor people who have not enough food to eat?

**PJ** : So you are saying, sir, that the starting point of inquiry is in the outer.

**K** : Absolutely. You see, Pupul, if I don't have the obvious common sense criteria, then how can I ever have a clear perception of myself? Do you understand?

**PJ** : Yes, I understand.

**K** : Because the outer is a manifestation of myself. I'm part of nature. Without understanding the beauty of the land, the rivers and every part of this extraordinary world we live in, this brutal world we live in, with all the cruelty, the terrorism, and so on, how can I ever have a clear perception of myself? What is my relationship to all that? Am I blind to it all? Am I silent to it all? Or do I have certain conclusions which dominate me? And conclusions are a product of thought, nature is not.

**PJ** : Sir, we all think that we look at nature. We think that we look at the trees, that we look at the flowers, and at the rocks. We feel that we look. We feel that as we have eyes, we look. But there is something in the looking and in the relationship that you are talking about, which obviously is not the looking which we are used to.

**K** : How do you look at nature? Do you look at it only with your eyes? Is the perception of the long evening shadows and the very small shadow of the midday sun merely a visual perception? That is, do you look at those marvellous shadows only with your eyes? Or do you look at them with your whole being, with all your senses? How do you look at all this? How do you perceive all this? Do you perceive it as though it was something outside you or as something of which you are a part?

**PJ :** I think one can actually say that there *is* a looking in which the seer does not exist. But I don't want to start there. That's why I'm coming to you as a beginner, a beginner who says, 'I look with my eyes'. I want to start from there.

**K :** I would reply to that: Do you only look? Or do you also hear—hear the sound of the whisper among the deep shadows of the trees, the sound of the breeze and of running water? My question is: Do you listen, see and feel?

**PJ :** Sir, if you are seeing, listening, feeling, then it is a state where everything exists. But I don't know anything about that. So, I would like to approach it from the point of view of a beginner rather than of any other.

**K :** Would you agree that human beings have lost touch with nature?

**PJ :** Yes, completely; because when they see, their eyes move over. They never look directly. They never look—period. They consider it too trivial.

**K :** That's just it. They consider viewing nature as something trivial. They consider nature as something that can be exploited.

**PJ :** You see, sir, the mind has divided itself. It considers looking at a leaf or a leaf's movement as something unimportant; what is important is something vast.

**K :** So, let's begin. What is important? For the average man, for the ordinary person, what is important? Food, clothes, shelter— that's all that he is concerned with.

**PJ :** No, sir. Beyond that there is the sacred, the divine, God.

**K :** Of course, but I'll come to that later. I'm just beginning with needs—food, clothes, shelter. When he has that, then he begins to think about God as something extraordinary . . . .

**PJ :** And he wants to think of it in a vast . . . .

**K** : He sees the evening sky and the sun rising and sees the immensity of this marvellous world, and he says, 'Who created all this?' Right?

**PJ** : The capacity to see that the small and the vast are at the same level of importance . . . .

**K** : Yes, there's no vast and small.

**QUESTIONER (Q)** : My senses have been very deeply dominated by my thinking. I see for myself that when I go for a walk, I'm not really looking, I'm not really listening. I am all the time thinking, and from that thinking I occasionally glance at something or the other. So in a sense there is no looking, no seeing, the actuality of a tree.

**PJ** : If you were to try to get someone to look at one leaf, at one single leaf, you will find out how difficult it is. But why take someone else? When one does it oneself, one realizes how difficult it is to look at a thing.

**Q** : As you said, we glance at it and move away.

**K** : Would you blame religion? Would you blame the orthodox, established religions that have prevented man from considering nature as part of himself? You see, religions have said, 'Suppress all your senses. Don't look out there; always look inside you'.

**Q** : Krishnaji, would you say that the modern urban man is to a great extent not influenced by religions?

**K** : No, we are not talking about an urban man or about a rural man, a man who lives in a big town or in a little town or village. We are talking about the ordinary man who has seen the sannyasis, the monks, the Trappists who never speak. And all these so-called religious people have maintained that desire is to be suppressed, that the senses are to be suppressed because they distract.

**Q** : Yes, this has been upheld not only by religion but also by society.

**K** : Of course. You see, the religious leaders have not said, 'Look at all the wonders of this world. Look at its beauty; feel it; absorb it; be of it'. What they have done is to create images—images that are made by the hand and by the mind. And images that are made by the mind are more important than the other. Sir, you have a temple nearby—Tirupati. Thousands go there; millions are spent on it—why?

Now, if I were an ordinary man and I were to hear all this, as Pupulji pointed out, where would I begin?

**Q** : But, wouldn't you say, Krishnaji, to even ask that question, the ordinary man must have seen somewhere, somehow, that his world is limited?

**K** : Yes, he knows death.

**Q** : He has to be already a little bit discontented with his God, with his . . . .

**K** : I question that, sir. I question whether he is discontented or sceptical about his Gods.

**Q** : Then what makes him ask the question, 'Where do I begin?'

**K** : He doesn't ask this question.

**PJ** : He does. He does when he is in sorrow; he does when he is suffering; he does when there is death.

**K** : He does when there is sorrow. He does when there is death. He does when he sees a rich man go by in a marvellous car and he has to walk ten miles to go to that same place. It is then that he will begin to say, 'What is all this? Why should I not be as rich as that man?'

**Q** : But that is not asking the same question.

**K** : It is part of that, sir.

**PJ** : Otherwise how does one start?

**Q :** Sir, but you see, there are a number of people who generally live very happy lives. They have no sorrow—at least the sorrow that is common to most people: poverty, ill-health, lack of education, and so on. Yet they come upon these questions, and they go, very seriously, into them.

**K :** You are talking of those people who are exceptional. We began by asking, 'If I were an *ordinary* man where would I begin?' Let us say that I am an ordinary man, fairly educated, and surrounded by the very complex problems of existence—suffering, pain, anxiety, and all the other activities of thought—where would I begin to understand the very complex society in which I lived? That is a real question, and that is the question with which Mrs Jayakar began.

**PJ :** You see, we take it for granted—when we listen to Krishnaji—that the beginning must start within. We have all taken it that way, namely, that the beginning has to start within, with the discovery of 'what is'. We have never looked at the outside and seen the outside as the same movement as the movement within. Therefore the callousness, therefore the corruption . . . .

**K :** Why have we neglected or discarded or despised all the things from nature?

**PJ :** Because we divide. We divide the outer world as the world of desire and the inner world as the real world.

**K :** And also because for both the Buddhists and the Hindus the outside world is *māyā*, an illusion. K, however, is saying quite the contrary. And that's why I feel it's important to understand one's relationship to nature, to the outer world. That's why I feel it is important to understand one's relationship to the world in which all the misery, confusion, brutality, and corruption is going on. Look at that first and, then, from the outer, move to the inner. But if you start and stop at the inner, you will have no measure. You stay with worship; you follow Jesus or some guru. That is what you call religion. Right? The rituals, the paraphernalia—that is what you call religion.

I feel, personally, that we must start with what we see, with what we hear, and what we feel outside. You see, the question is: How do I look at my wife, my children, my parents, and all the rest who are outside?

Take death. When I see somebody carrying a dead body—in this country it's simple; just two or three people carrying a corpse— I begin to ask, 'What is death?' Death is there outside of me, but I begin to inquire. I can't just go off by myself into a mountain cave and there inquire what death or God is. Of course, I can imagine a lot of things, but if I have not established a right relationship with nature, with another person—wife, husband, anyone—how can I ever establish the right relationship with the immensity of the universe?

**Q :** Krishnaji, in looking at the outer, you're saying that the brain quickens.

**K :** Of course; it becomes more sensitive.

**Q :** And, therefore, it can look at the inner without distortion.

**K :** Yes, without distortion.

**Q :** But, sir, half the world—the West—has always treated the outer as very, very concrete. All their energies have moved outward. But that doesn't seem to have brought about the inwardness either.

**K :** So we come to a much more serious question. What makes a man change? Would you begin with that? I'm envious, I'm brutal, I'm violent, I'm uncertain, I'm confused and jealous. There is hatred in me. I'm the result of thousands of years of evolution. Why have I not changed? That is one of the basic questions.

**Q :** And isn't it too early to ask that question?

**K :** Yes, it is early.

**Q :** But you are saying that, all the same, we have to come to it.

**K** : I have been through all this and I have come to it. And, also, I appreciate nature; I am in constant touch with it. So I begin; I look. But ultimately, I must ask myself—I, who am a human being, who suffers, who has fear and who is in turmoil, just like the rest of mankind—'Why have I not radically changed?' That is my question.

**Q** : It is interesting that the ordinary man is much more concerned with gaining the object of his greed or with running away from the object of his fear, than with asking the question, 'Why am I greedy?' or 'Why am I afraid?'

**K** : What is your question, sir?

**Q** : It is this question that you have raised: Why have I not changed?

**K** : Ask yourself, sir; ask yourself. I'm not being personal or disrespectful or impudent. Ask yourself why after thirty or forty years you are exactly as you were—modified, of course, but with no radical change. Why? I suggest that any rational and thoughtful person would ask this question.

Sir, do you understand what I mean by 'change'?

**Q** : No, sir, I do not understand.

**K** : By 'change' I don't mean, for example, the rejection of Hinduism and the acceptance of Buddhism, or vice versa. For that would merely be the repetition of the same pattern over and over and over again.

**Q** : Yes, sir, but we don't see it as the same pattern; we see it as a different pattern.

**K** : Take envy. That is a common factor for everybody, and it has produced a great deal of trouble in the world. You see the consequences of envy, but you remain envious. Why is it that you don't—radically—wipe it out of your brain? Please don't make it complex. To watch the brain being envious, and to wipe it out—

why hasn't that been possible? Why haven't you done it? You talk about it endlessly.

**Q** : Sir, there seems to be a kind of paradox, for I feel that suffering seems to be necessary in some ways for this 'radical' change that you are talking about. Yet when one suffers and keeps on suffering, it has a blunting effect on the individual who suffers. So where do we go from there?

**K** : Sir, first of all, there is no division between the outer and the inner; they are one. Do you see that? Do you actually see the fact that the outer, that is, the society in which we live, and which we have created, and the inner, the 'me', are the same? I am part of society. Society is not different from me. That is one of the most fundamental facts. Do you, actually, recognize that fact, and not just agree with it?

Secondly, there is division between you and me. You belong to one group or community or religion, and I belong to another group, another community, another religion, and so on. This division is created by thought and, therefore, it is tremendously complex.

Now, you say, 'I suffer, you suffer, the rest of humanity suffers'. But you never ask, 'Can this suffering end'?

**Q** : Sir, would you say that the two questions—'Can suffering end'? and 'Why have I not changed'?—are the same?

**K** : They are the same.

**Q** : Is the answer to both the questions the fact that we don't have enough energy?

**K** : I would not say that you haven't got enough energy. You have plenty of energy when you want to do something. Right? When you want to make money, you work tremendously to get it. So I don't think it is a matter of energy.

**Q** : Is it that we do not want to change with our whole being?

Why is it that the desire 'not to suffer' or the desire to 'change radically'—as you put it—is so easily dissipated in us?

**K** : Is it because there is no profit in that? We are profit-motivated, aren't we? We always want a reward. Our brains are conditioned to reward and punishment. Right? We work like the blazes if we can have a reward at the end of it—money, position, status, happiness, whatever it is.

**PJ** : Sir, I think we have moved away slightly. We were talking of the senses and their operation and . . . .

**K** : Yes.

**PJ** : Now, the senses are energy. That which is outside is energy.

**K** : Have you seen the way grass grows through the cement?

**PJ** : But what is it that thwarts the energy of the senses? What is it that comes in the way of their real capacity?

**K** : Is it our conditioning? Is it our education? Because, as you know, we are always told to control.

**PJ** : Yes, sir, but I think that there must be some seed, some insight, that has been responsible for this teaching, namely, that we have to not only be very careful with our energy but also channelize it properly. The whole of life and the whole of education is, I feel, merely a channelling of this energy and, so, perhaps in itself it is an incorrect approach.

**K** : Yes.

**PJ** : Because what is necessary is the conservation of energy. Now, how does one conserve energy? How does one create energy?

**K** : Would you conserve energy? Or is it that the more you expend energy the more there is?

**PJ** : But you can also allow energy to fritter away.

**K :** That's just it. You see, for a person like 'K', there is no distraction or attraction.

**PJ :** This is the magical thing. For 'K' there is no distraction in the mind; there is no triviality.

**Q :** Also, there is no preoccupation.

**K :** That's right.

**Q :** In the very saying, 'I will conserve energy', there is a channelling of energy.

**PJ :** No. What I said was from a different viewpoint. We see that energy disperses. Whatever energy a human being has, he is dispersing it all the time. There must be something at the root of it.

**K :** No, Pupul, just look. You are conditioned from childhood to this idea of reward and punishment. Right? Your mother says, 'If you do this, I'll give you a sweet. If you don't do that, I will punish you'. When you enter school, the same principle is carried on: better marks in the examinations, and so on—you follow? Our brains are conditioned to reward and punishment. Right? So you expend all your energy to avoid punishment and gain a reward. And a reward gives you tremendous energy.

**PJ :** But, sir, of a different quality.

**K :** Wait, wait. I say that a reward gives me tremendous energy to work, work, work. And then you come along and tell me that this reward and punishment is a conditioning, and that in that there is no freedom. Heaven isn't a reward; enlightenment isn't a reward. But I have been trained from childhood to seek reward. So there is a battle and I waste my energy in that battle. I want happiness; I want peace. And I do everything to accelerate that.

**PJ :** Sir, life is so complex that if I ever try to solve it, 1 never will. But you have given us a key. The key is this total operation of the senses. Can we explore and go into that?

243

**K :** Yes, let's do it. *(Laughing, asks)* Aren't we doing that?

**PJ :** Because that wipes out everything, and there is nothing to be done.

**K :** Are seeing and hearing separate, or are they one? Do you understand my question? When you perceive something, for example, this question, is the seeing of it and the hearing of it separate, and also is there a thinking about it? You see, the moment you think about it, you are not listening to the question.

The point is, can you see, that is, perceive, and hear at the same time?—Not as two separate things. You see, I was talking to a scientist last year—a biologist who is concerned with nature, and so on. He asked me, 'Do you hear the sound of a tree? Do you hear the sound of a tree, not when it is moving with the wind, but when it is absolutely quiet, for example, early in the morning or as the sun is setting? Have you heard a tree when there is no breeze? A tree has a peculiar quality of sound'. And I said, 'Yes, a tree has a peculiar quality of sound'.

Can you hear and see that sound at the same time? Or do you divide it? Do you follow what I'm saying?

**PJ :** I follow, sir.

**K :** Sound is an extraordinary thing by itself, but I don't want to enter into that now.

The question is whether you can see something without division. That's all I'm asking. See, hear, feel, smell, taste—without any division. It's as though you were completely immersed in it.

**Q :** Sir, you have frequently said that meditation is a sixth or seventh sense, and that if one doesn't have it, one is missing a lot. What exactly is the essential nature of meditation according to you?

**K :** The essential nature of meditation is never to be conscious that you are meditating. Do you understand what I am saying? If you attempt to meditate—sit in a certain posture, sit back quietly, breathe and all the rest of the tricks you play—then it is like any other business. You merely want to achieve. And *meditation is not an achievement*. If you meditate according to a system, a method, and so on, then it is an achievement. At the end of it all—your endeavour, and so on—you say, 'Ah, at last I have got peace!' *(Laughs)* It is the same as saying, 'At last, I have a million dollars in the bank'. In the business world you do this, this and this to get money, but you can't *do* anything to get this. You see, meditation, to K, is something that cannot be consciously achieved.

**PJ :** Is it separate from the state of seeing-listening?

**K :** That is in itself meditation.

**Q :** You speak of 'a contact with nature'. There seems, to me, meditation going on in a very sensitive way when there is a contact with nature—especially the kind of contact that you describe. Unfortunately, many people, however intelligent they may be, feel that a posture or an approach is very relevant to meditation.

**K :** I know.

**Q :** So when you talk about meditation, a meditation in which all these things are eliminated, one is lost.

**K :** Be lost!

**Q :** But we are not lost in the way you mean.

**K :** Be lost, be lost.

**Q :** We are lost in confusion.

**K :** Sir, doing all this *is* confusion!

**Q :** How would you further guide us so that meditation becomes an actuality?

**K :** I don't know what you mean by meditation and actuality. Sorry, I'm not being facetious, but I really don't know what you mean by those two words: meditation and the actual. And also, perhaps, we are going off from what Pupulji started with.

**Q** : I asked the question in relation to the full operation of the senses; because the quality is very different from the scientific, technological attitude. The scientist or technologist is concerned only with the outer.

**K** : No, sir. They are also asking these questions. As I told you the other day, we were invited to Los Alamos which is the National Laboratory of America. They're concerned not only about meditation, but also about what creativity in science is. Do you follow? They're going beyond a merely technological approach to life.

**PJ** : Sir, there can be no other ground of the creative—the operation of the senses are themselves the ground of the creative.

**K** : When you're watching this whole universe, watching, not seeking a reward or evading punishment but watching—the suffering of those villagers, of those little boys who walk twelve miles a day to school—in that very watching there is great perception, great love, great care. You see, watching is not merely with the senses, for in watching there is this quality of love, this quality of care.

**PJ** : Yes. Now we are getting to it.

**K** : Yes.

**PJ** : What awakens? I think there is a possibility for observing— I am speaking for myself—with all the senses . . . .

**K** : The awakening of all the senses and the fullness of it—there's a quality of something totally different in that.

**PJ** : There must be something missing because—let me put it in other words—that explosion of the heart . . . .

**K** : That is a good phrase—'explosion of the heart'.

**PJ** : That does not happen, sir. The explosion of the heart does not take place. That is really the crux.

**K** : Would you say that the brain is the centre of all our nervous, electrical responses? It is the centre of all thought. It is the centre of all confusion, of all pain, of all sorrow, anxiety, depression, aspiration, achievement, and so on. In the brain there is a great activity of confusion and of contradiction.

Love is not that. Therefore it must be something outside the brain. Just follow it logically. And we look at nature, or other human beings . . . .

**PJ** : From inside the brain.

**K** : Yes, we look from inside the brain. We were walking yesterday with some of the people here, and there was complete silence even though there were bullock carts, children cycling, you know, all the other noises. There was nothing, just immense silence. And it was not silence out there. It was silence; the entire world was silent. And you were silent. And you felt the whole earth as part of you.

**PJ** : You see, sir, this is *your* statement, and I am listening.

**K** : Of course, it may be silly nonsense.

**PJ** : But the fact is that I do not wipe the tear of another.

**K** : No.

**PJ** : You see, sir, the senses working simultaneously give the brain great clarity, a great living, germinating creativity, but it doesn't wipe the tear of another.

**K** : No.

**PJ** : I am concerned with what it is that wipes the tear of another. Because unless that is there . . . .

**K** : Just a minute. Can the brain—that is my question—be so

247

quiet that the activity of thought has completely ended in that second or in that period? Or is the brain always chattering?

**PJ :** Is it, sir, that the only thing which is legitimate is to be totally awake, that is, for the senses to operate fully and, then, never even query the other?

**K :** Of course. You don't even know the other. How can you question . . . ?

**PJ :** . . . what is outside the skull.

**K :** Yes. All I know is what is within the skull. Right? And you come along and say, 'As long as you're in there, you will solve nothing'. You point this out to me. And I listen to you because I see the logic of all this, the common sense of all this, and I say, 'Quite right'. So I want to know what it is to make the brain quiet—though it has its own rhythms. We have tried everything, but the brain has never become quiet.

Meditation is not quietness. You try to bring quietness through control, through all kinds of tricks. But that's not the stillness and the beauty of silence. So where do we end up?

**PJ :** You see, sir, everything else is man made. Only *that* is divinity and, unfortunately, we just don't know how to reach it, how to touch it.

**K :** I met a man the other day. He was a great painter. He said to me, 'What man has made is the most beautiful thing'. That was the end of it for him. Then I pointed to a tree and said, 'No one made that', and he began to see. 'Yes', he said, 'that's interesting'.

*Rishi Valley*
*19 December 1984*

# Is There a Time of Non-Movement?

**J. KRISHNAMURTI (K)** : At lunch this afternoon we were talking not only about time but also about the nature of dialogue. As far as I understand, a dialogue is a conversation between two people. A dialogue can be a discussion that is very, very superficial. It can also be a conversation that takes place between two very religious people—people who are religious, not in the usual sense of that word but in the sense that they are totally free from all tradition, from all systems and from all authority.

We are talking about this kind of dialogue—a dialogue that is not just a conversation between two people, but a questioning and an answering where the very answering provokes a further questioning and so on. In this kind of dialogue the two people, you and I, disappear altogether, and only the question and the answer remain. Do we agree with that?

**PUPUL JAYAKAR (PJ)** : I looked up the word 'dialogue' in the dictionary, and found that it can be a conversation between a group of people. It is not restricted, necessarily, to two people.

**K** : Yes.

**PJ** : But the essential nature of a dialogue is a probing into something. Now, it seems to me, that all problems of the mind . . . .

**K** : Of the brain; let us stick to that one word.

**PJ** : All right. I would like to start with this, namely, that all problems of the brain are born of time.

**K** : Are born from the process of time.

**PJ** : Problems arise because the brain changes 'what is' into something different, and the movement of the brain which wants to change 'what is' into something else, creates time.

**K** : Could we say this very simply? There is both physical time and psychological time. Just a minute. Let me go into it a little bit. Physical time is going from here to there; it is covering a certain distance from one point to another point. Physical time is by sunrise and by sunset. All movement is a matter of time. Right?

**PJ** : Yes.

**K** : Now, there is also psychological time—the time of *becoming* something. 'I am this, I will be that.'

**PJ** : Yes.

**K** : There is also this whole process of evolution—both psychological and physical. All this is fairly simple and clear, and we all accept this. Right? Now, my question is: Is there a time outside this movement which we know and call time? That is, is there a time of non-movement?

Let us go slowly into this. Time as we know it is a movement. The division or the gap between one action and another, between one understanding and another, is time. Time is a movement of fear Time is also hope. The whole movement from the past to the present to the future is generally acknowledged as time. Right? Movement—of evolution, of growth, of achievement, of fulfilment, of becoming something—involves time. The interval between seeing something, thinking about it and acting is time.

And I question whether there is a time—I am using that word for the time being till we find another word—which doesn't belong to this category at all.

**PJ :** When you use the word 'time' and say that it does not belong to the category of movement, does it belong to the category of matter?

**K :** Matter as I understand it—I've discussed the matter with Dr Bohm and others—is solidified energy; matter is manifested energy. The body is manifested energy.

**PJ :** You see, sir, the brain is matter.

**K :** Yes, the brain is matter. And thought is a material process.

**PJ :** Let us leave aside thought for the moment; let us take the brain. The brain is matter. Now, in that matter evolution *must* exist.

**K :** Of course. We were monkeys at one time. Gradually, through a million years of evolution, we became *Homo sapiens*—what we are now.

**PJ :** Yes, but we link that evolution with the content which the brain cells hold.

**K :** I don't quite follow this. *(Turns to the others present)* Come and join us. Come and discuss.

**PJ :** Let me put it this way: You accept that the brain is matter. Therefore you must accept that evolution is inherent in the brain itself, *because* it is matter.

**K :** Just a minute! I want to be clear on this. The brain is matter. That's a statement. What is the next statement?

**PJ :** The next step is, there is a content in the brain cells.

**K :** Which is memory.

**PJ :** Yes. Now, we link the evolution which is in the brain with the evolution in memory.

251

**K :** I see what you are trying to get at. Is memory a process of evolution?

**PJ :** I don't say that it *is* a process of evolution. I say that the problem arises because we apply to memory the same rules as exist for matter.

**K :** I don't understand.

**PJ :** Sir, you say that the brain is a material thing.

**K :** We all agree to that.

**PJ :** Therefore evolution should be inherent in it.

**K :** I question whether evolution is inherent in matter.

**PJ :** How can you question that?

**K :** I'm sorry, I don't quite understand.

**PJ :** The brain of the ape has evolved to the brain of the human being. So evolution is inherent in the material brain.

**K :** All right, I understand. The brain which is matter, has evolved
. . . .

**PJ :** Within that brain is the content of a million years.

**K :** Yes, millions of years of memory. Pupul, just hold it. Is memory which is knowledge, which is experience, the gathering process, a process of time?

**PJ :** Yes. But why do you bring time into it at this moment?

**K :** We are discussing, I thought, the whole idea of . . . .

**PJ :** That is why I said, Krishnaji, that the problem is that we take the content of the brain which is memory and feel that there is an entity which can change that content of the brain. The whole process of becoming is that; that is the time of the within, the time of the interior.

**K** : Yes. Time as becoming; time as accumulating more knowledge—advancing more and more . . . .

**PJ** : And becoming better.

**K** : I understand that all that is implied in time.

**PJ** : We apply the process of evolution which exists in the brain to the content in the brain. My question is: Is there evolution in time?

**K** : Evolution is time.

**PJ** : If evolution is time, then why should it not be applicable to becoming?

**K** : Just go slowly, I may be dull this afternoon, but I don't quite follow. Becoming implies time. Right? 'I am this, I will be that.'

**PJ** : Sir, I am saying that the brain has evolved through time. My question is: Is the content of the brain which is nothing but a gathering of experiences and knowledge, identical with the nature of the brain itself?

**K** : I see.

**PJ** : You see, we all know that becoming is illusion. That is very simple to understand. But there is something much more than that, and the 'much more than that' is that you make a statement that there is an outward time of the watch and that there is an inward time of becoming. You then ask: Is there another time which doesn't belong to these two categories?

**K** : That's my question.

**PJ** : Now, time and space are one; time and matter are one.

**K** : Time *is* matter. Time is manifested energy. The very manifestation is a process of time.

**PJ** : Time cannot exist without manifestation.

**K** : That's what I want to inquire into. Is there a time which is not manifest?

**PJ** : This interior time that you are talking about . . . .

**K** : Do go slowly.

**PJ** : When you say that it is not the outcome of manifestation, why do you then use the word 'time'?

**K** : I have no other word for the moment.

**SUNANDA PATWARDHAN (SP)** : Are you saying that the very ground from which manifestation arises is another time?

**K** : Partly. Probably. I am inquiring into that . . . . Could we move to something else? Love is not of time.

**PJ** : You see, forgive me for saying so, sir, the moment you use the word 'love', you have cut the ground from under our feet.

**K** : Why?

**PJ** : Because it is an absolute statement. And with absolute statements, no discussion is possible.

**K** : Wait, Pupul. That's rather an unfair statement. We are trying to find out what eternity is. We are trying to find out a reality which is not of time. We know that what is mortal grows and dies. We are asking whether there is a state or a movement which is not of time and which is beyond time. Do you understand?

**PJ** : I understand, sir.

**K** : Which means, is there a timeless activity which is infinite and measureless? You see, we are using words to measure the immeasurable, and our words have become time. Do you get what I am saying? Let's proceed slowly. Words have become time and with those words we are measuring a state which is not measurable, and *that which is not measurable is not of time.*

**PJ** : Now let us go into it. We know time as the past, as the present and as the future. We project the future. What is the nature or, in other words, what is the perception of that instant which is the only reality?

**K** : Wait. Let us examine that—the seeing and the doing, the 'I must do'. There is the seeing which is the future—'I must do', 'I will become'. Now, the future is the past modifying itself. That is time. Now, there is also a timeless action, an action which is perception-action. In timeless action, that is, in perception-action there is no interval. Right? Do go slowly, if you want to understand it.

**PJ** : Before I can even go into this, I want to go into what this 'modifying in the present' is.

**K** : What is this modification in the present? That is very simple.

**PJ** : What is the actual instant of . . . ?

**K** : Thought? I am afraid of the past and I meet the present. Thought modifies itself and goes on, but it's still 'fear'.

**PJ** : But can we examine that instant where this modification takes place?

**K** : Yes. I am afraid of what might happen tomorrow, but tomorrow is both in the today and in the yesterday. Just a minute. Let's make it very clear. The present, the 'now', is the past and the future. The present contains that.

**PJ** : But a perception in the present negates both the past and the future.

**K** : That's what I am saying. But perception requires a state without the past. Perception is timeless. That's it.

I perceive. I am full of prejudices, knowledge, conclusions, convictions, beliefs, and with that I look at the present. And that present is modified by the challenge—I might alter certain beliefs but I still remain in the same field. The present is modified, and so the future is the modification.

**PJ** : Yes, but this is a state where the point of perception . . . .

**K** : There is no point of perception here.

**PJ** : When you speak of a time which does not belong to these two—the past and the future—it is obviously the essential element of this perception of the 'now'.

**K** : Yes, and that perception is not of time. Because that perception doesn't contain the past.

**PJ** : What is the 'now'?

**K** : The 'now' is the past and the present.

**PJ** : Is it actually that?

**K** : Yes, that is the 'now'.

**PJ** : I want to question that.

**K** : The 'now' is all time: past time, future time and the present time.

**PJ** : Now, you see, you can experience past time, and you can experience future time because you project, but what is the experiencing of 'all time'?

**K** : You can't experience it.

**PJ** : You see this is exactly what I am trying to get at—the past you can experience . . . .

**K** : You can project the future and experience it without going through it.

**PJ** : Yes; but this experience of 'all time' is not an experience.

**K** : No; I am saying that. Experience implies the experiencer who is experiencing. The experiencer is of time.

**PJ :** Therefore when you say that the 'now' contains the past and the future, what does it exactly mean? How do you contact it? What I am trying to say is, we can use words to describe this.

**K :** I've got it.

**PJ :** But is there ever an actual contact with this?

**K :** Ah ha. *(Denying)* You are using the word 'contact' in the sense of contacting *me,* contacting *you.*

**PJ :** No, I am not. I am saying that it can't be contacted by me or without me.

**K :** No, no, no.

**PJ :** Just see this, sir, please. You say that the past and the present are both contained in the 'now'. I ask: What is this 'now'?

**K :** I'll tell you what the 'now' is.

**SP :** Can I say something?

**K :** Of course, everybody can.

**SP :** Pupul, 'what is' is the present. Let me put it this way. Fear is the 'what is'. It is the 'now'. Though it is the 'what is', the whole mass is in the 'what is'.

**PJ :** But what is 'what is'?

**K :** Pupul is asking: How does one see or assert that the past is contained in the present? Does one actually experience this, does one actually see it or is it a theory?

**SP :** I think . . . .

**K :** Listen to the question first.

**SP :** I understand it.

**K :** Wait, careful; don't say 'I understand'; go into it a little more. Pupul is asking: What makes you certain that the past is contained

257

in the present? Is it an idea, is it a theory or do you see the whole implication of that? Do you have an insight into that?

**SP** : Normally we don't get insight.

**K** : Therefore you are talking theoretically.

**PJ** : Krishnaji is asking whether there is a time which is not the linear time of the outside or the time of becoming. He asks a question: Is there a time which is independent of both these times?

**K** : That's all.

**PJ** : The only, at least to me, perception where the revelation of this or the insight into this can come about is in the present. Now, how do I come to this 'now' of existence?

**K** : You cannot come to it.

**PJ** : Yes. You cannot come to it—then?

**K** : You cannot experience it; you cannot conceive of it.

**PJ** : Yes.

**K** : See what has happened. Pupul, see what has happened. You can't experience it, but your brain is conditioned to experience. Your brain is conditioned to knowledge, is conditioned to measurement in words. But *this* cannot be approached that way. And this is where religious minds meet—do you follow?—because they have wiped away the theories, they have wiped away ideas and concepts. They deal with the actual state. And that is where the religious inquiry begins. But you are inquiring into theories and, so, you will play around with it infinitely.

**PJ** : Is it possible to probe into this time which is not of this . . . ?

**K** : Yes, it is possible. Possible in the sense, you may use words, but the words are not the thing. You can't measure *this* with words.

**PJ** : Because there are no words, the moment words cease . . . .

**K** : No, no; careful, careful. The question remains.

**PJ** : This is something quite extraordinary, because if the question remains, but the questioners do not remain . . . .

**K** : Yes. The question remains and the questioners don't exist.

**RADHIKA HERZBERGER (RH)** : Then, is it a verbal question at all?

**K** : No.

**ASIT CHANDMAL (AC)** : What does the question operate upon?

**K** : I said: Perception means that there is no perceiver. See what the implication of that is. The perceiver is the past and the future. But the perception is now. Therefore it is timeless just as action is timeless.

**PJ** : Therefore, in that perception, the past and the future are totally annihilated.

**SP** : I want to ask a question: What is the relationship of perception to the perceived?

**K** : There is no relationship.

**PJ** : You asked a question: What is the 'now'? Krishnaji started by saying that it contains the past, the present and the future. Then the next question was: How do I contact it? To that question, Krishnaji answered: It cannot be contacted; there can only be perception. Now the listening taking place in this state of perception, in this state of dialogue—that's why I brought in dialogue—wipes out this . . . .

**K** : Do you see what is happening now? Listening is not of time. If I listen, it is now. Do you understand, sir?

**AC** : I understand that, sir.

**K :** So attention has no time. And, therefore, there is no linear or horizontal time.

**AC :** I understand. In that state what is there a perception of? Who or what is listening or inquiring into that state? How can you ask a question?

**K :** You can. I am going to show it to you in a minute.

**PJ :** It is possible. Out of the listening itself the question arises.

**AC :** Does the question arise out of itself?

**K :** Careful, Pupul, careful. Please don't theorize.

**PJ :** I am not theorizing, sir.

**K :** I am not saying that you are theorizing. I am only saying be very careful; theory and speculation don't enter into this at all. I am saying that perception is timeless.

**PJ :** Yes, then I asked you a question: Is it possible to probe?

**K :** Yes. I say, yes. But, please, realize what has happened before we probe. The mind has rid itself of all concepts, all theories, all hopes, all desires. It is now in a state of clarity. Right? So in that state, you can inquire non-verbally. That's what I want to get at.

**AC :** I don't understand.

**K :** Look, sir, I tell you—just listen—love is not of time. Right? I tell you that. How do you listen to that? What is your response to that? First you hear the words—those words have a certain meaning and those words are interpreted according to your background, according to your intellectual capacity, your emotional capacity, your feeling of affection, and so on. You hear all this. But can you listen, listen to the truth of it? Do you understand what I am saying?

**AC :** I don't think I can listen. I am listening to the words. How can you separate the words from the rest of it?

**K :** Oh yes, you can. The word is not the thing.

**AC :** Yes, and therefore while listening to the words, I can't listen to the thing said. How can I?

**K :** Sir, don't you understand the simple truth of it? Love is not of time.

**AC :** It cannot have any meaning.

**K :** Now, have a dialogue with me. Don't categorically state that it has no meaning.

**AC :** Sir, the next question is: What do you mean by 'love'? What do you mean by . . . .

**K :** We can go into all that. But we must remember that the verbal description is not the fact.

**PJ :** I ask: How do you listen? Isn't that the crucial question?

**SP :** No, this question is not answerable.

**PJ :** I will answer his question: How do you listen? Without translating everything into memory.

I say that in a dialogue with Krishnaji you can listen without thought operating and, yet, comprehend fully what he is saying. It is in listening at such depths that it—the statement, the question, 'what is'—opens up, it tells you; there is no other action.

**SP :** Pupulji, what is the comprehension of the statement 'Love is not of time'?

**PJ :** There is no comprehension . . . .

**K :** Love is not of time.

**PJ :** You take a perfume . . . .

**K :** Wait, wait. I can't explain it to you. Have a dialogue regarding that. Here is a statement K makes: Love is not of time.

Do you understand the beauty, the depth of it? Have a dialogue regarding that.

**SP :** I understand that love is not attachment. I understand that where jealousy is, love is not.

**K :** That's analysing.

**SP :** No, I know that. But, in spite of all this dialogue, this state of love which is not of time . . . .

**PJ :** Sunanda, you can never use words to open up this statement. Forgive me for saying it.

**K :** You are using your intellect. You are not using a totally different capacity. We all have been trained, forgive me for saying so, to be highly intellectual. A poor man who is not so bright, who has not passed exams and secured professorships, will understand a simple statement like this. At least I *think* he will.

**AC :** Sir, may I come back? How can there be an inquiry into the state of perception?

**K :** Sir, just listen, I will show it to you. I tell you, 'Love is not of time'. To me that's a tremendous fact; it is the truth. You say, 'I really don't understand you'. And I tell you, 'You won't understand it the way you want to understand it, because you want to understand it through the intellectual process'. Do you get what I am saying?

You won't understand it because you want to understand it through the intellectual process: through argument, through a reactionary process, a constant back and forth of words. I say that you won't understand it that way. You might say that that is the only instrument you have—there is a dialogue going on now—and I reply, 'Look, there is a totally different instrument. I will tell you what that instrument is if you can put aside the enormous weight of knowledge which is of time'.

**AC** : Do you put aside your intellectual instrument, instead of knowledge?

**K** : No, of course not. I said knowledge. Knowledge is evolution.

**AC** : I understand that—which means you are saying that the intellectual instrument . . . .

**K** : This interests me. Is there a comprehension, an insight, an immediate perception without the word, without analysis, without bringing all your knowledge into it? Oh yes, sir.

**AC** : I understand that, sir.

**K** : So, if you understand that there is a state where words have lost their meaning, but that there *is* pure perception of something, you will probe into that perception. I will show it to you.

**AC** : How can I inquire into that state?

**K** : I will show it to you.

**PJ** : Can you discuss that?

**K** : You can't discuss it.

**AC** : Yes. You cannot, for how does one inquire without the word? You see, this state, to me, is the end of inquiry, not the beginning of inquiry.

**K** : All right, if it is the end of inquiry, do you stop there? The brain—does it see this? Then that's finished. Do you follow?

**AC** : Yes, I follow.

**K** : Do you get it?

**AC** : Yes.

**K** : Do you get it? Do you get it that the brain says, 'Yes, that's finished'?

**AC** : No, the brain doesn't say it. Energy lapses. The brain cannot maintain that level of energy—it lapses.

**K** : On the contrary.

**AC** : Sir, as long as there is energy, there is no further inquiry or question.

**K** : I agree.

*Madras*
*28 December 1985*

# PART II

PART II

# Biological Survival and Intelligence

**PUPUL JAYAKAR (PJ) :** There was something which Krishnaji said in his talk yesterday; I do not know whether it will bear discussion. The question he posed was whether the brain cells could strip themselves of everything except the movement of survival or, to put it in other words, the pure biological necessity which alone makes the organism exist. It was a very startling question. Krishnaji seemed to suggest that before any movement in the new dimension could take place, this total stripping to the bare bedrock was essential. In a sense he was back to a totally materialistic position.

**P.Y. DESHPANDE (PYD) :** If you have survival as the dimension of existence, then there is no other dimension. Can this bear investigation? Is such a stripping of every element of consciousness, as we have understood it, possible? We have always claimed that the human being is more than the urge for survival.

**MAURICE FRIEDMAN (MF) :** Are the brain cells not the repository of culture?

Previously published in *Tradition and Revolution,* ed. Pupul Jayakar and Sunanda Patwardhan, Madras: Krishnamurti Foundation India, 1972, pp 229–242.

**PJ** : If you strip man of every psychological element except the urge for physical survival, how is he different from the animal?

**J. KRISHNAMURTI (K)** : We know both biological and psychological survival. But the factors for psychological survival, like nationalism, make biological survival almost impossible. Psychological fragmentation is destroying the beauty of survival. Can one strip man of the psychological factors?

**PJ** : Apart from the biological and psychological, is there anything else? You spoke of stripping yourself of all factors. I am asking you if there is any other element apart from the biological and the psychological.

**K** : As far as we know these are the only two factors that operate in man.

**MF** : Is there not, apart from the physiological factor, such a thing as psychological survival?

**K** : Which means the survival of the psyche. The psyche is the result of the environment and of heritage. Last evening, when we used the word 'consciousness', we said that the whole of consciousness is its content. The content of consciousness is conflict, pain; the whole of that is consciousness.

**PYD** : You also said that intelligence is more than consciousness.

**K** : Wait. We said that understanding the fact of consciousness and going beyond it is intelligence. You cannot come to that intelligence if this consciousness is in conflict. All that we know now is biological survival and the survival of psychological consciousness. What is the next question?

**PJ** : You implied yesterday that there was a necessity to strip consciousness of everything save the factors which ensure biological survival.

**K** : Can you strip that whole content of consciousness which is psychological? In that stripping, intelligence operates. Then there remain only the factors which ensure biological survival and intelligence—there is no other.

**PJ :** You did not speak about intelligence yesterday. You said: When there is a total stripping of consciousness and nothing else remains, that operation is the biological movement of survival; it is the movement which perceives. Is there such a seeing?

**K :** Then the mind is not merely the survival-element, but there is another quality in it which perceives.

**PJ :** What is that quality?

**K :** What did K say yesterday?

**PJ :** He said that there is a stripping away of consciousness, and that there is only the movement of survival in silence. And that silence sees.

**K :** Perfectly true. Now what is silence? What is the nature of silence?

**PJ :** No, sir, something was said yesterday and, so, we cannot help asking: If man is stripped of everything which we consider the element which makes him human . . . .

**K :** Which is conflict, pain.

**PJ :** Not only that, but compassion . . . .

**S. BALASUNDARAM (SB) :** We consider that man, as opposed to animal, is human. What are the things which differentiate man from animals? Intelligence, the capacity to analyse, speech.

**PYD :** Man is an animal that uses language. And this is the mark which distinguishes him from the rest of the animal world. Language enables man to say, 'I am I'. And the moment he goes beyond that, he speculates, he projects, he says, 'I am I, and in that "I" you can contain the whole cosmos'.

**SB :** And one more thing. Because of language, man has been able to evolve culture, and he cannot go back to the biological stage.

**PYD :** In twenty-five thousand years of evolution, of thinking, of speaking and so on, there is very little change in man; the environment has changed but, fundamentally, there is very little change in man.

**K :** Yes.

**PJ :** I accept what Balasundaram or Deshpande say, but still I am aware that I am. That statement is where it is.

**K :** Balasundaram is saying very simply: Strip man of all the psychological factors, then what is the difference between animal and man? Oh, there is a vast difference.

**PJ :** The moment you posit a difference, you are investigating something else.

**SB :** Man is aware of himself and the animal is not; that is the only distinction.

**K :** Let us go back. We want to survive psychologically and also biologically.

**PYD :** I say that there is something else.

**K :** We will have to find out. Merely to posit that there is something else has no meaning.

**PYD :** But you say that all other aspects of the human being have ended.

**K :** When conflict, misery, and pain have ended . . . .

**PJ :** As also fantasy, wonder, imagination—all that which has made man reach out, reach in.

**K :** K said both the outer and the inner.

**PJ :** Yes, it is the same movement. When you say that all this is to be stripped, what happens? Is it legitimate to ask that? Can we, in discussion, in going through this, get the feeling of that stripping, that seeing?

**K :** We have said that intelligence is beyond consciousness and that when the mind is stripped of the psychological elements, in the very stripping, there is the uncovering of this intelligence; intelligence comes into being in the very stripping. There is biological survival, and there is intelligence. That is all.

Intelligence has no heritage; consciousness has heritage. Within the field of consciousness, we are caught in becoming; we are trying to become something within that field. Strip all that. Empty all that. Let the mind empty itself of all that. In the very emptying comes intelligence. Therefore there are only two things left: the highest form of intelligence and survival, which is very different from living like an animal. Man is not merely an animal; he is able to think, design, construct.

**PJ :** Do you mean to say that there is an intelligence which manifests itself in the action of stripping consciousness?

**K :** Listen carefully. My consciousness is all the time trying to become, to change, to modify, to struggle, and so on. That and biological survival are all that I know. Everybody operates within these two. And within that struggle, we project something beyond consciousness; but that is still within consciousness because it is projected.

The mind that really wants to be free from the wrangle, from the back-chattering asks: Can the mind strip itself of its own content? That is all. *(Pause)* And intelligence comes to be in that asking.

**PJ :** Is emptying an endless process?

**K :** Certainly not. Because if it were an endless process, I would be caught in the same phenomenon.

**PJ :** Let us pause here. Is it not an endless process?

**K** : It is not an endless process.

**PJ** : You mean, once it is done, it is done?

**K** : Let us go slowly. You must first understand this verbally. My consciousness is made up of all that we have talked about.

**PJ** : Does the emptying of consciousness take time or is it free of time? Is it piecemeal? Or, is it an emptying of the whole?

**K** : Is the question whether the emptying is piecemeal or whether it is whole?

**PJ** : Putting the question that way reveals the whole which contains the piece.

**SB** : Stripping has to be a joint process which includes the part and the whole.

**K** : Discuss it.

**PJ** : What is it that one strips? Or, what is it that one perceives? Or, is there a dissolution of that which emerges, which is thought?

**PYD** : If all these go, what remains?

**PJ** : When you say that all goes, what do you mean?

**SB** : Only awareness remains. Is complete awareness the whole?

**PJ** : Yes.

**K** : She says yes, but what is the question?

**PJ** : Is the awareness of a point of consciousness, of one thing such as jealousy, the totality of consciousness?

**K** : When you use the word 'aware', what do you mean? If you mean aware of the implications—a state where there is no choice, no will, no compulsion, no resistance—obviously it is so.

**PJ** : So, at any point this is possible.

**K** : Of course.

**PJ** : Yes, because that is the door—the door of dissolution.

**K** : No. Hold it a minute.

**PJ** : I used that word 'door' deliberately.

**K** : Hold on. Let us begin slowly, because I want to go step by step. My consciousness is made up of all this. My consciousness is part of the whole, both at the superficial and at the deeper level. You are asking: Is there any awareness which is so penetrating that in that very awareness the whole is present? Or, is it present bit by bit? Is there a search, is there a looking in, an analysing?

**PYD** : The yogic position is that nature. It is a flowing river. In that flow, man's organism comes into being. As soon as it comes into being, it has also the capacity to choose. And the moment it chooses, it separates itself from the flow, from the river. This is a process of separation from the flow, and the only thing which brings this into being is choice. Therefore, they say that the dissolution of choice may bring you to total emptiness and that in that emptiness you see.

**K** : Right sir, that is one point. Pupul's question was: Is this awareness a gradual process of stripping bit by bit? Does this awareness, in which there is no choice, empty the whole of consciousness? Does it go beyond consciousness?

**MF** : Supposing I cease to choose, is that stripping?

**PJ** : Is there an end to stripping?

**K** : Or, is it a constant process?

**PJ** : And the second question was: Where there is intelligence, is there stripping?

**K** : Let us start with the first question, it is good enough. What do you say?

**PJ** : It is one of those extraordinary questions to which you cannot either say yes or say no.

273

**PYD :** It hangs on time or no time. If it is invited, it is time.

**PJ :** If you say that it is not a question of time, then it is not a process. Five minutes later it will emerge again. So this question cannot be answered.

**K :** I am not sure. Let us begin again. My consciousness is made up of all this; my consciousness is used to the process of time; my consciousness thinks in terms of gradualness; my consciousness is: practice, and through practice achieve—which is time; my consciousness is a process of time.

Now I am asking that consciousness whether it can go beyond this. Can we, who are caught in the movement of time, go beyond time? Consciousness cannot answer that question. Consciousness does not know what it means to go beyond time because it only thinks in terms of time. So, when questioned whether the process can end—leading to a state in which there is no time—it cannot answer, can it?

Now, since consciousness cannot answer the question, we say: Let us see what awareness is and investigate whether that awareness can bring about a timeless state. But this brings in new elements: What is awareness? Is it within the field of time, or is it outside the field of time? Is there in awareness any choice, any explanation, justification or condemnation? In awareness is there an observer, or the one who chooses? And if there is an observer, is that awareness? So, is there an awareness in which the observer is totally absent? Obviously there is. I am aware of that lamp; I do not have to choose when I am aware of it. Is there an awareness in which the observer is totally absent?—Not a continuous state of awareness in which the observer is absent, which again is a fallacious statement.

**ACHYUT PATWARDHAN (AP) :** The term for this is *svarūpa s'ūnyata*—the observer becomes empty; he is stripped.

**K :** Now, is that awareness to be cultivated? And cultivation implies time. How does this awareness in which there is no observer come into being? Is this awareness to be cultivated? If it is to be cultivated, it is the result of time, and also a part of that consciousness in which choice exists.

And you say that awareness is not choice; you say that it is observation in which there is no observer. Now, how is that to come about without consciousness interfering? Does it come out of consciousness, flower out of it? Or, is it free of consciousness?

**PYD :** It is free of consciousness.

**PJ :** Does it come about when I ask the question: Who am I?

**K :** All the traditionalists have asked that question.

**PJ :** But it is an essential question. Does it come about when I try to investigate the source of the ego itself? Or, does awareness come about when one tries to discover the observer?

**K :** No. The moment you try, you are in time.

**PJ :** It is a question of semantics. You can strip consciousness at any point—where is the observer? We are taking it for granted that the observer is.

**K :** Let us begin slowly. One sees what consciousness is. Any movement within that field is still a process of time: it may try to be or not to be; it may try to go beyond; it may try to invent something beyond consciousness, but it is still part of time. So I am stuck.

**PJ :** I want to use words which are not yours. So I have rejected all your words. I have to use my own instruments. What is the element in me which seems to me the most potent and powerful? It is the sense of the 'I'.

**K :** Which is the past.

**PJ :** I will not use your language. It is very interesting not to use your language. I say that the most potent thing is the sense of the 'I'. Now can there be a perception of the 'I'?

275

**MF** : That is a wrong question. I will tell you why. You ask: Can I perceive the 'I'? Now the 'I' is nothing but an insatiable hunger for experience.

**K** : Pupul began by asking: Who am I? Is the 'I' an act of consciousness?

**PJ** : Let us look; let us investigate.

**K** : When I ask myself: Who am I, is the 'I' the central factor in consciousness?

**PJ** : It seems so. And then I say: Let me see the 'I', let me find it, perceive it, touch it.

**K** : So you are asking: Is this central factor perceivable by the senses? Is the central factor tangible? Is it to be felt, to be tasted? Or, is that central factor, the 'I', something which the senses have invented?

**PJ** : That comes later. First of all, I see whether it can be touched.

**K** : When I ask the question: Who am I? I must also question who is investigating, who is asking the question.

**PJ** : I do not ask that question now. I have asked that question over and over again; I have discussed awareness endlessly. I discard it because you have said: Do not accept one word which is not your own. I start looking. Is this 'I' which is the central core of myself, tangible? I observe it in the surface layers, in the deeper layers of my consciousness, in the hidden darkness, and as I unfold it what takes place is a light, an explosion, an extension within.

Another factor that operates is that that which had been exclusive—now becomes inclusive. So far I have been exclusive, now the world flows in.

**K** : We see that.

**PJ** : And I find that this is not something which can be touched or perceived. What can be perceived is that which has been; it is a manifestation of this 'I'. I see that I had a thought of this 'I' in action, but it is already over. Then I explore: From where does thought emerge? Can I pursue a thought? How far can I go with a thought? How far can I hold a thought? Can thought be held in consciousness? These are tangible things which the individual has to completely feel for himself.

**K** : Let us be simple. When I ask: Who am I—who is asking the question? One finds on investigation that the 'I' is not observable. And so, is the 'I' within the field of the senses? Or, have the senses created the 'I'?

**PJ** : The very fact that it is not within the field of the senses . . . .

**K** : Do not move away from that. Is it not also within the field of the senses? We jump too quickly.

**PJ** : I want to put aside everything Krishnaji has said, and I find that the very inquiry, the very investigation into the 'I' creates light; it creates intelligence.

**K** : You are saying that the very inquiry brings about awareness. Obviously. I did not say that it did not.

**PJ** : And, in the inquiry, one can only use certain instruments, which are the senses. Whether the inquiry is outside or within, the only instruments which can be used are the senses, because that is all we know: the seeing, listening, feeling—and the field is illuminated. The field of the without and the field of the within are illuminated. Now, in this state of illumination, you suddenly find that there has been a thought, but that it is already over. If you now ask: Is the stripping partial or total, the question is irrelevant; it has no meaning.

**K** : Wait a minute. I am not sure. Is perception partial? I have investigated through the senses—the senses creating the 'I', investigating the 'I'. The activity brings a lightness, a clarity. Not entire clarity, but some clarity.

**PJ** : I would not use the words 'some clarity', but 'clarity'.

**K** : It brings clarity. We will stick to that. Is that clarity expandable?

**PJ** : The nature of seeing is such—I can see here, and I can see there, depending on the power of the eye.

**K** : We said that perception is not only visual but also non-visual. We said that perception is that which illuminates.

**PJ** : I would like to ask you something. You have said that seeing is not only visual but also non-visual. What is the nature of this non-visual seeing?

**K** : The non-visual is the non-thinkable. The non-visual does not pertain to the word; it does not pertain to thought. That is all. It is without meaning, without expression, without thought. Is there a perception without thought? Now proceed.

**PJ** : There is a perception that can see close, that can see far.

**K** : Wait. We are talking only of perception—not duration, length, size or breadth of perception, but of perception which is non-visual, which is neither deep nor shallow. Shallow perception or deep perception comes only when thought interferes.

**PJ** : Now, in that, is there partial or total stripping? We started with that question.

**MF** : She is asking this: In every perception, there is the non-verbal element of mere sensation; then there is the psychological superimposition. Is there a state of mind in which superimposition does not occur and there is no stripping?

**PJ** : That is right. Perception is perception. We are asking: Is there a perception in which stripping is not necessary?

**K** : There is no such thing as an everlasting perception.

**PJ :** Is it identical with what you call intelligence?

**K :** I do not know. Why are you asking that?

**PJ :** Because it is timeless.

**K :** Timeless means timeless. Why do you ask this? Isn't perception which is non-verbal also non-thought, non-time? If you have answered this question, you have answered that one also. A mind which is perceiving is not asking this question; it is perceiving. And each perception is perception; it is not carrying over perception. Where does the question of stripping or not stripping arise?

**PJ :** Perception is never carried into another thought. I see that lamp. The seeing has not been carried. Only thought is being carried.

**K :** That is obvious. My consciousness is my mind, which is the result of sensory perception. It is also the result of evolution and time. It is expandable and contractible. And thought is part of consciousness. Now somebody comes along and asks: Who am I? Is the 'I' a permanent entity in this consciousness?

**PYD :** It is not permanent.

**K :** Is this 'I' consciousness?

**PYD :** It cannot be.

**K :** Consciousness is heritage. Of course it is.

**MF :** We are mixing the concept of consciousness with the experience of consciousness.

**K :** This is very clear—'I' is that consciousness.

**PJ :** The 'I' has a great reality for me until I begin to investigate.

**K :** Of course. The fact is that after looking, after observing, I see that I am the whole of this consciousness. This is not a verbal statement. I am the heritage—I am all that. Is this 'I' observable?

Can it be felt, can it be twisted? Is it the result of perception and heritage?

**MF** : It is not the result of the inherited; it is the inherited.

**K** : And then she asks: Who is that 'I'? Is that 'I' part of consciousness, part of thought? I say yes. Thought is part of the 'I', except where thought is functioning technologically, where there is no 'I'. The moment you move away from the scientific field, you come to the 'I', which is part of the biological heritage.

**MF** : The 'I' is the centre of perception; it is a working centre of perception, an *ad hoc* centre, and the 'other' is an effective centre.

**K** : Be simple. We see that consciousness is the 'I'; the whole of that field is the 'I'. The 'I' is the centre of the field.

**PJ** : I want to put aside everything and tackle it in a new way. I see that the most important element in me is the 'I'. Now what is the 'I'? What is its nature? One investigates that, and in the very process of observation there is clarity.

**K** : Full stop.

**PJ** : Clarity being non-eternal . . . .

**K** : But it can be picked up again.

**PJ** : I say, maybe.

**K** : Because I have an idea that perception is whole.

**PJ** : Can the question whether clarity is eternal legitimately arise in this state?

**K** : It does not arise in the state of perception. It only arises or exists when I ask: Is this process everlasting?

**PJ** : And what would you say?

**K** : You are being asked. Answer. You have to answer this question. At the moment of perception, the question does not arise. The next moment, I do not perceive so clearly.

**PJ** : If I am alert to see that I am not perceiving so clearly, I will investigate that.

**K** : So what am I doing? There is perception. That is all.

**PJ** : The key to the doorway is in that question.

**K** : Let us be simple about this. There is perception. In that perception there is no question of duration. There is only perception. The next minute I do not see clearly, there is no clear perception; it is muddled. Then there is the investigation of pollution, and so clarity. Muddle and again perception, covering and uncovering—this goes on. This is going on. Right?

**MF** : Is it a movement of time?

**PJ** : Something very interesting takes place. The very nature of this awareness is that it operates on the other.

**K** : What do you mean by the 'other'?

**PJ** : Inattention.

**K** : Wait. There is attention followed by inattention. Then be aware of inattention, which then becomes attention. This balancing is going on all the time.

**PJ** : Now I make a statement: Awareness lessens inattention. It would be incorrect for me to say this. The only thing I can observe is that there is an action of attention on inattention.

**K** : Does that action on inattention wipe away inattention, so that inattention does not come again?

**PYD** : It is attentive to the inattentive.

**PJ** : I am going further than being attentive to the inattentive. I say that the nature of this attention is such that it operates on the brain cells. I am very, very hesitant when I say this. It is the nature of attention to operate on the brain cells. That which is dormant in the brain cells re-emerges when it is exposed to attention, and the very nature of dormancy undergoes a change. I would like this area to be investigated.

**K :** Let us begin again. If there is choice in that awareness, we are back again in consciousness. Awareness is non-verbal; it has no relationship to thought. We call that awareness attention. When there is inattention there is inattention, why do you mix up the two? I am inattentive; there is no attention. That is all.

In that inattention there are certain actions going on. And those activities bring further misery, confusion, trouble. So I say to myself: I must be attentive all the time so as to prevent this disturbance taking place. And I say: I have to cultivate attention. That very cultivation becomes inattention. The seeing of that inattention brings attention.

Attention affects the brain cells. Look at what has happened. There is attention, and then inattention. In inattention there is confusion, misery, and all the rest of it. Now what takes place?

**PYD :** The dispelling of inattention has gone down in the unconscious.

**PJ :** Is it not really that you can do nothing about it?

**K :** I agree Pupul, but hold on a minute. Do not say that there is nothing. We will find out. We are investigating. There is attention and there is inattention. In inattention everything is confusion. Why do I want to put the two together? When there is the urge to put the two together, there is an action of the will, which is choice: I prefer attention to inattention. And so I am back again in the field of consciousness. So what is the action where the two are never brought together? I want to explore that a little bit.

When there is attention, thought as memory does not operate; there is no thinking process in attention, there is only attention. I am only aware that I have been inattentive when the action produces discomfort, misery or danger. Then I say to myself: I have been inattentive. And as inattention has left a mark on the brain, I am concerned with the misery inattention has brought about. Then, in investigating that misery, attention comes again, leaving no mark. So what is taking place? Each time there is inattention, there is the quick and instant perception of it. Perception has an immediacy; it has no duration. It is not of time. Perception and attention leave no mark: The immediacy of perception is always taking place.

*Bombay*
*18 February 1971*

# The Mind and the Heart

**PUPUL JAYAKAR (PJ)** : Sir, so far our discussions have been related to the mind and its problems. What we have not discussed is the movement of the heart.

**J. KRISHNAMURTI (K)** : I am glad you have raised that.

**PJ** : Is the movement of the heart a different movement from that of the mind? Do they constitute one movement or two movements? And if they are two movements, what are the elements which make these two movements different? I use the words 'mind' and 'heart' because these are the two focal points around which certain sensory responses appear to focus. Are the two movements in fact one movement?

**K** : Let us begin. What do you mean by 'movement'?

**PJ** : Any kind of emotional response which we call love, affection, goodwill, compassion, seems to ripple, to move from a focal point which we identify as the region of the heart. These ripples affect the heart; they make it, physically, beat faster.

---

Previously published in *Tradition and Revolution,* ed. Pupul Jayakar and Sunanda Patwardhan, Madras: Krishnamurti Foundation India, 1972, pp 243–253.

**K** : This is the physiological movement of the brain cells.

**P.Y. DESHPANDE (PYD)** : Or is it the nerves which have an impact on the heart?

**K** : It is a response of the nerves, the heart, the brain, the whole psychosomatic organism. Now, is the movement of the mind separate from the movement of what is generally called the heart? We are not speaking of the physical heart, but of the emotions: the sentiments, the anger, the jealousy, the feeling of guilt—all the emotions that make the heart throb and beat faster. Are the movements of the mind and heart separate? Let us discuss it.

**PJ** : In the context of what we have been saying all along, that is, of stripping the mind until nothing except the movement of survival remains, the only factor which would distinguish man would be this strange movement of the heart.

**K** : I think this division is artificial. First of all, we should not start that way.

**PJ** : While we have been discussing with you, there has been a silencing of the brain cells, there has been a tremendous clarity, yet there has been no response from the heart; there have been no ripples.

**K** : So you are separating the two: there is the movement of the mind and there is the movement of the heart. Let us question whether they are separate. And also, if they are not separate, when the mind is emptied of consciousness, in the sense in which we have used that word, what is the quality of the mind that is compassion, that is love, that has empathy? Let us begin by asking whether the movement of the heart is separate.

**PJ** : What identity has anger with the movement of affection?

**K** : I am asking: Is any movement separate?

**PJ** : Separate from what?

**K :** Is any movement separate, or is all movement unitary, like all energy is unitary, though we may divide it up and fragment it? One has broken up movement into different categories, as the movement of the heart and the movement of the mind. We are asking: Is there a movement of the heart separate from the movement of the mind? I do not know if I can verbalize this: Are the mind, the heart and the brain one unit?—And from that unit, movement flows, a movement which is unitary. But we divide the emotions, the sentiments of devotion, tenderness, compassion, enthusiasm, from their opposites.

**PJ :** As evil, cruelty, vanity. But there is a purely intellectual movement which is neither the one nor the other—the purely technological movement.

**K :** Is the technological movement different from the movement of the mind?

**PJ :** I think thought has its own technology. It has its own momentum, it has its own reason for existence, its own direction, its own speed, its own motives and its own energy.

**MAURICE FRIEDMAN (MF) :** You cannot measure thought. Do not call it technology.

**PYD :** Thought waves have been measured. Technology implies measurability.

**K :** We said just now that compassion, love, tenderness, care, consideration and politeness are one movement. The opposite movement is contrary to that; it is the movement of violence and so on. So there is the movement of the mind, the movement of affection, love, compassion, and there is the movement of violence. So there are now three movements. Then there is another movement which asserts that this must be and this must not be. Has the assertion that this must be or this must not be anything whatsoever to do with the other mental movements?

**PYD :** Apart from the three there is the movement of the co-ordinator.

**K :** Now we have the fourth movement, that of the co-ordinator. The four movements are: the movement of the heart which has affection; the movement of violence, callousness, depression, vulgarity and all that; then the intellectual movement and, finally, the movement of the co-ordinator. Now, each one of these movements has its own sub-divisions. And each of the sub-divisions is in contradiction with its opposite. And so it multiplies. See how complex it becomes. This psychosomatic organism has many contradictions, not just intellectual and emotional movements. These movements are multitudinous and contradictory. And there is the co-ordinator trying to arrange things so that he can operate.

**MF :** Is there not a selective mechanism which picks out and names it 'thought', 'mind', 'heart' and so on? Is that not the co-ordinator?

**K :** Co-ordinator, chooser, integrator, selector, call it what you will—they are all in contradiction with each other.

**MF :** Why do you say that they are in contradiction? Is it because each one is an independent movement?

**PYD :** In the way one lives, they seem to be in contradiction.

**MF :** But each one is moving on its own.

**PJ :** As Friedman says: If, at any given point, one is, then the other is not.

**MF :** Then there cannot be contradiction.

**K :** When one is, the other is not. But the co-ordinator weighs these two: I want this, and I do not want that.

**MF :** That is the whole movement of life.

**PJ :** We started this discussion by asking whether there is such a thing as a movement of the heart. So far we have investigated the movement of the mind.

**S. BALASUNDARAM (SB) :** Is the heart's movement a nourishing movement? Is it a movement of sustenance? And is it not necessary, in order that the movement of the brain does not remain sterile?

**PYD :** We are not in the field of contradiction at all.

**K :** There is no contradiction when one is and the other is not. Contradiction comes in when the co-ordinator says: I would rather have this and not that. Then contradiction, the opposition as choice, begins.

**ACHYUT PATWARDHAN (AP) :** If I am full of hate, etc., I cannot take two steps beyond. The question is: Is the movement of the heart distinct from that of the mind? Or, does it have its own quality?

**K :** That is what Pupul is saying. There is the movement of the mind—the intellectual, technological movement; there is the movement of the heart; and there is the movement of violence. There are multitudinous movements in us, and the co-ordinator selects one or two to sustain himself. From there, what is the next question?

**PJ :** Are these movements parallel to each other? Ultimately they are either the one movement or the other.

**K :** I am not sure.

**PJ :** Is the movement of the brain basically that which excites emotions?

**AP :** Though one may not have personal hate or anger, when I read about Bengal, certain emotions arise, and they are social responses; I do not do a thing about it. Whereas to have love, affection, is a definite quality of enrichment; it is a sustenance which the mind cannot give you.

**PYD :** We have already agreed that the perception of the brain is thought.

**K** : Let us get the meaning of the words clear. The response to various forms of stimuli is what we call emotion. Is perception an emotion?

Now what is the next question? Are the two movements with their sub-divisions parallel?

**PJ** : A parallel movement means a separate movement; they never meet.

**K** : Or, are they really one movement, which we do not know?

**PJ** : Take the example of desire—which category, thought or emotion, would you put it in?

**SB** : Desire is from the heart.

**PJ** : After a while desire becomes thought. So where will you put it?

**AP** : It arises only as thought.

**MF** : The arising of desire as an immediate emotional response of the heart is not separate from thought: when one is angry the heart beats faster. All that is one movement.

**K** : Desire, hate, love are mental and emotive movements. You ask whether they are parallel and, therefore, separate. I myself am not saying that they are or that they are not.

**PJ** : I don't think that that is a valid question. The valid question is: If they are two separate movements, is it possible for them ever to come together? Or, is the very cause of our misfortune that we keep them separate?

**MF** : That which perceives the pattern is thought; that which perceives without the pattern is emotion.

**PJ** : When you make such a statement, either this is so for us and, therefore, the duality has ceased in us, or it is a theory.

**K** : It is a theory. Conclusions and formulas mean nothing. I say: I do not know. I know only these two movements—the intellectual or rational movement and the feeling of kindliness, gentleness. That is all. Are these separate movements? Or, does our present misfortune and confusion arise because we have treated them as separate movements? You see, Pupul, we have divided the body and the soul. The religious tendency in both the East and in the West has been to divide. But it is really a single psychosomatic state which invents the soul. And so the question is: Are there two movements, or have we accustomed ourselves to the thought that the two, the body and the soul, are separate?

**PJ** : But how can you ignore the fact that an emotional intensity brings a new quality of being, a complete experience of what the other person feels—a sense of unspoken understanding?

**K** : Do not bring that in yet. We are asking: Are these two movements separate? Or, is it because we are so driven by habit that we have accepted these two as separate movements? If they are not separate, what is the one unitary movement that includes thought as the movement of the brain and the movement of the heart?

How do you investigate this question? I can only investigate it from fact to fact; I can have no theories about it. I see the fact of perception; I see the fact of the movement of thought; and I ask: When there is no movement of thought, is there a movement which is non-verbal? Have I explained myself?

If there is complete cessation of thought, which is movement, is there a movement which is an emotive movement—as love, devotion, tenderness, care? Is there a movement separate from thought; thought being verbal—meaning, explanation, description, etc.? When the movement of thought comes to an end without any compulsion, is there not a totally different movement which is not that or this?

**PJ** : That is so, sir, and I am saying this very, very hesitantly.

There is a state when it is as if an elixir is released, when one is overflowing; there is a state in which the heart is the only thing that there is. I am using metaphors. There can be action in that state, there can be doing, thinking; there can be everything. There is also a state when thought has ceased and the mind is very clear and alert, but the elixir is not present.

**K :** Let us stick to one thing. Just what is the factor of division?

**PJ :** What divides is an actual physical sense; it is not mental. There is a certain ripple; a ripple is very real.

**K :** I am not talking about that. What is the factor in us that divides one as the emotive movement and the other as the intellectual movement of thought? Why is there the division between soul and body?

**PYD :** Would you admit that the very faculty of the intellect sees that there is a movement which emerges from thought and another that emerges from the heart? It is observable.

**K :** I ask: Why is there a division?

**PYD :** The hand is different from the leg.

**K :** They have different functions.

**PYD :** There is the function of the brain and there is the function of the heart.

**AP :** As far as my experience goes, when the verbal movement ceases, there is an awareness of the entire body in which emotional content is pure feeling. It is not thinking any more, but pure feeling.

**PJ :** In the Indian tradition there is a word called *rasā*, which is very close to what Krishnaji says. Tradition recognizes different types of *rasā*: *rasā* is essence; it is that which fills; it is that which permeates. But *rasā* is a word which needs to be investigated.

**PYD** : It is emotion.

**PJ** : It is much more; *rasā* is essence.

**K** : Keep to that word: 'essence', 'perfume'. Essence means 'what is'. Now what happens? In observing the whole movement of thought, in observing the content of consciousness, the essence comes out of it. And in observing the movement of the heart, in that perception, there is the essence. Essence is the same whether it is this or that.

**AP** : That is what the Buddhists also say.

**K** : In perceiving the whole movement of thought as consciousness—consciousness with its content, which is consciousness—and in observing it, in that very observation is the external refinement, which is the essence. Right? In the same way, there is the perception of the whole movement of the body, of love, joy. When you perceive all that, there is the essence. And in that there are no two essences.

When you use the word 'essence', what does it imply? You see, it is the essence of the flower which makes the perfume. The essence has to come into being. Now, how do you produce it? Do you distil it? When flowers are distilled, the essence of the flowers is the perfume.

**PYD** : When the pollution goes, it is essence.

**MF** : There is the essence of friendship, of affection.

**K** : No, no. I would not use 'essence' in that way—as 'essence of friendship', 'essence of jealousy'. No. No.

**MF** : What do you mean by 'essence'?

**K** : Just look. I have watched what we have been doing during these discussions. We have observed the movement of thought as consciousness; we have observed the whole of it—the content of the movement is consciousness. There is the perception of that.

The perception is the distillation of that; and that we call 'essence' which is pure intelligence. It is not my intelligence or your intelligence—it is intelligence; it is essence. And when we observe the movement of love, hate, pleasure, fear, which are all emotive, there is perception. And, as you perceive, the essence comes out of that. There are no two essences.

**PYD :** Here comes my question. What is the relationship between essence as you perceive it and uniqueness? I think they are interchangeable.

**K :** I think I would rather use the word 'essence'.

**PJ :** The great masters of alchemy were called *rasāsiddhas*.

**PYD :** 'They who are established in *rasā*', that is, those who have attained, who have their being in that.

**K :** During these days and even earlier, one has watched the movement of thought. One has watched it, and watched it without any choice; and in that is the essence. Out of that choiceless observation comes the essence of the one and the essence of the other. Therefore what is the essence? Is it a refinement of emotions, or is it totally unrelated to emotion? And yet it is related, because it has been observed. Right?

**PJ :** So energy which is attention . . . .

**K :** Energy is essence.

**PJ :** Though operating on matter, essence is unrelated to both.

**K :** Let us begin again slowly with essence. Is it unrelated to consciousness? I am assuming that one has observed consciousness. There has been a perception of the movement of consciousness as thought, and as the content of that consciousness, which is time. The very observation of that—the flame of observation—distils. Right?

In the same way, the flame of perception brings the essence of emotive movement. Now your question was: Having this essence, what is its relationship to the emotion? None whatsoever; essence has nothing to do with the flower. Though the essence is part of the flower, it is not of it. I do not know if you see this.

**MF** : 'Although it is part of the flower, the essence is not of it'— how can that be so, even grammatically?

**K** : Look, sir, the other day I saw them taking the bark of a tree to produce some kind of alcohol; that essence is not the bark.

**MF** : But it is in the bark.

**PYD** : Which is realized because of the heat.

**K** : The heat of perception produces the essence. So what is the question?—Is essence related to consciousness? Obviously not. The whole point here is the flame of perception; the flame of perception is the essence.

**PYD** : It creates the essence and it is the essence.

**K** : It is the essence.

**PJ** : Is perception the moment of creation?

**PYD** : Do we create what we perceive?

**K** : I do not know what you mean by creation.

**PJ** : Bringing into being something which was not there before.

**K** : Is perception creation? What do you mean by creation? I know what perception means. Let us stick to that word. I do not know what the meaning of creation is. Producing a baby? Baking bread?

**PYD** : No, I would not say that. Moving from here to there is also producing.

**K** : Do not reduce everything to creation; going to the office is not creation. What does it mean to create, to produce something which has not existed before? What does it mean, for example, to create a statue? What is brought into being? Is it essence? There are only two things which can be brought about: thought or emotion.

**PYD :** Bringing into being means 'essence manifested'.

**K :** I ask of you: What is creation? I do not know. Is it bringing into being something new which is not in the mould of the known?

**PJ :** Creation is bringing into being something new, something not of the old.

**K :** Therefore let us be clear. 'Bringing into being something totally new'—at what level? Watch it. At the sensory level, at the intellectual level, at the level of memory—where? 'Bringing into being something new'—so that you see it, so that you can visualize it? So, when you speak of bringing into being something totally new, at what level is it brought about?

**PJ :** The sensory.

**K :** At the sensory level? Take a picture which is non-verbal—can you paint something that is totally new? That is, can you bring something into being which is not an expression of the self? It is not new if it is self-expression.

**PJ :** If creation is something entirely new, which is unrelated to any self-expression, then probably all self-expression ceases, all manifestation ceases.

**K :** Wait. Wait.

**PJ :** I will say that because there does not exist anything which is not an expression of the self . . . .

**K :** That is what I want to get at. The man who discovered the jet—at the moment of discovery there was no self-expression. He translated it into self-expression. It is something discovered, then it is put into a formula. I only know that the flame of perception has brought about the essence, and now the question is: Has that essence any expression? Does it create anything new?

**PYD** : It creates a new perception.

**K** : No. There is no new perception; the flame is the perception. The flame is a flame all the time. One moment there is the pure flame of perception, then it is forgotten, and again the pure flame of perception, then forgotten. Each time the flame is new.

**PYD** : Perception touches matter, and there is an explosion and mutation. Now, you cannot postulate that which emerges out of it. It is the discovery of the jet engine.

**K** : Let us put it this way. In that essence when there is action, there is no concern with self-expression. It is concerned with action. Action then is total, not partial.

**PJ** : I want to ask one more question. The manifestation of this . . . .

**K** : Is action.

**PJ** : Has it contact with matter?

**AP** : We go with you as far as perception.

**K** : No, sir, you have gone further. There is a perception which is a flame, which has distilled the essence. Now that perception acts or may not act. If it acts, it has no frontiers at all; there is no 'me' acting. Obviously.

**PJ** : That itself is creation. Creation is not something apart from that.

**K** : The very expression of that essence is creation in action—not new action or old action. The essence is expression.

**PJ** : Then is perception also action?

**K :** Of course. See the beauty of it. Forget about action. See what has taken place in you. Perception without any qualification is a flame. It distils whatever it perçeives; it distils whatever it perceives, because it is the flame.

There is that perception which distils at every moment: When you say I am a fool to perceive that. And in that perception there is the essence. That essence acts, or it does not act—depending upon the environment, depending upon where it is. But in that action there is no 'me'; there is no motive at all.

*Bombay*
*19 February 1971*

# Compassion as Boundless Energy

**PUPUL JAYAKAR (PJ)** : Rinpocheji has asked a question: In listening to you over the years, one feels that the door is about to open but it does not. Is there something inhibiting us?

**ACHYUT PATWARDHAN (AP)** : Do we find that the door to perception is closed to us because we live in time and perception is not of time?

**PJ** : Many of us have had this feeling that we are at the threshold.

**BRIJ KHARE (BK)** : It is true for all of us, but part of the problem also—and perhaps it is implied in the question—is that we are afraid to open the door because of what we might find behind it.

**PJ** : I did not say that.

**AP** : What you say implies that there is somebody who opens the door; but it is not like that.

**J. KRISHNAMURTI (K)** : After exercising a great deal of intelligence, reason, rational thinking and watching one's daily

Previously published as 'In Listening is Transformation—III' in *The Way of Intelligence,* Madras: Krishnamurti Foundation India, 1985, pp 47–61.

life, what is it that prevents or blocks us all? That is the question, isn't it?

**PJ** : I would go beyond that. I would say that there has been diligence, seriousness and we have discussed this over the years . . . .

**K** : But yet something does not click—right? It is the same thing. I am an average man, fairly well-educated, with the capacity to express myself, to think intellectually, rationally, and so on, yet there is something totally missing in all this and I can't go any further—is that the point? Further, do I perceive that my whole life is so terribly limited?

**PJ** : I say that we have done what has to be done. We have taken the decisions.

**K** : All right. What is it that a man or a woman can do? What is it that a person who has studied K, who has discussed all this these many years, but finds himself or herself up against a wall, to do?

**PJ** : I am neither here nor there; I am in-between. I am in the middle of the stream. I can't say that I am there nor can I say that I have not started. You must take this into account, sir, even though you say that there is no gradual approach.

**K** : So what is the question?

**PJ** : It is as if something is at the point of opening, but it does not open.

**K** : Are you like the bud which has moved through the earth?—The sun has shone on it, and continues to shine on it, but the bud never opens to become a flower. Are you like that? Let us talk about it.

**G. NARAYAN (GN)** : Biological time propels action because of the innate energy in it. You say that in the same way psychological time also propels a certain kind of action. Is psychological time a deposit like biological time?

**K :** You are mixing up the two questions. Pupulji says this: I have done most things. I have read, I have listened to K, and I have come to a certain point where I am not entirely with the world nor with the other; I am caught in-between; I am half way and I don't seem to be able to move any further.

**BK :** I think, sir, that for several years now you have—in your talks, in your dialogues—suggested, hinted, at the answer. And we say the same thing—intellectually.

**PJ :** I am not prepared to accept that. When I put this question to K, I have seen and gone through all this.

**K :** The rational part of the mind is repressed.

**PJ :** No, it is not so. I have observed time. I have gone into the process of time—psychological time. I have seen its movement. Some of the things that K says seem so to me. I can't say that they are totally unknown to me. But there seems to be a point at which some leap is necessary.

**K :** In Christian terminology, you are waiting for 'grace' to descend on you.

**PJ :** Perhaps.

**K :** Or are you looking for some outside agency to break this? Do you ever come to the point where your brain is no longer seeking, searching, asking, but is absolutely in a state of not-knowing? Do you understand what I am saying? Do you come to the point when the brain realizes that it doesn't know a thing—except for things in the technological world, of course?

**PJ :** I do not say that, but I do know a state in which the brain ceases to function. It is not that it says, 'I don't know', but all movement ends.

**K :** You are missing my point.

**PJ :** I am not.

**K :** I am afraid I am not making myself clear. A state of not-knowing—I think that that is one of the first things that is demanded. We are always arguing, searching; we never come to the point of utter emptiness, of not-knowing. Do we ever come to that, so that the brain is really at a standstill? The brain is always active, searching, asking, arguing, occupied. I am asking: Is there a state of the brain when it is not occupied with itself? Is that the blockage?

**MARY ZIMBALIST (MZ) :** In emptiness, there is a tremendous openness where nothing is being stored, where there isn't any movement, where the state of openness of the brain is at its greatest.

**K :** I would not introduce all these words for the moment. I am just asking: Is there a moment when the brain is totally unoccupied?

**SUNANDA PATWARDHAN (SP) :** What do you mean by 'totally unoccupied'?

**BK :** It does not think at that moment; it is blank.

**K :** Please see the danger, because you are all translating what I have said.

**JAGANNATH UPADHYAYA (JU) :** All action is bound within a time-space framework. Are you trying to bring us to the point where we see that all action as we know it is not only bound by time and space but is also illusion and, so, has to be negated?

**K :** Yes, it is negated. Is that a theory or an actuality?

**JU :** Are you speaking of that state which lies between two actions?

**K :** Shall we begin by inquiring into action? What is action?

**JU :** In reality, there is no action.

**K :** You are all theorizing. I want to know what action is, not according to some theory but in reality. What is action itself, *per* *se*—the doing?

**JU** : Action is the movement of thought from one point in space to another or one moment of time to another . . . .

**K** : I am not talking about thought moving from one point to another point, but of action, of the doing.

**PJ** : What is the fundamental question?

**K** : I am trying to ask the fundamental question which you raised at the beginning: What is keeping us from flowering? (I am using the word 'flowering' with all the beauty, the perfume and the delight that is associated with it.) Is it basically thought? I am just inquiring. Is it time, or is it action, or have I really, deeply, not read the book which is myself? I have read certain pages of one chapter, perhaps, but I have not totally finished with the book.

**PJ** : At this point, I say that I have read the book. There is no saying that I have read the book completely because every day, every minute, a chapter is being added.

**K** : No, no. Here we are—at last. I am asking a question: Have you ever read the book, not according to Vedanta or Buddhism or Islam, or even according to modern psychologists, but have you *actually read* the book?

**PJ** : Can one ever ask: Has one read the whole book of life?

**K** : You will find, if you have read the book at all, that there is nothing to read.

**JU** : You have been saying that if there is perception of the instant in its totality, then the whole instant is.

**K** : But that is just a theory. I am not criticizing, sir. Pupulji said: I have listened to K; I have also met various gurus; I have meditated. At the end of it, there are just ashes in my hand, in my mouth.

**PJ** : No, I won't say that there are ashes in my hand.

**K :** Why?

**PJ :** Because I don't see them as ashes.

**MZ :** We have come to a certain point. We have explored.

**K :** Yes, I admit it. You have come to a certain point and you are stuck there. Is that it?

**PJ :** I have come to a certain point and I do not know what to do, where to go, how to turn.

**RADHA BURNIER (RB) :** You mean that the breakthrough does not come?

**K :** Why don't you be simple? I have reached a point and that point is all that we have said, and from there I will start.

**PJ :** You must understand one thing. There is a difference, Krishnaji—to take a journey and then say we are in despair. I do not say that.

**K :** You are not in despair?

**PJ :** No. I am also awake enough to see that having travelled, the flower has not blossomed.

**K :** So you are asking why the flower does not blossom, why the bud does not open up—put it any way.

**AP :** Just to take it out of the personal context—when you speak to us, there is something within us which responds and says that this is the true, this is the right note, but we are not able to catch it.

**PJ :** I have wept in my time. I have had despair in my time. I have seen darkness in my time. But I have also had the resources to move out and, having moved out of this, I have come to a point when I say, 'Tell me, I have done all this. What next?'

**K :** I come to you and ask you this question: With all that you have said just now, what would be your answer? Instead of asking me, what would you tell me? How would *you* answer?

**PJ** : The answer is *tapas.*

**AP** : *Tapas* means that you have to keep on, and 'to keep on' involves time.

**PJ** : It means to burn the impurities which are clouding your sight.

**K** : Do you understand the question? 'Thought is impure'—can we go into this?

**RB** : This is very interesting. Thought is impure—but there is no impurity.

**K** : When you admit that thought is impure, impure in the sense that it is not whole . . . .

**RB** : Yes, that is what corrupts.

**K** : No. Thought is not whole. It is fragmented, therefore it is 'corrupt', therefore it is 'impure' or whatever word you would like to use. That which is whole is beyond the impure and the pure, the shameful and the fearful. When Pupulji says, 'Burn impurity', do please listen that way. Why is the brain incapable of perception of the whole and from that wholeness, of action? Is the root of it— the block, the inhibition, the not flowering—thought that is incapable of perceiving the whole? Thought is going round and round in circles.

Now I am asking myself: Suppose I was in that position. Suppose that I saw, that I recognized, that I observed that my actions were incomplete and that thought itself could never be complete and that therefore whatever thought did would be impure, corrupt and not beautiful . . . .

You see, why is the brain incapable of perceiving the whole? If you can answer that question, perhaps you will be able to answer the other question.

**RINPOCHE SAMDHONG (RS)** : You have correctly interpreted our question.

**K** : So, could we move from there, or is it not possible to move from there? That is, we have exercised thought all our lives. Thought has become the most important thing in our lives, and I feel that that is the very reason there is corruption. Is that the block, the factor that prevents this marvellous flowering of the human being? If that is the factor, then is there the possibility of a perception which has nothing to do with time, with thought? Have you understood what I am saying? I realize, not only intellectually but actually, that thought is the source of all ugliness, immorality, degeneration. Do I actually see that and feel it in my blood? If I do, my next question is: Since thought is fragmented, broken, limited, is there a perception which is whole? Is that the block?

**JU** : My mind has been trained in the discipline of sequence. So there is no possibility of saying, 'Can this be?' Either it is so or it is not.

**K** : I have been trained in the sequence of thought—thought which is logic. And my brain is conditioned to cause-effect.

**JU** : I agree that thought is not complete.

**K** : Sir, it is not a case of agreeing or of disagreeing. Do you actually see that thought is incomplete and that whatever it does is incomplete? Sir, whatever thought does will—must—create sorrow, mischief, agony, conflict.

**AP** : Thought will only take you up to a point. It will only move to a degree.

**JU** : We have certain other instruments, certain processes, but you seem to dispense with them. You dissolve whatever we have acquired. Supposing we have a disease, you cannot heal it; no outside agency can do that; we ourselves have to be free of the disease. So we have to discover an instrument which can open the door from disease to good health. That instrument is only thought which, in one instant, breaks the grip of the false, and in the very breaking, another illusion or the unreal comes into being. Thought again breaks that, and in this fashion, negates the false again and again. There is a process of the dissolution of thought and thought itself accepts this and goes on negating. Thus the nature of thought itself is to perceive that it can dissolve itself.

The whole process of thought is discrimination. It leaves a thing the moment it discovers that it is false. But that which perceived it as false is also thought.

**K** : Of course.

**JU** : Therefore the process of perception is still riding the instrumentality of thought.

**K** : You are saying that perception is still thought. We are saying something different. We are saying that there is a perception which is not of time, not of thought.

**RS** : We want to know your position more clearly. Please elaborate.

**K** : First of all, we know the ordinary perception of thought: discriminating, balancing, constructing, destroying, moving in all the human activities of choice, freedom, obedience, authority, and all that. That is the movement of thought which perceives. We are asking—not stating—is there a perception which is not thought?

**PJ** : I often wonder what the value of a question like that really is. You see, you pose a question and you say that no answer is possible.

**K** : No, no.

**PJ** : Is an answer possible?

**K** : Yes. We know the nature of thought. Thought discerns, distinguishes, chooses; thought creates the structure. There is a movement of thought in perception to distinguish between the right and the wrong, the true and the false, the lovable and the hateful, the good and the bad. We know that and, as we said, that is time-binding. Now, do we remain there, which means, do we remain in perpetual conflict? So you ask: Is there an inquiry which will lead us to a state of non-conflict? Which is what? Is there a perceiving which is not born of knowledge—knowledge being experience, memory, thought, action? I am asking: Is there an action which is not based on remembrance—remembrance being the past? Is there a perception which is totally independent of the past? Would you inquire with me that way? I know this, and I realize that this implies everlasting conflict.

**AP :** This process of thinking in the field of cause and effect has no way of escaping the chain reaction. It is only a bondage. Therefore, observing this, we let go of it here and now. Next we ask the question: Is there a perception which does not touch the past, which does not get involved in the past—the past being all that we have done and been concerned with?

**K :** It is a rational question to ask whether this can end; not an illogical question.

**AP :** Because we have learnt by experience that thinking through the medium of cause and effect cannot free us from the wheel of sorrow.

**JU :** Whatever instrument we had, you have broken that. Before an ailment afflicts us, you have removed it; which means, before a disease grips you, it is removed. The sick man will continue to live. Therefore, when he wants to be free from disease, it is necessary to point out to him some process by which he achieves this. Even after renouncing the chain of cause-effect, he needs to be shown its futility. I accept that it is difficult to do this.

**AP :** No. What you are saying amounts to an assertion that we cannot let go the wheel of time.

**JU :** No, this is not what I am saying. Cause and effect is a movement in time and if you say that at the end of this a 'process' still remains, it must be a form of mental activity. Whatever that

307

may be, the question is: Can the patient be allowed to die before the ailment is cured? I accept the fact that the cause and effect chain is incomplete. I also understand that till we can break that, this dilemma cannot be broken; but the point is very simple, namely, that the patient has to be restored to health and not be allowed to die. The disease will have to be cured without killing the patient.

**K :** If you say that life is conflict, then you will remain where you are.

**PJ :** Upadhyayaji understands the whole movement of conflict in time and sees the inadequacy of it. But according to the metaphor that he uses, the man who is ill, the suffering man who wants to be cured, cannot kill himself before he is cured. What you are asking for is that he kill himself.

**K :** You are making a case which is untenable.

**PJ :** He may put it in a different way. Don't also forget that conflict is the 'I'. Ultimately society and everything else can go down the drain. Ultimately it is the 'I'. All experience, all search, centres around that which is thought caught in time as conflict.

**K :** So the 'I' is conflict.

**PJ :** I see it is so in an abstract way.

**K :** No, it is not so in an abstract way; it *is* so.

**PJ :** Maybe this is the ultimate thing which is stopping us . . . .

**K :** Let us be very simple. I recognize that conflict is my life. Conflict is 'me'.

**AP :** After accepting the futility of cause and effect, what remains is an identification with a certain habit reflex. Does that identification break or not? If it does not break, then our dialogue is only at the theoretical level.

**K :** Don't introduce more words. When you say that conflict ends, does the 'me' end? Or is there a block?

**PJ** : I know conflict.

**K** : You don't know it. You can't know it.

**PJ** : How can you say that?

**K** : That is just a theory. Do you actually realize that you are conflict? Do I realize in my blood, in my heart, in the depth of the 'me' that 'I am conflict', or is it just an idea which I am trying to fit into?

**JU** : If you accept that the chain of causality includes the impact of time, space and circumstance, we must recognize that this is a major problem. This is like a wheel and any movement of this wheel is not going to dissolve the problem. We accept this by logic and experience. What I was seeking to explain by the simile is that a process must remain which is within the wheel of sorrow. If the disease is not, and the wheel of sorrow is not, still some life principle must remain.

**AP** : A process is continuity.

**JU** : Then what is it? Is it immutable?

**AP** : When perception and action are not related to the past, then there is a cessation of continuity.

**K** : I only know that my life is a series of conflicts until I die. This is our life. Can man admit this?

I am a reasonable man, a thinking man, and I say, 'Must I go on this way?' Now you come along and say to me, 'Find out if there is a different way of looking, acting, which does not contain this—for this is the continuity'. You also tell me that there is a different way which is not this and you say that you will show it to me.

**JU** : I accept that this circle of continuity in which I am moving is not taking us anywhere. I come with you up to there. Where it is a matter of experience, I clear my position with the help of an example. But you cut the ground under my feet by saying that I must discard the continuity. If continuity is cut, the question itself disappears. So how can I accept the proposition that I renounce continuity altogether?

**AP** : Therefore you must let go of examples or similes. Let go of all anchorages of the past.

**JU** : If I give up the simile, it does not bring a termination; unless there is an ending, how can there be a new beginning?

**K** : Who is saying that?

**AP** : You have said that this is time; you say negate time.

**RB** : What Upadhyayaji is saying is this: Life is conflict, time, thought, and he accepts that they have to go.

**K** : I am not asking anything to go.

**JU** : If that goes, then what is the connection between that and what is to be?

**K** : I am not talking about any connection. I am a man who is suffering, who is in conflict, in despair, and I say that I have been with this for sixty years; please show me a different way of living. Would you accept that very simple fact? If you accept it, then the next question is: Is there a way of looking at or observing life without bringing in all the past? Is there a way of acting without the operation of thought which is remembrance? I say that I am going to find out what perception is. I have perceived life as conflict; that is all I know.

He comes along and tells me, 'Let us find out what true perception is'. I don't know it, but I am listening to what he says. This is important. I have not brought into listening my logical mind; I am listening to him. Is that happening now? The speaker is saying that there is a perception without remembrance. Are you listening to it or are you saying that there is a contradiction? If you are saying anything at all it means that you are not listening at all. I hope you have got it. I say, 'Achyutji, there is a way of living without conflict'. Will he listen to me? Will he listen, and not translate it immediately into a reaction? Are you doing that?

**AP** : When a question is asked or when you are faced with a challenge, there must be a listening without any reaction, for only in such a state can there be no relationship whatsoever with that which is the past.

**K** : Therefore there is no reaction, which means—what?—that you are already seeing. Do you get it?

**JU** : I have not understood the state. For instance, if one observes, in a single moment and with attention, all illusions, then in the light of that attention the whole process of illusion will be dispelled, and that same moment of attention will be the moment of true observation. Is that so? For that would mean that one would observe 'what is' as is.

**PJ** : Krishnaji is asking us whether we can listen without the past, that is, without bringing in the projections of the past. Only then, in such listening, is there perception.

**JU** : That is why I was saying that if the moment which is loaded with illusion can be seen with full attention, then it becomes the true moment of perception because the illusion is seen for what it is. To give an example: I see a coin on which there is the seal of the Ashoka Chakra. The other side of the coin is different, but they are two sides of the same coin. Is the seeing, the perception which was caught in the past, the same seeing?

**K** : No. Now sir, you are a great Buddhist scholar. You know and you have read a great deal of Buddhism. You know what the Buddha has said; you know all the intricacies of Buddhist analysis, Buddhist exploration and the extraordinary Buddhist structures. Now, if the Buddha came to you and said 'Listen', would you listen to him? Please don't laugh; this is much too serious. Sir, answer my question: If the Buddha came to you today, if he was sitting there in front of you now, and said, 'Please sir, listen—for

if you listened to me, that would be your transformation', would
you listen? Just listen. That listening is the listening to the truth.
*(Pause)* You can't argue with the Buddha.

**JU** : This pure attention is the Buddha and this attention is action,
which itself is the Buddha. That is why I gave you the instance of
the coin, which has one seal on one side and another seal on the
other side.

**K** : Would you listen? If the Buddha talked to me, I would say,
'Sir, I listen to you because I love you. I don't want to get
anywhere because I see what you say is true, and I love you'. That
is all. That has transformed everything.

**AP** : When I am aware that this is the word of the Buddha, it is
the truth. This truth wipes out every other impression.

**K** : Nobody listened to him; that is why there is Buddhism.

**JU** : There is no Buddha; there is no speaking of the Buddha.
There is only listening and in the right listening, there is the
quintessence of that wisdom which transforms. The word Buddha
or the word of the Buddha is not the truth. Buddha is not the truth.
This attention itself is the Buddha. The Buddha is not a person; he
is not an *avatāra* and there is no such thing as the word of the
Buddha. Attention is the only reality. In this attention, there is pure
perception. This is *prajñā*, intelligence; this is knowledge. That
moment which was surrounded by the past, that moment itself,
under the beam of attention, becomes the moment of perception.

**K** : Now, just listen to me. There is conflict. A man like me
comes along and says that there is a way of living without
knowledge. Don't argue; just listen. To listen without knowledge
means to listen *without* the operation of thought.

**AP** : That moment of attention is totally unrelated to the thought
process; it is totally unrelated to causality.

**K** : I know that my life is conflict. And I am asking: Is there a way of looking, of listening, of seeing, which has no relationship to knowledge? I say that there is. And the next question is: As the brain is full of knowledge, how can such a brain understand this statement? I say that the brain cannot answer this question. The brain is used to conflict, it is habituated to it, and you are putting a new question to it. So the brain is in revolt; it cannot answer it.

**JU** : I want to know this. The question that you have put is my question. You have posed it with clarity.

**K** : The speaker says: Don't be in revolt; listen. Try to listen without the movement of thought, which means, to see something without naming. The naming is the movement of thought. Then find out what the state of the brain when it has not used the word in seeing—the word which is the movement of thought—is. Do it.

**RS** : That is very important.

**AP** : Your perception is that.

**JU** : That is right.

**PJ** : The truth is to see the brain's incapacity.

**K** : My whole life has changed. Therefore there is a totally different learning process going on, which is creation.

**PJ** : If this is itself the learning process, this is creativity.

**K** : I realize that my life is wrong. Nobody has to point that out; it is so. That is a fact and you come along and tell me that I can do something instantly. I don't believe you. I feel it can never happen. You come and tell me that this whole struggle, this monstrous way of living, can be ended immediately. My brain says, 'Sorry, you are cuckoo; I don't believe you. You may be God, you may be the Buddha, but I don't believe you'. But K says, 'Look, I will show it to you step by step. Listen; take time'. I am using the word 'time' here in the sense of having patience, but actually patience is not time; impatience is time. Patience has no time.

**SP :** What is patience which is not time?

**K :** I said—we all said—that life is conflict. I come along and tell you that there is an ending to conflict and the brain resists. I tell you to let it resist, but to please keep on listening to me. I tell you not to bring in more and more resistance. I tell you to just listen, to move, and not to remain with resistance. To watch your resistance and keep moving—that is patience. To know the resistance and to move along, that is patience. So I say: Don't react but listen to the fact that your brain is a network of words and that you cannot see anything new if you are all the time using words, words, words.

So, can you look at something, anything—your wife, a tree, the sky, a cloud—without a single word? Don't say, 'It is a cloud'; just look. When you so look, what has happened to the brain?

**AP :** Our understanding, our total comprehension, is verbal. When I see this, then I put aside the word. That which I see now is non-verbal. What happens then to the accumulated knowledge?

**K :** What happens, not theoretically but actually, when you are looking without the word? The word is the symbol, the memory, the knowledge and all that.

**AP :** This is only a perception. When I am observing something, keeping aside verbal knowledge and watching that which is non-verbal, what reaction does the mind have? It feels that its whole existence is threatened.

**K :** Watch it in yourself. What happens? It is in a state of shock; it is staggering. So have patience. Watch it staggering—that is patience. See the brain in a staggering state and be with it. As you are watching it, the brain quietens down. Then look with that quiet brain at things; observe. That is learning.

**AP :** Upadhyayaji, K is saying that when you observe the instability of the mind, when you see that that is its nature, then that state disappears.

**K** : Has it happened? The bond is broken. The chain is broken. That is the test. So, sir, let us proceed. There is a listening, there is a seeing and there is a learning without knowledge. Then what happens? What is learning? Is there anything to learn at all? Which means you have wiped away the whole self. I wonder if you see this. Because the self is knowledge. The self is made up of experience, knowledge, thought, memory; memory, thought, action—that is the cycle. Now has this happened? If it has not happened, let us begin again. That is patience. That patience has no time. Impatience has time.

**JU** : What will come out of this observing-listening? Does this state go on, or will something come out of it which will transform the world?

**K** : The world is me, the world is the self, the world is different selves. That self is me. Now what happens when this takes place, actually, not theoretically? First of all, there is tremendous energy, boundless energy—not the energy created by thought, the energy that is born out of this knowledge, but a totally different kind of energy, which then acts. That energy is compassion; that energy is love. Then that love and compassion are intelligence and that intelligence acts.

**AP** : That action has no root in the 'I'.

**K** : No, no. His question is: If this really takes place, what is the next step? What happens? What actually happens is that he has got this energy which is compassion and love and intelligence. That intelligence acts in life. When the self is not, the 'other' is. The 'other' is compassion, love and this enormous, boundless energy. That intelligence acts. And that intelligence is naturally not yours or mine.

*Madras*
*16 January 1981*

# Can the Brain be Free of its Own Limitation?

**J. KRISHNAMURTI (K)** : As Asit is involved in the manufacture of computers we—he and I—have, whenever and wherever we met in different parts of the world, been talking about the relationship of the human mind to the computer. We have been trying to find out what intelligence is, and whether there is an action which the computer cannot possibly do—some action that is far more penetrating than anything man can do externally.

I thought that this morning we could go further into this matter.

**ASIT CHANDMAL (AC)** : You see, sir, the Americans are developing super computers. Now we, as human beings, have to, in a sense, be more intelligent than the technology of the Americans to counteract the threat of that technology. And the technology is not only in computers, it is also in genetic engineering, biochemistry, etc. They are trying to control genetic characteristics completely. I'm sure it's only a matter of time before computer-brain interfaces are created. Then, in Russia, there is a great deal of research being

Previously published in *The Way of Intelligence*, Madras: Krishnamurti Foundation India, 1985, pp 194–205.

done on the ability to read thoughts and transmit them to someone else.

I would like to speculate a little bit. I am using the word 'speculate' in the sense of seeing certain problems now which will be, in the next few years, solvable technologically. I think it is important to do this because you are not merely talking to us, but you are also talking to those in the centuries to come, to whom all this will be a reality. For example, consider the role of the teacher today. You can get a small computer, put a magnetic strip in it and it will communicate with you in French. If you were to put another strip in, it would communicate, fluently, in Arabic, Japanese, or whatever, instantaneously. Suppose the strip could be put into a human brain; the problem is only the interface between the brain and the strip, because the brain operates as an electrical circuit. The question is: What then happens to the role of the teacher?

The next point is that in affluent societies, because of the tremendous increase in physical appliances like motor cars and washing machines, the body has deteriorated. Now, since more and more mental functions are going to be taken over by the computer, the mind is going to deteriorate not only at the level of what you are talking about, but even in ordinary functioning. I see this as an enormous problem. How does one cope with the problem in a world which is moving in this direction?

**K :** If learning can be done instantaneously, say, for example, if I can be a linguist when I wake up in the morning, then what is the function of the brain? What is the function of the human being?

**PUPUL JAYAKAR (PJ) :** Is it not a problem of what humanness is? Is it not a question of what it is to be a human being apart from all this?

**K :** Apparently a human being, as he is, is a mass of accumulated knowledge and reactions according to that knowledge. Would you agree with that? If the machine, the computer, is going to take charge of all that, what then will the human being—man—be? And, what is the function of a school then? Please, think a great deal about this. This is not something that needs a quick response. This is tremendously serious. What is a human being if his fears, his sorrows, his anxieties are all wiped away by chemicals or by some implanted electric circuitry? Then what am I? I don't think we get the fullness of it.

**PJ** : If you take a strong tranquillizer, your anxieties are temporarily over. That is not arguable. But if you can clone, you can do anything. We are missing something in all this. I don't think we are getting to the central thing. There is something else also involved in this.

**K** : Look, Pupul, if my anxieties, if my fears and my suffering can be allayed and my pleasure increased, I ask: What then is a human being? What is our mind?

**ACHYUT PATWARDHAN (AP)** : Do I understand that while on the one hand man has developed these extraordinary capacities, there is also a corresponding process of deterioration in the mind which is a side-effect of super mechanization?

**AC** : If you have a car and you stop walking, your body will deteriorate. So if the computer takes over mental functions, the mind will deteriorate. I mean just that.

**K** : I don't think we understand the depth of what is happening. We are arguing over whether it can happen. It is going to happen. Then what are we? What is a human being then? And then, when the computer—I am using the word 'computer' to include the chemicals and so on—takes us over completely and we no longer exercise our brains, they—our brains—will physically deteriorate. The question is: How shall we prevent that? What shall we do? We must exercise our brains. At present, the brain is being exercised through pain, through pleasure, through suffering, through anxiety, and all the rest of it. Through pain, through pleasure—it is working. It is working because we have problems. But when the machine and chemicals take over, it will cease to work. And if it is not working, it will deteriorate.

Can we start with the assumption that these things are going to happen, whether we like it or not? In fact, they are happening right now. Unless we are blind or uninformed, and we don't, therefore, know about it. So let us inquire whether the mind can survive at all if it is deprived of its problems either chemically or by the computer.

**AP :** I am not quite clear about one point. There is in each human being a feeling of a void, of emptiness, which needs to be filled.

**K :** It will be filled by chemicals.

**AP :** It cannot be filled; no, sir.

**K :** Oh yes, it can be.

**AP :** I am questioning that. There is a strange void in every human being.

**RADHA BURNIER (RB) :** What he is saying is that there will be other forms of LSD, other drugs without the side-effects which will fill that gap.

**K :** Take a pill and you will never feel the void.

**AP :** At some point you have to see that there is something which will remain untouched.

**AC :** What if you don't find that?

**AP :** Before you come to that, the finding of that, at least you must posit a need for that.

**K :** I am positing a need.

**AP :** What is the need?

**K :** The need is for chemicals, for the computer, both of which are going to destroy me, my brain.

319

**AC :** I am saying something slightly different, and that is, if this technology continues, there won't be any void in any human being because eventually they—human beings—may die out as a species. At the same time, as a human being, I feel that there is something else which I don't know but which I want to find out. Is there something which is different, which needs to be preserved? Can I understand intelligence? How am I going to preserve that against all these dangers?

**K :** Asit, it may not be preservation at all. Look, sir, let us take for granted that chemicals—the computer—is going to take man over. And if the brain is not exercised as it is being exercised with problems, anxieties, fears, etc., then it will inevitably deteriorate. And deterioration means man gradually becoming a robot. Then I say to myself, as a human being who has survived several million years: Is he—man—to end like this? It may be so, and probably he will.

**AC :** It seems to me that the movement of this technology is a very evil thing because there is a certain goodness which is being destroyed.

**K :** Agreed.

**AC :** The technology is created by human beings. There seems to be a movement of evil, and the evil thing is going to take over.

**K :** Why do you call it evil?

**AC :** Evil because it is destroying the world.

**K :** But we are destroying ourselves. The machine is not destroying us. We are destroying ourselves.

**AC :** So the question is: How is man to create this technology and yet not be destroyed by it?

**K :** That is right. The mind is deteriorating because it will not allow anything to penetrate its values, its dogmas. It is stuck there. If I have a strong conviction or opinion, I am deteriorating. And the machine is going to help us deteriorate faster. That is all. So what is a human being to do? Then I ask: What is a human being deprived of all this? In other words, if he has no problems, and is only pursuing pleasure, what is he? I think that is the root of it. This is what man seeks now, pleasures in different forms. And he will be nothing. He will only be involved in the pursuit of pleasure.

**AC :** And the computer and television will provide the pleasure right in his home. Sir, right now there are not only computer scientists but also genetic scientists and multinationals engaged in entertainment electronics and they are going to converge at a point where man will end up either by destroying the capacity of the human brain or as a human being in a constant state of pleasure without any side-effects. And the pleasure will be obtained through the computer and chemicals, and a direct relationship with other human beings will gradually disappear.

**K :** Perhaps no chemist, no computer expert has gone so far as yet but we have to be ahead of them. That is what I feel. So what is it that man has pursued all through his existence? From time immemorial, what is the stream he has always followed? Pleasure.

**AC :** Pleasure, yes, but also the ending of sorrow.

**K :** No, pleasure. Avoid the other, but essentially pursue pleasure.

**AC :** He pursues pleasure and at some point he sees the need not merely for pleasure, but in the negative sense, the ending of suffering.

**K :** Which means pleasure.

**AC :** Is the ending of suffering pleasure?

**K :** No. You are missing my point. I want pleasure at any price and suffering is an indication to me that I am not having pleasure. Dispute it; don't accept it.

**AC :** What I am saying is that historically man has always pursued pleasure.

**K** : Which means—what? Go on, analyse it.

**AC** : The self has pursued it.

**AP** : When you say the 'self', are you talking of the physical self or of the psychological self?

**K** : Both. I want to survive physically and psychologically, and to survive, I must do certain things, and to do certain things, they must be pleasurable. Sir, please look into this very carefully. Ultimately man wants pleasure. The pursuit of God is pleasure. Right? Is that what is going to be encouraged by the machine, by drugs? And will man be merely an entity that is concerned with pleasure? Is the conflict to find a balance between the two? Pleasure is the most destructive thing in life.

I don't think you understand the significance of this. The conflict between good and evil has existed from time immemorial. The problem is to find a balance or a state where this conflict does not exist, which is pleasure. And pleasure is the most destructive thing in life. Right?

**AP** : In terms of what you are saying, does the search for freeing the mind from bondage fall in the realm of pleasure?

**AC** : We in fact reduce everything to that: that is what human beings have done. Attachment, bondage, create suffering. That is why we want freedom. Can we see that all human action ultimately ends in wanting happiness or pleasure, and that they are enormously destructive? They have ended up in a technology which is also a pursuit of pleasure, which is self-destructive. There must be some other movement of the mind which is not seeking pleasure, which is not self-destructive. I don't know if there is, but there must be.

**K** : Asit, let us get this clear between ourselves, you and I. It is a fact that human beings, historically, have always been in conflict; there has always been the conflict between the good and the bad; their ancient paintings indicate a struggle. The spirit of conquering pervades, which ends up in pleasure. I have looked at it and I realize instantly that the whole movement of man has been this. I don't think anybody can dispute this. I am saying that the whole of it, not only physical but also psychological self-preservation is part of that movement. That is a fact. Is that destructive of the mind, of the brain?

**RB** : Sir, what do you mean by 'good' and what do you mean by 'evil' when you say that pleasure is nothing but trying to balance the good and the evil?

**K** : You have seen those paintings in the caves of France and Spain. They are thousands and thousands of years old. And in those ancient paintings you see man struggling against the bull.

**RB** : Yes. It exists everywhere in some form or other.

**K** : Yes. This conflict between the two—what is called good, and what is called evil—has existed from time immemorial. Right? And man has invented good and evil. Watch it, watch your own mind. Don't theorize. Look at yourself if you can, and see what good and evil are. The fact is never evil. Right? Anger is anger. But I say that it is evil and that I must, therefore, get rid of anger. But anger is a fact. Why do you want to name it either 'bad' or 'good'?

**RB** : Whether you name it bad or not, it can be terribly destructive.

**K** : It can be very destructive, but the moment I have called it bad, it is something to be avoided—right? And then the conflict begins. But it is a fact. Why do you call it anything else?

**PJ** : Take the pursuit of black magic. Would you or would you not say that the pursuit of that in its very nature is evil?

**K** : What do you call 'black magic'?

**PJ** : Black magic is the pursuit of something with the intention of destroying another.

**K** : Which is what we are doing, though we may not call it black magic. You see, Pupul, what is war after all?

**PJ** : Let me go slowly; you are rushing us. What I speak about brings into operation, supposedly, powers which are not physical powers.

**K** : I had seen here at Rishi Valley some years ago, stuck under a tree, a figurine of a man, or a woman, in which they had put pins. I asked what it was about, and they explained it to me. Now, there was the intention to hurt somebody. Between that and the intention to go to war, what is the difference?

You are losing, missing, an awful lot. You are all so damn clever, that is what is wrong with you. Light is neither good nor bad. Which means—what? Look, sir, the computer, the chemicals, are taking over man. This is neither good nor bad—it is happening. Of course, there is cruelty; of course, there is kindness. It is obvious. The mother beating up a child and somebody with compassion who says 'Don't hurt anyone'—there is a difference, that is obvious. Why do you call it good or bad? Why do you call it evil? I am objecting to the word, that is all.

Can we move to something else? Pleasure is always in the known. I have no pleasure today but the day after tomorrow it might happen. I like to think that it will happen. I don't know if you see what I mean. Pleasure is a time-movement. Is there pleasure that is not based on knowledge? My whole life is the known. I project the known into the future. The future is the present modified, but it is still the known. I have no pleasure in the unknown. And the computer, etc., is in the field of the known. Now the real question is whether there is freedom from the known. That is the real question because there is pleasure, there is suffering, there is fear. The whole movement of the mind is the known. And it—the mind—may project the unknown, it may theorize, but that is not a fact. So computers, chemicals, genetics, cloning are all the known. So can there be freedom from the known? The known is destroying man. The astrophysicists are going to space from the known. They are pursuing the investigation of the heavens, the cosmos, through instruments constructed by thought, and they are looking through those instruments and discovering the universe, they are watching but all that is still the known.

**PJ :** The mind of man at present is threatened, is being destroyed, because of the way in which it is functioning. A very interesting thing has struck me just now, namely, that the present functioning of the mind—as we know it—will be destroyed either by the machine which will take it over or by the other, namely, freedom from the known. So you see, sir, the challenge is much deeper.

**K :** Yes. That is what I said. You've got it. What Pupul is saying is, if I understand rightly, that the known in which our minds are functioning is destroying us. The known is also future projections such as machines, drugs, genetics, cloning; all that is born out of these. So both are destroying us.

**AC :** She is also saying that the mind of man has always moved in the known, in pursuit of pleasure. That has resulted in technology which will destroy the mind. Then she is saying that the other movement, which is freedom from the known, will also destroy the mind as we know it now.

**K :** What are you saying?

**AC :** There are two movements, she says. The movement of the known is leading to greater and greater destruction of the mind. The way out is freedom from the known, which is also destroying the movement of the known.

**K :** Wait. Freedom is not *from* something. Freedom is an ending. Do you follow?

**AC :** Are you saying, sir, that this freedom from the known is of such a nature that you are not destroying this movement? Are you saying that in this freedom from the known thought has its place, that the mind has its place? Are you saying in that there is freedom?

**K :** I say that there is only freedom, but not from the known.

**PJ** : I say that what we call the mind operates, functions, in a particular way. That human mind is put under pressure by technological advances. This other, namely, the freedom from the known, is also totally destructive of this function of the mind. Therefore, a new mind—whether born of technology or one which is free of the known—is inevitable. They are the only two things; the present position is out.

**K** : Let us be clear. Either there must be a new mind or the present thing is going to destroy the mind. Right? But the new mind can only exist actually, not theoretically, when knowledge ends. Knowledge has created the machine and we live on knowledge. We are machines; but we are now separating the two. The machine is destroying us. The machine is the product of knowledge; we are the product of knowledge. Therefore, knowledge is destroying us, not the machine. So the question then is whether knowledge can end and not whether there can be freedom from knowledge.

**AC** : The question is: Can knowledge or the action born of knowledge end? Action out of knowledge can end. Knowledge can't end.

**K** : It can. You see, action is freedom from knowledge.

**AC** : Knowledge can't end.

**K** : Yes, sir.

**PJ** : What do you mean when you say that all knowledge ends?

**K** : Knowledge is the known. Can knowledge end? We are now not talking of technological knowledge. Who is to end knowledge? The person who ends knowledge is still a part of knowledge. So there is no entity apart from knowledge which can end knowledge. Please go slowly.

**AC** : There is only knowledge?

**K** : There is only knowledge, not the ending of knowledge. I don't know if I am making myself clear.

**AC :** So, sir, there is the tremendous force of self-preservation and there is only knowledge. And you are asking: Can knowledge end—which means self-annihilation?

**K :** No, I understand what you are saying. I am leaving now, for the moment, the ending of the self. I am saying that both—the computer and my life—are based on knowledge. So there is no division between the two.

**AC :** I follow that.

**K :** This is a tremendous thing. And so long as we are living in knowledge, our brains are being destroyed through routine, the machine, etc. So the mind is knowledge. There is no question of saying that it must free itself from knowledge. See that. There is only the mind which is knowledge.

I am going to tell you something. You see, you have blocked yourself. Don't say that it is impossible. If you had said that it is impossible, you couldn't have invented computers. Move from there. Whatever the mind does—including saying that it must be free—will always be within the field of knowledge. So what is the state of the mind that is completely aware, or knows, or is cognizant that it is entirely knowledge?

I have moved. Don't you see it? Now what has taken place? Apparently knowledge is movement. Knowledge has been acquired through movement. So knowledge is movement. So time, and all that, is movement.

**AC :** You are speaking of the state of mind when time comes to a stop.

**K :** That is freedom. Time is movement. Which means—what? It is very interesting, sir. Let me put it together. The mind has invented the computer. I have used the word 'computer' to include all technology—genetics, cloning, chemicals, and so on. All that is born from the knowledge which man has acquired. It is still the known, the product of the known, with its hypotheses, theories and refutals and so on. Man has also done exactly the same thing as the machine. So there is no division between the two. The mind is knowledge. Whatever it does will be born of knowledge—his Gods, his temples are born of knowledge. Knowledge is a movement. Can the movement stop?

That is really freedom. That means, perception is free from knowledge and action is not of perception, not out of knowledge. The perception of the snake is based on centuries of conditioning about the snake. The perception that I am a Hindu, with all that has gone on in that name for three thousand years is the same movement. And we are living in the field all the time. That is destructive, not the machine. Unless that machine of the mind stops—not the computer—we are going to destroy ourselves.

So is there a perception which is not born out of knowledge? Because when this movement stops, there must be action.

**AC** : In other words, it is to act in the world, but nothing sticks, no marks are left. Nothing takes root.

**K** : Which means—what?—a perception which is not of knowledge. Is there such perception? Of course; there is perception which cannot be computerized. Is this inquiry born out of the instinct for pleasure? We are all inquiring.

**PJ** : I don't know whether it is for pleasure or for something else.

**AC** : It doesn't matter whether the computer can do it or not. It is essential that we do it.

**PJ** : Which leads to the position that there is something to inquire into.

**K** : You see how deep-rooted it is!

**AC** : The question is: What is the mechanism of the mind, what is the structure of the mind which operates with perception, with insight, and with absolutely no accumulation?

**K :** But look at what we have done—to come to that point, which is perception without record, how long it has taken! Why? Because we function in time.

**AC :** In other words, what you are saying is that you don't have to go through this process. If we have come to this point, and do not act, it is very dangerous, much more dangerous than not having a discussion at all.

**K :** That is what I am saying. It is a tremendous danger. Have you come to a point where you see what the mind has invented?—The machine which is the computer, drugs, chemicals, cloning—all this? And do you see that all that is the same as our minds? Our minds are as mechanical as that. And we are acting always in that area. And therefore we are destroying ourselves. It is not the machine that is destroying us.

**PJ :** One can say at the end of it, *tapas, tapas, tapas.* It means we have not done our homework.

**K :** I am not sure if you are not back in time. You know, sir, a pianist once said, 'If you practice, you are practicing the wrong thing'.

**PJ :** It is not a question of practice.

**K :** Pupulji, all the teachers are sitting there. What are they going to do?—Put a bomb here? Do you follow what I mean? We are handling a bomb, and it may go off at any moment. I don't know if you realize this. It is a tremendous thing.

**AC :** It is far more dangerous.

**K :** This is really frightening. I wonder if you realize it. What will you do? This is real revolution.

**AC :** And not only for teachers and students.

**K :** Of course, of course.

**AC :** I wanted to ask you: Does the mind which has gone with you up to a point, the mind which reaches this point, become much more vulnerable to evil?

**K :** I understand what you mean. We won't discuss it now. So, sir, the question is stopping movement, ending movement, and not ending knowledge. That is the real question.

*Rishi Valley*
*4 December 1980*

# Intelligence, Computers and the Mechanical Mind

**ASIT CHANDMAL (AC) :** Sir, for the last two and a half years we have been talking about computers, about the way they are progressing and the impact technology could have on the human mind and, therefore, on the species. We have discussed not only the sociological impact of computer technology, but also whether the computer can ever be like the human mind. In Japan, the government and top computer scientists have decided to create a computer which will replicate the processes of the human brain, and hundreds of millions of dollars have been earmarked for this project. They say that what they term the fifth generation of computers will, by 1990, speak and understand many languages. Now, the problem they are facing is this: They don't know what intelligence is.

The brain is matter made up of hydrogen, carbon and other molecules and it operates essentially as an electrical circuit through chemical reactions. The computer is made of silicon molecules and it also operates essentially as a collection of electrical circuits of chips. Man can now make these chips smaller and smaller and

Previously published in *The Way of Intelligence*, Madras: Krishnamurti Foundation India, 1985, pp 169–185.

make them work faster and faster; the computers can now put away more memory, and function more logically than human beings ever can. But you see, sir, even though a tremendous number of logic-circuits can be installed in the computer, it cannot, it does not, respond the way a human being does. And this is because the computer thinks out things sequentially; it cannot perceive immediately.

So they—the scientists and other computer personnel—said that if they could only understand how the human mind works, they would be able to simulate it in a computer. They admit that they do not understand the human mind, the brain or intelligence. They say that in order to understand intelligence they must understand the thinking process. The scientists also do not understand what creativity is and how it operates. Now, most people say that the human mind has the ability to make a leap. So they are looking into what intelligence, the thinking process and creativity are, because they feel that if they can only understand this, they can reproduce it in a computer and that would give it—the computer—intelligence and creativity.

You, sir, are saying that intelligence has nothing to do with thought. Man knows only the thinking process and, so, the scientists are going to find out about that and put it into a computer.

**J. KRISHNAMURTI (K)** : You are almost certain they will do it?

**AC** : They call it a major attack on the unknown, which is the mind, and they say that this is their perception of the future—future industry, future technology and all that. The Americans are very worried about it. So IBM and all the other American companies are putting hundreds of millions of dollars in similar research.

**K** : The Americans are doing it too?

**AC** : Oh yes, they are. You know, sir, there is an organization in America which most people don't know about—the National

Security Agency. It sprawls over ten square miles and is covered with computers. It is so big that it has its own university. It has more PhDs than all the universities in Europe, and they are all geared towards defence work. The people in the Agency are also working on such computers but they don't get publicity. There is an incredible amount of money, and highly educated specialists are working on creating a machine which will perform like the human mind.

Now my question is: If they succeed in doing this, namely, creating a computer which will perform like the human mind, then, as I see it, the present human mind has to eventually die out; it will become obsolete; it will not be able to compete. In terms of evolution it just can't survive. So what is our response to this? Then again, if the present human mind is different from merely being a thinking machine, what is the difference? Is it creativity, is it intelligence, and if so, then what is creativity and what is intelligence? So shall we take the first question sir: Are our minds merely programmed thinking machines? Are our minds mechanical?

**K :** Where do we start discussing, exploring, this?

**AC :** I think we should start from the way we actually operate in our daily life. All action is based on thought and thought is a material process. It seems to me fairly clear that such a mind has to die out because it will be replaced by superior technology.

**K :** Would you differentiate between the mind and the brain or would you only use the word 'mind' to convey the wholeness of the human mind?

**AC :** I am using the word 'mind' in terms of what a human being is. He has a brain with thought, emotions and all kinds of reactions.

**K :** So you are using the word 'mind' in the sense that it includes all reactions, emotions, remembrances, confusion, desire, pleasure, sorrow, affection. If all that is the mind, then what is the relationship between that and the brain?

**AC** : What do you mean by the brain?

**K** : Is that brain an individual entity, or a result of the entire process of evolution of the human being?

**AC** : Physically, it is a separate brain. But are you saying that the cells in my brain or someone else's brain have the same content?

**K** : Is the brain which has evolved my brain or the brain of this tremendous evolution?

**AC** : It is obviously the product of evolution.

**K** : So it is not *my* brain; it is not *my* thinking. It is *thinking*. Whether it is a poor man or a rich man or a professor, it is thinking. You may think differently, I may think differently, but it is still thinking. Are you saying then that thinking is an integral part of the brain?

**AC** : It seems to be.

**K** : Thinking has created problems. It has created all the human, psychological problems as well as the technological problems. And thinking tries to solve these problems and it finds that it cannot.

**AC** : And it says that it cannot because 'I am not thinking well enough'.

**K** : Yes, thinking itself says that. Now, thinking is common to all mankind. A top scientist or a poor, ignorant villager thinks. And that thinking has created war. It has created churches, temples, mosques. It has created all kinds of divisions between people, and then it tries to overcome those divisions by creating one God—a God who is not divisible. Thought has created every kind of problem in human relationships, and thought has not been able to solve them. It cannot, because thought itself is limited. Thought is the result of experience, knowledge, memory. Knowledge is never complete. Therefore thought can never be complete. As knowledge is limited, thought must be limited and that limited thought creates the problems. All limitations must create problems and so, you see, thought which is limited and which has created the problem can never solve the problem.

**AC :** Are you saying that problems are created because knowledge is limited and that the instruments of knowledge are limited?

**K :** And thought is limited because of knowledge.

**AC :** Are you saying that thought is limited because it has not been able to know everything?

**K :** Thought is the result of vast experience, memory, all that. You have seen the computer. Thought is a form of computer which has had a great deal of experience, a great deal of knowledge. And thought and knowledge are limited.

**PUPUL JAYAKAR (PJ) :** What is the distinction between thought and the mind?

**K :** They are both the same movements.

**AC :** In other words, you are saying that all new knowledge is essentially contained in old knowledge and is a result of thought.

**K :** Of course. All knowledge is the result of thought.

**AC :** Are you saying that discovering a new thing in physics or mathematics is not creativity but is merely the same limited knowledge increasing?

**K :** Look, we must keep creation out for the moment, for it may have a different meaning to you or to her. Let us be clear. All knowledge is limited. Scientists are adding to our store of knowledge; that will go on for the next thousand years, but whatever is being added must still be limited because there is always something more to be added.

335

**AC** : It is limited at any given point of time.

**K** : Of course. So, knowledge must always go with ignorance. Thought is born of knowledge. If you have no knowledge, you wouldn't think.

**AC** : As you are saying that all knowledge is limited, I have to ask a question regarding creativity as we know it. If somebody composes a new symphony or writes a new equation in physics, would you say that it is not creativity in the true sense?

**K** : I won't call that creativity. I may be wrong; I am not laying down the law.

**AC** : In that case, sir, you are in fact saying that our minds as we know them and as they operate in our daily lives, are entirely mechanical. In which case, that is what the Japanese are going to do: build a computer which has a vast storehouse of knowledge, and an extremely 'intelligent', logical—deductive and inductive— brain which is much better than the human brain. So, what happens to our brain?

**PJ** : The human mind—which Krishnaji says is both the individual mind and the mind of mankind—has itself been a storehouse for the mind of mankind to probe into and draw out of. The memory bank of the computer can never be the memory bank of the racial mind.

**AC** : Why do you say that?

**PJ** : The racial mind is the result of a millennia of evolution. So in a sense, while all the options within it may still be limited, all the options of the memory of mankind are available to it.

**AC** : It may have more options, more memory than the computer, but essentially it is still doing the same thing—operating out of memory and knowledge.

**K** : Of course, of course.

**AC :** Computer scientists are saying that we can put a much vaster storehouse of knowledge in the computer by networking computers. Now, superficially, that is true; no human being can remember everything in the encyclopaedia. So, outwardly, the memory of the computer is much better. In a much deeper sense, since it does not have subconscious or racial memories, the human brain can have much more access to knowledge and more memory, but it is still the same thing—access to more memory.

**K :** Yes sir, move from there.

**AC :** And you say that any act of that mind—including the composing of symphonies, Einstein's discovery, writing poetry— is not creative. It is all a projection of knowledge, memory; at best just permutations and combinations.

**K :** Of course, of course.

**AC :** The moment you accept that, the computer will definitely become superior to man, the human mind, in this function.

**ACHYUT PATWARDHAN (AP) :** What you say is tantamount to saying that the evolutionary process of the brain has come to an end.

**AC :** That is correct.

**AP :** Now I question this.

**AC :** I am saying that the mind as it is, the brain as it is, has come to an end because that particular brain is going to be replaced by a brain, the computer, which can perform these functions.

**AP :** This is just a hypothesis.

**AC :** It is not a hypothesis. Already it is performing a lot of functions far better than the human mind. It can't do all of them, so they are working on that. Why should you believe that matter made of hydrogen and carbon molecules is inherently superior to something made of silicon molecules or that the human brain's electrical circuits are inherently and forever superior to those of computers?

**K :** Achyutji, Asit, would you agree on one point—that the computer has a cause just as the human brain has a cause, and that which has a cause has an end? Now, is there something which is causeless? If there is such a thing as a movement which is causeless, that is creation.

**RAVI RAVINDRA (RR) :** What you are saying is that there is an extraordinary mind.

**K :** No. I have not gone into it yet. After forty or fifty thousand years, we have reached this point—the brain. The computer has reached this point. Between the two, there is not much difference; both are created by thought.

**AP :** I am not willing to concede that that which the human brain has created has come into total possession of all the faculties of its creator. Is that what you are saying, Asit?

**K :** No, sir. He does not say that. The computer cannot see the stars and look at the beauty of the stars.

**RR :** But it can simulate it.

**K :** Of course. But it hasn't the perception of the human eye; it cannot look at the heavens and say 'What a marvellous night this is'!

Now, is there a perception which is not the product of thought?

**AC :** Does the human mind have such a thing?

**K :** Probably not.

**AC :** The computer hasn't got it either. But they will have in twenty or thirty years' time—the computer will be superior to human beings.

**K :** Of course, I am inclined to agree with you.

**PJ** : I am inclined to question you, sir.

**AP** : We are observing the human mind which has gone into the making of the computer, and you are assuming that the human mind has exhausted its potential by creating the computer. Having created, having given birth to the baby, the mother dies. That is what you are saying.

**K** : No, no.

**AP** : I refuse to accept that.

**AC** : Why do you refuse to accept it? Having given birth to a nuclear weapon, those weapons will wipe out human beings.

**AP** : Agreed.

**AC** : So, having given birth to computers which are now designing and making new computers which will make better and faster computers, why do you say that they won't be able to destroy man who has made them?

**RR** : And even if they did not destroy, why cannot the baby have all the potentialities of the mother?

**RUPERT SHELDRAKE (RS)** : So why do I or the Japanese or all the other top computer scientists, the various governments and international companies, need to produce these computers if computers can already do it—produce better, newer, faster computers, that is?

**AC** : No, no; that is the target. Computers cannot already do it.

**RS** : The fact is that it is a target; in reality it is nothing. Alchemists for the past so many years have tried to create gold but they have failed. We are talking about what, in my mind, amounts to fantasy.

**AC** : Do you know what they are trying to do? Genetic scientists have got together with computer scientists. They are saying: Why are you using silicon? The human brain has hydrogen and carbon molecules. So let us take hydrogen and carbon molecules, let us use brain cells and make computers. Another approach is: Our genes are programmed so that some cells become eyes, others become the nose, and so on. If you can break that genetic code, you could programme it to become a brain or a computer. There is a lot of research going on in that.

**RS** : I know about this research. I regard that as fantasy too because I think that the whole thing is based on false premises about the nature of the brain, about the nature of life and so on. But this would be sidetracking the main issue. I think I would rather come back to the point that in relation to producing bigger and better computers which may supersede certain powers of human beings, what is involved is human activity—call it thought or whatever you like. And these computers are the product of human activity. There is no doubt that many things human beings make exceed human capacities, but there is a limit. Machines can do many things which human beings can't do. Nevertheless they are the products of human beings and it seems to me unlikely in any sense that these things would supersede human beings. They may, however, supersede particular faculties of human beings.

**AC** : What are the things they will not be able to supersede?

**RS** : They have not yet superseded the ability to invent the fifth generation of computers.

**AC** : Yes, but the Japanese cannot do it without computers. It is being done by the Japanese and by computers. And if you actually measure it, perhaps twenty per cent of the effort will be human, eighty per cent will be that of the computer.

**RS** : Well, everything that we do today in the modern world is aided by the machine.

**AC** : What is it that a human being can do that you think cannot be done by machines in the next twenty-five or fifty years?

**RS** : Well, it is a subject which we are now coming to—creativity.

Let us take a smaller point—humour. And one of the most striking things is that most of us are not behaving like desiccated calculating machines. Most people lead their lives with a certain sense of humour. You see people laughing about all sorts of things. I have never seen a computer laugh.

**AC :** If you heard the computer laugh, would you accept that it can do what human beings can?

**RS :** No. You can get a tape recorder to laugh.

**AC :** What will convince you?

**RS :** Nothing.

**AC :** You have made up your mind.

**RS :** I am prejudiced.

**AC :** Why are you prejudiced? If you see a baby, you will say that the baby will be capable, when it grows, of doing a lot of things which computers cannot do. But if a group of people design a new type of computer, you will say *a priori* that computers will never be able to do what the baby can do. Why? What is it in that baby that prejudices you in its favour?

**RS :** You see, there are a lot of things which we recognize and understand directly without putting everything into explicitly stored-up recognition programmes. I can recognize many different kinds of flowers, trees and animals. If I have to say how I recognize them, what it is that makes me recognize them, it will be very difficult for me to tell you. I think it will be difficult for you, too.

**K :** But sir, when you recognize, it is based on memory.

**AC :** They are working on pattern recognition. There is tremendous research going into it today. Computers are beginning to recognize some things visually.

**RS :** But there is a certain intuitive sense . . . .

**AC :** What is intuition?

**RS :** It is notoriously difficult to say what intuition is.

**AC :** It is just a word. Unless you know what it means, you cannot use that word.

**RS :** No. You don't have to be able to spell out in mathematical formula what a word means.

**AC :** Spell it out in words. What is intuition?

**RS :** Intuition is grasping something more, seeing something more; it is insight; it involves a direct kind of knowledge which does not have to go through a process of words, thought and action.

**AC :** How do you know that it has not gone through the process of word or thought? It could have done it subconsciously in your mind. The brain has been working on it and it emerges instantaneously, and you call it intuition. It does not mean that it has not gone through the process of thought.

**RS :** It may have gone through such processes. If for everything I say, you are going to postulate hidden processes . . . .

**AC :** I am not postulating.

**RS :** Yes, you are.

**PJ :** Sir, the point seems to be that if the brain is nothing but a closed circuit, then what Asit says is true. However the 'but' comes in because the question is: Is the brain a closed circuit? Can there be an acceleration of the very capacity of the brain so that it ceases to be a process?

**RS :** The trouble is that it takes a long time to answer these questions. I have my own theory about biology which would deny most of these basic premises. You see, the conventional theory of biology including the conventional theory of the brain starts from the assumption that there are simple mechanical, chemical or physical processes within the organism. Now, ninety-nine per cent of biology is based on this assumption, and therefore the kind of language in which we speak is based on that kind of thinking.

I disagree with the assumption: firstly, that the brain is a closed circuit; secondly, that it works entirely mechanically or chemically or electrically, and so on. So, I think we have a theory of life which says that living organisms are nothing but machines, and then we have a theory which says that it has nothing to do with machines. Why can't we model them on machines? This is the basis of your argument, and it seems quite reasonable on the face of it, but there are a number of assumptions.

**PJ** : There are three things: Is the brain as it is today a closed circuit; what is intelligence; and what is creativity?

**AC** : I didn't say that the brain was a closed circuit.

**K** : May I ask a question, sir? Would you say that the brain has infinite capacity? Don't say 'No' right away. Let us use the word 'capacity'. I don't like the word capacity because for us capacity is educated knowledge and all that. But if I can use that word, the brain has infinite capacity. Look at what it has done in the technological world, and this includes the computer.

**AC** : You can't say that thought is limited and then say that the brain has infinite capacity.

**K** : Yes, I am going to come to that. Thought has limited the brain, has conditioned the brain. Would you agree? I am a Hindu, I believe in all kinds of superstitions, and so on. Right?

**AC** : You are separating thought and the brain.

**K** : No, no. I want to find out if the brain can ever be free of its own limitations—thought, knowledge, emotion. All right, call it thought. If that conditioning is somehow freed, it has got to have infinite capacity.

**AC** : You can't say that.

**K :** It may. You understand now? You have been to the moon, the brain has created cruise missiles, it has had extraordinary technological movement. Agreed? Now, is there an instrument which is not thought? This is not romantic speculation. I am just asking; I am not saying that there is or that there is not. Do you understand my question? Thought is a worn-out instrument. I think it has reached its limit, its tether, because it has not solved the human problem. So, is there a way of looking which is not thought but which can instead of going out there—to the heavens and all that—turn inwards? That inward movement is the infinite.

**RR :** Still it has not solved the human problem.

**K :** No, thought will not solve human problems. On the contrary, it is increasing human problems. Right?

**QUESTIONER (Q) :** Your question is: Is there anything other than thought which could be an instrument?

**K :** Yes, though you may not agree with what I am going to say presently. Yes, and perhaps that instrument can look both outward and inward and is infinite.

**Q :** Psychologists try to discover what is within; at least they profess to do this.

**K :** I know, sir; but what they say is all mechanical.

**Q :** I accept what you say.

**K :** Don't accept, sir. I hesitate to accept what I say too. I want first to be quite clear that thought has not solved human problems. It has solved technological problems but not human problems—my relationship with my wife, my relationship with the community, my relationship with the heavens, and all the rest of it. And thought tries to resolve these problems and it has made things worse. It is so obvious. So I am now asking: Is there something which is not thought, which is not mechanical?

**AC :** You are asking in other words what Pupulji was asking the other day: Is there a sensory perception without thought?

**K :** Yes. Will you listen to something? Life is a movement, going out and coming in, like the tide. I create the world, and the world then controls me. And I react to the world. It is movement. Would you agree to that? Now, if you see the same thing as I see it—not that you must—you will see that it is a movement out and in. This is our life—action and reaction, reward and punishment. Can this movement stop?

**PJ :** You have to move out of the closed circuit of your computer to even face that question.

**K :** No, not move out of the circuit. This is our life. Now, as long as this movement exists, I will be caught in time which is evolution.

**RS :** Why not just say that it is life, evolution?

**K :** Yes, and that is: I am evolving. This movement gets better, it gets worse; but it is always a movement. So, as long as this movement exists, I will be mechanical.

**Q :** Only mechanical?

**K :** Yes. I see a woman and I want her. I see a garden, I want it. It is action and reaction, reward and punishment, punishment and reward. Where is intelligence in that? As long as you are caught in that, your intelligence is out; it is a mechanical intelligence. You hate me and I hate you in turn.

**AC :** I follow that.

**K :** If you accept that, intelligence is something totally different from thought.

**RS :** If what you are saying is what I think it is, perhaps you could say that it is cause and effect, action and reaction, instead of 'mechanical'. . . .

**K** : Yes, yes.

**RS** : Now there is a certain kind of low level activity, what people ordinarily call intelligence, which perhaps we can better call ingenuity, where, in order to get something you want—but you may not be able to get it in a straightforward way—you may have to resort to some fairly original way, some new kind of competence, making some bogus documents and so on. There is a certain kind of ingenuity which is not purely mechanical. It is subsumed in a certain mechanical set of desires and within that is the framework of a certain inventiveness. So the framework may be one of action-reaction but within that we exhibit considerable ingenuity and inventiveness.

**K** : I would not call that intelligence.

**RS** : No. But in ordinary language it is often called intelligence. An intelligent businessman is one who would think of ways of getting more of what he wants.

**K** : Yes, but I would not call that intelligence.

**RS** : I would call it ingenuity or inventiveness.

**K** : Call it inventiveness. I won't call it intuition because that is a different thing.

**RS** : No, ingenuity.

**K** : To be ingenious is to solve problems of God, problems of heaven, problems of painting, etc. You see, all that is within the same area, the same field. I may move from one corner to the other corner of the field, but it remains the same field; I call that ingenuity and that has nothing to do with intelligence. Intelligence is something totally different.

**Q** : Will you elaborate on what we call intelligence?

**K** : I don't want to elaborate. Ingenuity, choice, cleverness, moving from one point to another, from one corner to another but within the same field—that is what we are doing.

**PJ :** That is the field of the known.

**K :** Yes, yes. I don't want to use that word for the moment.

**AC :** I was just wondering why we have evolved like that.

**K :** It is essentially based on reward and punishment.

**AC :** But I am asking: What is the reason, the particular reason, that we have evolved like that?

**K :** What was the cause of it?

**AC :** It must have had tremendous advantage.

**K :** Of course, it is completely secure. Secure in the sense—at least for the time being. Of course 'the time being' creates wars. Now, would you go along up to this point, namely that this is not intelligence?

**AC :** Yes.

**K :** Right. Then let us inquire as to what intelligence is. If this is not theory but a fact, that means the movement of reaction which is the movement of time has stopped. Agreed?

**AC :** When you say 'time', I don't understand.

**K :** Time in the sense I have evolved in this process.

**Q :** That is the movement of life.

**K :** Yes. And that is unintelligence. Therefore don't call it intelligence. So what is intelligence? As long as I am in this field there is no intelligence; it is adaptability.

**AC :** But one has to respond.

**K :** We will find out. If this is not intelligence, then we have to go into something quite different. Agreed? If I totally see, not verbally but actually, that this is not intelligence, then what happens to the mind which has been caught in this? Do you understand my question? As long as I am functioning in time, cause, effect, action, reaction, which is this movement of the tide going out and coming in, as long as my whole attitude to life is that and I refuse to move out of that, there is nothing to be said. But if I see that that will not solve the problems of humanity, then I have to look in another direction.

**PJ** : What is this looking?

**K** : My eyes have always been seeing in this direction only. And you come along and tell me, 'Look in other directions'. I can't because my eyesight has been so conditioned that I don't even turn around to look. So I must be first free of this. I can't look in any other direction if I am not free of this.

**PJ** : I want to ask you a question. Can I look at my own instrument? Can perception look at its own instrument? Can perception, which is a flow, see itself?

**K** : Don't call it an instrument.

**PJ** : A faculty . . . .

**K** : No, I won't even call it a faculty.

**PJ** : Can perception perceive itself?

**K** : You may be right. Can perception see itself as perceiving? Go slowly, Pupul. Perception seeing itself in action, is seeing itself as perception . . . .

**PJ** : Don't bring in action.

**K** : Perception seeing itself perceiving—then it is not perception.

**PJ** : You see, you have posed a question which is totally unanswerable . . . .

**K** : Would you say that this movement is the wandering of desire?

**PJ** : Yes. This movement is the wandering of desire.

**K :** Can this desire be seen as a whole? That is, can desire itself and not the object of desire be seen? Can it see itself as a movement of attraction?

**PJ :** Can desire see itself? Let us not even bring in attraction.

**K :** To understand if desire can see itself, one must go into desire. Desire exists only when thought comes into sensation.

**AC :** This question is very important. We are operating in that field. Anything operating in that field . . . .

**PJ :** Can never deny that field.

**K :** Of course. There is this movement. As long as I am in that movement, you cannot ask me to see it as the false and deny it.

**PJ :** Therefore, where do I look?

**K :** You don't have to look. The thing is, stop this movement. Find out, discover for yourself how to end this movement. Is that possible at all?

**PJ :** I think it is possible to cut . . . .

**K :** Be careful when you use the word 'cut'. Who is the cutter?

**PJ :** I think that it is possible to cut without the cutter.

**K :** Therefore, what does that mean? Go on. Don't complicate the issue. Just see who the cutter is. There is no cutter. Then what happens? If there is no entity who can cut, then . . . .

**PJ :** It is just perceiving.

**K :** That is all. There is only perceiving. There is not the perceiver perceiving nor the perceiver investigating what he is perceiving. There is only perception—right? Perception of that which is false.

**PJ :** The perceiving throws light on the false. There is only perceiving.

**K :** There is only perceiving. Stick to that. Then we will inquire into what perceiving is. What is perception without the word, without the name, without remembrances? What is perceiving something which one calls intuition? I don't like to use that word, forgive me. Perception is direct insight.

**PJ :** Is the question one of being completely awake?

**K :** Would you call that attention?

**PJ :** To be completely awake is attention.

**K :** That is all.

**PJ :** That the computer can never do.

**K :** Asit is taking it in, he is not answering. Sir, is there an end to thought? Time must have a stop. Right?

**AC :** I understand.

**RR :** Can I ask you a question: What happens when we perceive with insight?

**K :** There is this perception of insight and the brain cells themselves change. Can your thought ever stop when your brain has been conditioned in time, in this movement? What happens when cause, effect, action, reaction and all that suddenly stops? The brain undergoes a radical change. Of course it does.

**RR :** I have to ask you this question again. If there is such a seeing that the brain cells change, what happens after perceiving it?

**AC :** Only the physical brain has changed and I am afraid it dies.

**K :** That is why we are going into the question of consciousness.

**AC :** Does this end with death? Then all that will be different from the computer . . . .

**K :** Sir, how will you translate all this to your friends who are computer experts?

**AC :** They are going to continue doing what they are doing—trying to produce super-computers.

**PJ :** The question then arises: How can man so accelerate the other to bring into being this new perception?

**AC :** One can only see this movement and do nothing else.

**K :** That is all.

*Madras*
*31 December 1982*